i

Table of Contents

Foreword

We're all familiar with "Goodbye, Mr. Chips," the story of a British public school teacher who survives the joys and sorrows of several generations of students. Mickey Bergstein might not be Mr. Chips, but he comes as close to him as anybody I know at Penn State.

Mickey and I have been close friends since the day I started here 45 years ago. His memoirs make for warm, wonderful reading. For anyone who is interested in the Pennsylvania State University, I am sure fond memories will be evoked. For those who are not sentimentally attached to Penn State, I think you will learn what commitment, compassion, and persistence can mean to a person and the people around him.

I am very pleased and honored that Mickey asked me to do this foreword, and I know you will enjoy this book.

Joe Paterno

Introduction

■

It has been said many times that athletic competition is a metaphor for life. While that thought is a cliché, it's also true. And in my six decades of teaching at Penn State University and many years of involvement with its athletic teams as a broadcaster, I have seen people learn the life lessons that athletic competition teaches. They are lessons that have meaning for all of us, and that's why I wrote this book.

This book is not my autobiography. Rather, it tells of many people I have met and known whose experiences can teach us about life. Many of the people I've written about are well–known and familiar to you. Others you may have only heard or read about, and still others you probably never have heard of. I have included each of them because I believe they have stories worth writing about, stories worth remembering.

This book has stories about football, coaches, (including Joe Paterno), players, and others associated with that great sport, as well as stories devoted to interesting and memorable figures in other sports. There are stories about Penn State itself, including its growth from a college to a university, its growth in sports prowess, and its growth from an athletic independent to a member of the Big Ten. There also are stories about life in the Borough of State College and on the Penn State campus.

I have detailed here my participation in the invasion of Iwo Jima and have told about some of my personal heroes from that bloody battle.

My story does not tell you what I accomplished as a 22–year–old lieutenant responsible for 27 young men, because I could do little for them after being wounded early in the battle. I do try to describe what it was like to be there, and hope I have been able to convey to you a sense of that experience. I also tell you of more than a year recuperating at a naval hospital and introduce you to the men I lived with there and with whom I shared some amusing experiences, despite the grim setting.

I devote some space to my philosophy of teaching and what I have learned about educating young men and women since I began my teaching career in 1947.

Rather than being about *my* life, this book is about the people I have known and worked with at and through Penn State for the past 50 years. Their voices deserve to be heard and I am glad to be able to tell their stories.

Mickey Bergstein
State College, Pennsylvania
December 1997

Acknowledgements

■

In writing this book, I acknowledge the encouragement and assistance of:

Gerry Abrams, for his insistence that this book would prove worth writing and his help while writing it.

Ruth and Blair Seitz and the staff at RB Books for their willingness to work together to publish this book.

John Hope, for his professional abilities and insights as my editor.

Bill Campbell, for sharing his editorial experience.

The Penn State Sports Information Office, for granting permission to use photographs and for filling in some of the blanks in my sports memories.

Our sons, Andrew and Michael, for reversing our student–teacher roles and beginning to be my mentors.

Dedication

I dedicate this book with great love to:

Our daughter, Nan, (1962–1997) who was a role model for us all and who, during her life, showed and taught us the meaning of courage.

My wife, Betty, who, with unbelievable energy and effort, not only raised our sons and created a home for our family, but also gave Nan the most useful life possible for the past 35 years.

My Aunt and Uncle, Jenny and Morris Bergstein, who, lack of space and resources notwithstanding, were there when my two brothers and I needed them a long time ago.

1

Kickoff

■

Unless you have been there, it's not possible to imagine the atmosphere in a team locker room before a game. The room is full of somber and tense athletes and coaches. Until the coach sends them out to the field or gym, it is a very quiet place. I suspect the quiet has to do with each player's realization that <u>the time is now</u>.

Seemingly all of a sudden, the players realize the importance of this game to their entire season, maybe their entire career, and to any post–season rewards that a win could bring.

There is a tense, almost electric excitement, but it is a contained excitement bottled up within each player, waiting to erupt at the right moment.

A star football player once told me that you can't realize how, all of a sudden, the excitement and tension builds inside you, and that's why teams seem to explode out of the runway when it comes time to take the field.

Another player told me, "I have run down that tunnel and onto the field perhaps 20 or more times and still haven't gotten used to the feeling of running out onto the field and looking up and seeing more than 90,000 people and, if it is a television game, knowing that everything that I do for the next three hours will be watched by millions of people in addition to those in the stands, and will be recorded by all those writers who fill the huge press box. All of a sudden it seems to be more than a game."

During Curtis Enis' years at Penn State, the crowd saw a pre–game ritual develop. As the Penn State team leaves the tunnel and runs onto the field between the lines formed by the Blue Band and the cheerleaders, most players run directly to the area in front of the team's benches to stretch, run in place, jump up and down, and do all the other things they try to get rid of the pre–game jitters. But not Curtis Enis!

Enis ran the length of the field, through the end zone, and right to the fence that rings the field. He then talked to the crowd in the lower end zone seats, immediately back of the goal posts. He shook hands, exchanged high–fives with the crowd, and talked to the fans for a minute or two. He did this every game.

Curtis was a guest of the State College Quarterback Club mid–way through the 1997 season. When I interviewed him on stage, I asked why he began every game with a visit to the fans in the end zone. "The fans in those seats can't see the game very well," he explained, "and I want them to know how important their support is to me and to the team. So I tell them that their cheers are very important to us and that we know they are there and, even though they are low in the end zone, we need the noise and excitement the crowd creates and we appreciate them."

Usually we see the crowd making a fuss over the team. At Beaver Stadium on Saturday afternoons with Curtis Enis, we saw a key member of the team making a fuss over the crowd.

Because of the national attention it received, most Penn State fans realize that Curtis Enis' collegiate football career ended on a disappointing low note. Following the revelation that he had allowed a sports agent to purchase a suit and possibly other items for him, he was suspended by Coach Joe Paterno for the 1998 Citrus Bowl game and for the 1998 season; effectively ending his Penn State career. Acceptance of gifts from an agent is a violation of NCAA rules governing players with remaining eligibility. This was the first such violation by a football player during Paterno's 48 years on the Penn State coaching staff.

Enis had an extremely productive three–year career as the Lions' leading rusher from 1995 through the 1997 season. He is in the Penn State record books as the third most productive rusher in Lions history, with 3,256 career yards carrying the football. (In second place is All–American Blair Thomas, with 3,301 yards, while the leader is All–American Curt Warner, with 3,398 yards. It is obvious that if Enis had not lost his final season because of the rules violation he would, barring injury, have claimed the number one spot since he trails Warner by only 142 yards.)

Although I do not know Curtis on a personal level, I interviewed him on several occasions and had some personal conversations with him. Because he struck me as a well–spoken, polite, and seemingly mature and intelligent young man, he was one of the last athletes in all my years at Penn State that I would have guessed would violate the rules.

I have no information concerning Enis' suspension other than the details that have been reported in the news media. Was he aware of the "no gifts" rule? Knowing the careful attention that Penn State gives to the rules, and the information routinely given to the players, I believe he certainly should have been aware. Players meet regularly with advisors who talk with them about the regulations, interactions with agents, etc. Penn State has a full–time NCAA Compliance Coordinator, John Bove, and I believe that Penn State's spotless record until this year should speak for itself.

Curtis' outstanding football ability aside, the manner in which his productive Penn State career ended was a sad disappointment to his teammates and coaches and to Penn State alumni and admirers everywhere. And, I would guess, a sad disappointment to Curtis, himself.

They Always Seem to Get Better

Coach Joe Paterno traditionally tells his teams the same thing each season after their first game: "This team will get better or you will get worse. You can't stay at the same level and expect to win, because the teams we play will get better as the season progresses, and if we stay at this level, it won't be good enough for us to have a winning season."

Anyone who has followed Penn State football for very long knows that as most seasons move along, the Nittany Lions always seem to get better. As a result, athletic directors tell themselves, "Try not to play Penn State in late October or November. Late in the season, the Lions are always much tougher." And the record bears this out.

Since Joe Paterno became Penn State's head coach in 1966, the team has lost only 14 of 66 of the regular season's last two games. That's even more impressive when you realize that the year's toughest opponents traditionally are scheduled for late in the season.

Many theories have been advanced to explain why Penn State improves each year. Watching from the broadcast booth for many years, I think there are at least three reasons. First, the mark of a really good coach and an effective staff is that they are all good teachers. The players learn their lessons well as they have more and more coaching through the season.

Second, there is the matter of Penn State tradition. Penn State players *expect* to get better and they *expect* to win the tough, late–season games. On the other side of the line of scrimmage, our opponents are aware of the admonition to avoid playing the Lions late in the season if at all possible. There have been many games in which a Penn State opponent has found itself ahead in the late stages with a solid chance to win. All of a sudden, something seems to happen. As someone once said, "The other team suddenly realizes that they have a chance to beat Penn State, and they begin to look for reasons *not* to lose the game. It's almost as if they expect something bad is bound to happen to make them lose the game. Penn State, on the other hand, doesn't think about losing. It's almost as if they *expect* to win, and they usually do."

The third reason I see for the Lions' late–season strong finishes has to do with the fact that Joe Paterno moves many players around during spring practice and even during early fall practice. He never seems to hesitate to move a player from offense to defense or the other way around. He often fills a spot in the lineup by moving a player to a new position.

There are many college coaches who put a player at a position that he didn't play in high school. Paterno does that, too. Many high school players, especially the good ones, play multiple positions, often on both offense and defense. College coaches try to decide which is the strongest position for each player and slot him there. Paterno and his staff obviously do that, too.

But in addition, Penn State seems to be very successful at moving players to completely new positions. It takes a player some time to feel comfortable at a new position, especially if it is a drastic change. So, as the season progresses the players who are in new spots progress, and Joe's teams seem to become more efficient and more organized. This, of course, is a tribute to the players and also to the coaches and their teaching abilities.

If you think back through the seasons, you can remember some of those players who performed extremely well at new positions or more than one position. An All–America linebacker with Penn State's undefeated teams in 1967 and 1968, Denny Onkotz also returned punts. He returned 47 punts for 619 yards and two touchdowns. How many linebackers are also punt return men? Denny was a high draft choice of the New York Jets, but his pro career was cut short by a serious knee injury. Today he is a successful and respected financial consultant with a large firm in State College.

John Cappelletti, Penn State's great running back in the early 1970s and winner of the 1973 Heisman Trophy, played defense his sophomore year and also returned punts. Why defense in 1971? The Lions had a damn good tailback that year in Lydell Mitchell, and Joe apparently felt that Cappelletti was such a good athlete that he had to find a way to get him in the game somewhere. Incidentally, John's 1973 rushing total of 1,522 yards is third on the Penn State single season rushing yardage list to Lydell's 1971 total of 1,567 yards and Ki–Jana Carter's 1,539 yards in 1994.

Matt Suhey, who was a great tailback at State College High School and won All–State honors at that position, was switched to fullback by Paterno and ranks sixth on Penn State's career rushing list. Another multiple–position player was Rich Milot, who played defensive back and defensive end, and even started one game at tailback. Rich was drafted in the seventh round by the Washington Redskins in 1979 and started at linebacker for many years during the Redskins' 1980s successes.

Mike Guman not only was a running back for the Lions, but also a wideout and tight end. The Los Angeles Rams drafted him in 1980 and he had a long career with them as a running back and as a back split wide to become a receiver. On Penn State's 1986 national championship team, one of the starting defensive ends was Bob White, who was a high school standout at fullback on offense and linebacker on defense. For the Lions, he made a key sack during Miami's final series inside the Penn State 10–yard line that had threatened to win the game for the Hurricanes.

These are just a few of the position switches that have been successfully engineered by Joe Paterno over the years. Key to all of these opportunities is for a player to be ready when his chance comes. Two Penn State players best illustrate that need—one as a collegian and the other as a pro.

You've Got to be Ready to Play

Lydell Mitchell was drafted in the second round in 1972 by the Baltimore Colts. Despite his obvious abilities and great statis-

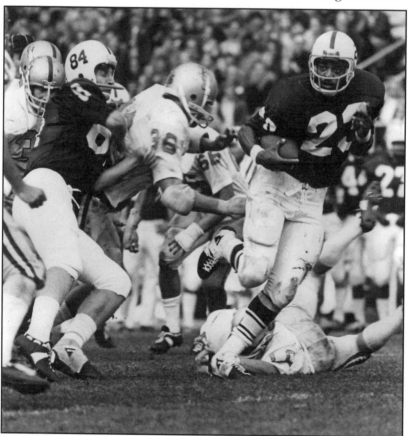

Penn State's Lydell Mitchell carries the ball in a 1971 game. He rushed that year for 1,567 yards, giving him the university record for most yards gained in a single season.

tics at Penn State, he didn't see much playing time with the Colts in his rookie season. Lydell had been a star everywhere he played—at high school in Salem, New Jersey, and, of course, at Penn State. It must have been very difficult and trying for him to sit on the Colts' bench.

Following his rookie pro season, he returned to Penn State for a visit. He was asked how he felt about being a reserve, sitting on the bench for the first time in his life. Lydell said, "It's very hard not to be playing, especially when you know you are good enough. But, I know three things now that I have had a chance to sit and watch. First, I know that I am good enough to play in that league. (Subsequent years as a star with the Colts proved him right.) Second, if I get a chance to play, I know that I can gain 1,000 yards. (Right again.) Third, when my chance comes, I'd better be ready." His chance finally *did* come and he *was* ready.

Probably the best example of a Penn State player being "ready" is John Hufnagel in the 1970 season. Penn State was coming off two 11–0 seasons and easily won the 1970 home opener against Navy, 55–7. Then Penn State went to Boulder, Colorado, to play the Buffaloes in a nationally–televised game. Penn State was on a 23–game winning streak, but was beaten easily, 41–13. The next game was at Wisconsin and Penn State lost again, this time 29–16.

At this point, the Lions had used two quarterbacks, Mike Cooper and Bob Parsons (who later would have a long career as the punter for the Chicago Bears). On the road for their third game in a row, they rebounded from their two losses to beat Boston College 28–3. Homecoming was next and the opponent was Syracuse. Penn State continued to get erratic play from the two quarterbacks and lost to Syracuse 24–7. Now with two wins and three defeats, coming up was a big game at Army.

For that game, Coach Paterno made a dramatic shift at quarterback. The third–string quarterback, who also was the third–string safety, was John Hufnagel. Nobody had heard of John, but he started the game with Army and led the Lions to 15 straight wins in the rest of that season and the next. John was named to the Associated Press and Walter Camp All–America teams. He played 12 seasons in the Canadian league and today is a coach in that league. When John was asked about turning around his career at Penn State, he always said, "I knew I was good enough to play. I also knew I had to be ready if I got the chance."

A final mark of a Penn State football team that has made a great contribution to the program's success over the years is that Penn State is able to keep its squad intact. While occasionally a player has transferred elsewhere, it is fairly rare, and most Penn State classes remain together throughout their college careers. Penn State players play out their eligibility because of what has become almost a trademark of Joe Paterno's teams, and you hear his players talk about it. The conversation goes something like this: "If you pay your dues playing for Penn State, you are fairly sure that, given reasonable ability and a good attitude, you'll get a chance to play."

"Go For It!"

Football fans would probably agree that it is a rare game in which one team or the other isn't faced with a fourth down and short yardage to go one or more times. When it's a team a fan is rooting for, the call is usually, "Go for it!" When the team doesn't get the first down, the fan's observation is usually, "Damn, the coach called the wrong play! If only he had...."

Have you ever wondered how the decision to go for short yardage, especially in the opponent's territory, usually works out? These statistics were gathered by the late John Miller of Bellefonte, a town approximately 10 miles from State College. For many years, John was coach of the Bellefonte High School football team and also was in charge of the first–down chains at Penn State home games. He also was a high school football official in his younger days.

Miller kept extensive statistics on all of the high school games he coached and all of the Penn State games he saw in person or on television. Here's what his many years of statistics show: Almost seven out of 10 times, when a team went for the first down and made it, they didn't make another first down on the next series and ended up punting the ball. John's observation was that if a team needed four downs to make 10 yards, it probably was struggling with its offense and wasn't likely to put together a drive then. Of the three times on average that a team didn't have to punt on the next series, twice they had to punt on the series after that and once they went on to score, tried a field goal, or left their opponent deep in their own territory. So 10 percent of the time that a team went for short yardage, it turned into something positive. The other 90 percent of the time, it didn't produce anything positive, unless taking time off the clock was important at that point in the game.

What happened if a team went for short yardage and didn't make it? John Miller's records show that if a team was in its own territory or no closer than the opponent's 40–yard line, the team that took over scored or tried a field goal 40 percent of the time. The other 60 percent of the time, they either turned the ball back deep into their opponent's territory or punted. When we talked about these findings, John concluded that unless a team was a couple of scores behind or was trying to reverse the game's momentum, the odds were strongly against going for the short yardage. An exception might be when a team would be close enough to try a field goal if it could pick up one more first down.

This, of course, is an informal survey and John didn't pretend that it was scientific. Also, the analysis doesn't attempt to assess the effect of penalties or what happened in the remainder of the game.

Some Penn State fans probably remember the 1967 Gator Bowl 17–17 tie with Florida State during Joe Paterno's second year as head coach. With Penn State ahead 17–0 in the third quarter, we tried for a first down in a short yardage situation to move into Florida State territory. The Lions came up short and Florida State, given new life, scored two touchdowns in the third quarter and kicked a field goal in the fourth quarter to tie the game. Penn State had called a time out right before the decision to go for the short yardage first down. We'll never know whether Joe made the decision or allowed his players to talk him into it. Either way, it turned the game around and turned a probable bowl win into a tie. You would have to say that the decision that backfired gave Florida State a life; you could almost feel the change in momentum.

It is pure speculation, of course, but would Joe Paterno elect to go for the first down today, given identical circumstances? You might find a clue in something that Joe said during a Quarterback Club luncheon in 1993. The game with Florida State was in his second year as head coach; when he spoke at the luncheon it was during his 27th year in the job. Someone in the audience asked Joe about a decision he had made during the previous week's game. Joe is not often asked about strategy. (I think you should know that in the question–and–answer session when I put the questions to Joe at those luncheons, it is my unbreakable rule never to second–guess the coach if his team lost the game we are talking about. I rarely second–guess him in any case, but if I do ask a question about decisions or strategy, it is always after a game the Lions have won. I think it's a cheap shot and not fair to ask a coach to justify his decisions if the game was lost. If the game was a win, the coach can talk about it more easily and always has the option of replying, "Well, we did *win* the game.")

In this instance, when a question about a decision Joe had made came from the audience, Joe said something like, "That was an easy decision to make. You know, I get paid a nice yearly salary, but I don't get paid that money to make easy decisions. For example, I don't get paid my salary to decide to punt the ball when we are in our own territory or just inside the 50 and ahead in the game. That's a really easy decision. I get paid to make tough decisions…a decision to go for one point or two points after a late–game touchdown. We're one point behind—go for one and a probable tie or go for two points and a possible win or possible loss. Let's say the game is early in the season and you won't know the effect of your decision until the end of the season when you might have made a decision that cost you a championship or an invitation to an attractive bowl game. If I made the right decision, I will have earned my salary. If I made the wrong one…."

Scouting Pays Off

The Penn State–Syracuse football games were always tough, for both the Lions and the Orange. It seemed to be a matter of styles, in addition to the intense rivalry. Penn State always stressed defense, both during the time of Coach Rip Engle and under Joe

Paterno, with the notable exception of the great 1982 team when the Lions won the national championship with Todd Blackledge at quarterback, and the 1994 team with Kerry Collins at quarterback, when Penn State was undefeated through 12 games. Syracuse always stressed ball control with their unbalanced offensive line set and with their trademark big tackles and strong inside-running fullbacks. Touchdowns never seemed to come easily when these two teams got together.

Syracuse had defeated Penn State three times in a row—1964, 1965, and 1966. Usually the assistant coach who scouts a team before its game with Penn State is responsible for the Lions' game plan. Although he was now head coach, Joe Paterno reportedly decided to make the 1967 Syracuse game almost a personal crusade and, with the help of the scouting reports, took responsibility for putting together the game plan to try to beat Syracuse. Joe's decision must have been a good one—the Lions defeated the Orange 29-20. Joe always credited the assistant coach who had been responsible for a particular opponent. Although he had taken on this game as a personal project, Joe seemed reluctant to take the credit. At the post–game press conference, he indicated that the win was due to the work of his staff and team, which had played so hard. Gordon White of the *New York Times* apparently had heard that Joe had personally developed the game plan and raised the issue at the press conference. After dodging the question, with White pursuing it, Joe finally admitted that he did, indeed, develop the game plan but insisted he wouldn't take personal credit for the win.

Why tell this story? As an assistant coach, Joe Paterno had a reputation for developing outstanding game plans. As a head coach, his game week schedule included many time–consuming things, but he apparently put all that on hold and proved he hadn't forgotten his game–planning skills. Perhaps another game plan also would have resulted in a win. We'll never know. But we do know that this one did!

Fifteen years later, Penn State played a very important game when scouting and the resultant game plan won not only the game but also a national championship.

Penn State was matched against the Miami Hurricanes in a

Fiesta Bowl game that would determine the national championship for the 1986 season. That game received as much pre–game attention as any bowl game ever played. It was the game that saw the Miami team arrive at the game site in combat uniforms, declaring themselves to be "ready for combat" as they descended from the plane. There were other pre–game incidents, especially the Miami walkout from a luncheon honoring both teams, because of what the Hurricanes had perceived as some slight. As game day approached, it had taken on aspects of a grudge match, at least for the 'Canes.

With the arrival of the computer age and the switch from old–fashioned film to videotape, pre–game preparation of a team at the level of Penn State has changed dramatically. Years ago, scouting mainly depended on coaches sitting in the press box at a future opponent's game and noting their defensive formations, their offensive sets and tendencies, and strengths and weaknesses of individual personnel. These scouting reports were put together with what the team saw on the game films supplied by the opponent, and a final game plan was developed.

For the past several years, however, live scouting of an opponent has been prohibited; instead, the rules call for an exchange of game videotapes, according to a set calendar.

The technology now employed by the top teams would astound the average fan. A computer programs the videotapes of an opponent's game and teams have almost limitless ways to study the opponent. They can separate the game video by offensive and defensive plays. They can break down the offensive plays into pass plays and running plays, plays in which the quarterback sprinted out or dropped back into the pocket, sprint–out draws or straight draws, screen passes to wideouts or to the backs, or any other category of offensive plays the coaches want to examine.

The computer can separate defensive plays by the various defensive sets a team uses and the down and distance when a certain defense is called, how the linebackers play the run or the pass, how deep the defensive backs play in certain situations, all the punt returns a team made during the game, and any other information a coaching staff desires or has time to watch and learn from. All that is from technology. How a team uses the information that technology provides in making a game plan comes from coaching.

When a team plays a bowl game, it has videos of the games their opponents played during the regular season. Since teams usually have more than a month between the last regular season game and the bowl game, preparation of that game plan can become more of a detailed exercise than for a regular season game, for which there is only a matter of days to get ready.

When Penn State played Miami in 1986, there were many who believed the Lions were overmatched. Miami was an especially well–balanced team, strong defensively with many outstanding players and a fine offense with strong and quick backs and an outstanding quarterback in Vinny Testaverde. Penn State came into the game with a 12–0 record and a team that was reasonably balanced between offense and defense, with the defense probably rated higher than offense, but without the highly touted personnel to match those that Miami put on the field. If you didn't know that Penn State won the game and had to guess the winner from the game's statistics, you would have been misled:

· Penn State had 8 first downs, Miami 22;
· Penn State passed for 53 yards, Miami passed for 285;
· Penn State ran for 109 yards, Miami ran for 160;
· Penn State completed 5 passes, Miami completed 26;
· Penn State was 5 for 16 passing, Miami was 26 for 50.

Penn State probably could not have won the game without two other meaningful statistics: the Lions intercepted Testaverde five times and sacked him four times.

The Lions' fourth interception was by linebacker Shane Conlan, who ran the ball to the Miami three–yard line and set up Penn State's final touchdown. The fifth interception was late in the game with Miami at the Penn State 13–yard line. Pete Giftopolous intercepted at the goal line and Miami lost its chance to win the game. These two statistics are evidence of a masterful scouting job and game plan by the Lions' coaching staff, and the win gave Penn State its second national championship in five years. How did the game plan, in addition to the hard work and intensive effort by the team, give Penn State the win?

When Penn State dissected all of Miami's plays for the season, one thing stood out and Joe Paterno and his staff jumped right on it. Even with two fine running backs in Alonzo Highsmith and Mel Bratton, Miami was, by far, a passing team. Whenever the Hurricanes needed yards, Testaverde usually passed for them. This obviously meant that Penn State had to shut him down if they were going to win. Further examination of the Miami game videos showed that Testaverde rarely called a running play three times in a row. Even if two running plays picked up good yardage, Miami threw on third down and Testaverde, more often than not, got a completion, despite his tendency to look directly at his intended receiver.

Joe Paterno and Jerry Sandusky, his defensive coordinator, decided to put as many people as possible in the defensive backfield and play two or three people on the defensive front to give Testaverde a look he probably hadn't seen all season long.

In addition, the strategy called for big hits on the receivers when Testaverde completed a throw. As the game wore on, the strategy began to pay off, and it seemed that the punishment meted out by the Lions' secondary resulted in enough dropped passes or timid pass routes to account for a Miami completion rate of 26 out of 50, far below their season average.

The strategy had another effect. The Miami offensive line seemed confused at times and unsure of their blocking assignments. With only two or three Penn State defenders on the line of scrimmage, they often weren't playing with someone across from them, and if Penn State was going to change up and blitz, the Miami offensive line wasn't sure where the rush would come from. The result was the four Penn State sacks to go along with the five interceptions.

The game remained close, and with the Lions leading 14-10 with the clock running down, everyone watching knew that Miami would somehow launch a final drive and move the ball against the Lions. Miami changed its pattern as the drive began. They went to a running game with Alonzo Highsmith doing most of the damage, and he began to pick up big chunks of yards on every carry.

On the sidelines, as Joe Paterno explained later, it appeared that Miami had decided to give up throwing against the loose Penn State defense and instead run the ball against the two or three men up front. Joe and Jerry kept talking it over on the sidelines. "Will Miami keep running the ball and if they do should we get out of this defense? If we go to a standard defense, can we stop Testaverde from throwing again?"

By this time, Miami had moved nearly to the Penn State 10–yard line and had a new set of downs coming up. If they scored, the game was about over and the great Penn State defensive effort would have been wasted. Joe and Jerry kept trying to outguess the Miami coach, Jimmy Johnson. Should they stay in their pass defense? If they did, and Miami decided to run the ball, they felt certain that the defense they were in wouldn't stop the Hurricanes.

The first play saw Miami throw a short pass out to the right flat for a small gain. On the next play, Testaverde was sacked at the 13 as he dropped back to pass. Third down was an incomplete pass. Now everything was on the line for one more play. Would Miami throw or try to run it in? We were into a big and important guessing game, the kind of decision for which the coaches are paid their salary.

As Joe told it later, the Penn State coaches were fairly sure that Miami could run against their defense if they decided to call a run on fourth down. They might call a quarterback draw, or a draw to Highsmith, or a quick pitch to Bratton, or any of a number of possible running plays. If Penn State changed defense and came forward to stop the run, could they keep Testaverde from successfully throwing into the end zone? He had thrown for at least one touchdown pass in every game that year, but so far had been shut out against the Lions.

Joe guessed that Miami would go with its strength, as they had all season long. He guessed that Testaverde could see the post–game news stories in his mind: "Testaverde drove his team down the field and on the fourth down threw an end–zone touchdown to win the game and the national championship." So Penn State stayed in their defense and it looked like every Lion was on the goal line or crowded into the end zone. Testaverde took a short drop back, had lots of time to throw, and then threw the ball directly to Penn State's Pete Giftopoulos, who was standing almost on the goal line. Pete cradled the ball in his stomach, ran the ball out just past the five–yard line, and then dropped down. A couple of plays later, the game was over and Penn State had won the 1986 national championship.

Who's On Your "Best" List?

Sports fans constantly argue over who is or was the best. Every so often a sportswriter or broadcaster will try to settle the argument by asking fans to nominate their all–star team. On our campus there often are discussions about who was the most outstanding player in his position for the Lions. Picking an all–time best player at any position is not an easy task.

From season to season, the rules change. Some players played two–platoon football, while others played both offense and defense. In addition, memories fade and sometimes you are likely to vote for a more recent player.

Penn State has had more than its share of outstanding football players at virtually every position and compares favorably to most schools in the total number of All–America nominees through the years. The most memorable Penn State player I've ever seen didn't make a single All–America team. He not only is the most memorable player I ever saw with the Lions, I think he is as good a football player as I ever saw play for anyone.

I have always believed that Lenny Moore did not get his share of recognition while he was at Penn State because not enough people saw him play. Those were the early days of television (1953 to 1955), before the pro draft, and the big intersectional and bowl games didn't command the attention they do today. Certainly the media was not as far–reaching as it is today. I also believe that Lenny made things look so easy that people didn't realize how good an athlete he really was.

There is still another big, big reason that kept Lenny from earning the college reputation he deserved—they hardly ever threw him the ball. In his three varsity years at Penn State (back then, freshmen were ineligible for varsity play), he gained a total of only <u>89 receiving yards</u>. I don't mean that he caught 89 passes, I mean that he gained only 89 yards from catching a pass and then running with it. I'm not sure how many passes they threw to Lenny but knowing the kind of athlete he was, it couldn't have been very many. The story around campus at that time was that Lenny had "small hands" and that Lenny "couldn't catch the ball very well." I like to believe that the story is apocryphal and that no one really ever said or believed that. I say that in view of the fact that Lenny Moore is fourth on the all–time Penn State punt return list and ninth on the all–time kickoff return list. As far as I know, even back in the early '50s you had to catch a punt or kickoff before you could run with the ball!

If you are ever inclined to question whether the best known college players go on to the most successful careers in the professional leagues, consider these Lenny Moore NFL career statistics:

· Played 12 seasons
· Totaled 11,000 offensive yards in his career
· Named to the All–Pro team five times
· Played in seven All-Star games
· Established an NFL record by scoring in 18 consecutive games
· Caught 50 passes in 1958 (not bad for a guy with bad hands!)
· Fourth in the NFL with 113 touchdowns
· Member of the NFL Hall of Fame

There may be other players with those statistics, but I'm sure there aren't many.

There are two Lenny Moore stories that have stayed with me all these years. One concerns Jack Sherry, who was the captain and one of the stars of the 1954 basketball team, the only Penn State team to reach the NCAA Final Four.

Jack and I have exchanged many stories over the years, and Jack never minds telling this one on himself. Many people have forgotten that Jack was one of the few two–sport athletes, playing end on the Penn State football team.

When Lenny Moore was still a freshman, one year away from playing varsity ball, everyone knew that he was an outstanding prospect, and we couldn't wait to see him run against the varsity in spring practice scrimmages prior to his sophomore year. I remind you that this was before two–platoon football, and that Lenny carried a great reputation not only as a running back, but also as an outstanding defensive safety.

As Jack tells the story, during one of the early scrimmages he lined up and decided to test Lenny. Jack says he ran a pattern at Lenny, put on a fake or two, and found himself running free! He couldn't believe how easily Lenny went for the fake. On the next play he decided to put a different move on Lenny, and again he found Lenny going for the fake and Jack was free again.

Jack went to the huddle and told the quarterback, "This Moore isn't much. I put two fakes on him and he bit both times and I was wide open. I'm going to make an inside move on him and I bet I'll be wide open to the sideline." They broke the huddle with Jack split out to the right. Jack had a long, loping stride and he ran right at Lenny, gave him an inside head fake, and then cut to the sideline.

As Jack tells it, he was wide open and Lenny was nowhere to

Penn State All-American Dave Robinson, Number 89, leads All-American Roger Kochman through a right end sweep. Note the ballet-like timing and form of both players.

be seen. The ball came and, as it floated down and Jack reached for it, all of a sudden, "Here came a pair of hands out of nowhere. It was Lenny!"

Jack said that Lenny never even made contact with him, snatched the ball, and was gone in the other direction with the easiest interception that Jack ever saw. In the locker room later, Lenny came over to Jack and said, "Hey, Sherry, don't feel bad. After I saw you run a couple of patterns, I knew I could intercept on you!"

Before his Penn State career was over, Lenny Moore would intercept on a lot of quarterbacks and receivers. He ranks tenth on the all–time Penn State interception list, in addition to his offensive records. Incidentally, Jack Sherry ranks fourth in one–season interceptions; he had eight in the 1952 season.

The other story about Lenny Moore doesn't even concern football, but it shows the kind of athlete Lenny was. In those days, the Penn State Athletic Department allowed the State College High School track team to use the college track facilities and equipment. At that time, the Penn State track occupied the space near the water tower and Nittany Lion Inn and circled the old Beaver Stadium.

Lenny Moore was not out for the track team and spring football practice was over for the year. I was standing talking with Yib Bolton, the high school track coach, when one of his broad jumpers came over and said, "Coach Bolton, I was beginning my jump the way you told me to and that guy down there wearing the sweat suit told me I was doing it all wrong." We looked and there was Lenny in an old sweat suit wearing sneakers instead of track shoes.

Bolton said to the young man, "That's Lenny Moore the football player and he isn't even on the track team. Don't listen to him!" The kid replied, "Coach, he told me he can jump over 22 feet." Bolton yelled to Lenny, "Hey, Moore, come on over here." As Lenny jogged over, Bolton asked, "Did you tell this fellow that you can jump 22 feet? I don't believe it."

Lenny replied, "Mr. Bolton, I haven't broad jumped in a long time. I didn't tell him I can jump 22 feet. I said I used to be able to jump 22 feet." "Well," said Bolton, "how many feet do you think you can jump now?" Lenny said, "About 22 feet." The coach said, "Okay, Lenny, I'll call your bluff. I'll bet you 10 Cokes to your one that you can't jump 22 feet."

We walked down to the jumping pit and marked off 22 feet and then the coach said, "I'll give you a break, Lenny, you get three jumps." Lenny replied, "That's okay, Mr. Bolton, one will be enough."

Down the runway he came (remember, he was wearing sneakers, not spikes) and cleared the mark with something to spare. We had just seen a highly respectable college jump by a jumper not in condition and wearing a sweat suit and sneakers. Lenny bounded out of the pit with a big smile on his face. Before we could say anything, Lenny started to run to Rec Hall, where he probably had his locker. As he did, he passed close to the high jump bar, which was set at 5'3" and, without even a run–up, jumped over the high jump bar, bounded out of the pit and yelled back to Bolton, "You still owe me only 10 Cokes, coach. That one's on the house!"

Lenny Moore might be not only the most memorable football player I ever saw up close, he might be the greatest athlete, period! I've wondered many times what would have happened if we could have put about 20 pounds on Lenny and found someone to teach him how to throw the discus and shot put and gotten him ready for the decathlon. The way he cleared the high jump bar, I think I could have taught him to pole vault myself.

My other nominee for the "Most Memorable Penn State Player I Ever Saw" award has to be Dave Robinson who, after an outstanding record at Penn State, was the number one draft choice of the Green Bay Packers in the 1963 NFL draft. As did Lenny Moore, Robinson played in the days of one–platoon football. While he made his reputation and four 1962 All–America teams as an end, he had a great career in the NFL as a linebacker.

There was nothing that Dave Robinson couldn't do on the football field. He was a quick and strong defensive end, caught 17 passes for 187 yards his senior year, and made what I think was the greatest defensive play I ever saw when we played Georgia Tech in the 1961 Gator Bowl. Playing defensive end at one point in the game, Dave ran through the first blocker, hurdled over the blockers protecting the Georgia Tech quarterback, grabbed the quarterback, causing him to fumble, and then recovered the fumble. I can't imagine a man as big as Robinson making a play calling for that much agility but he did, and also made dozens and dozens of other outstanding defensive plays through his varsity years. Robinson had an all–star career as a linebacker with the Packers. He was named All–NFL many times and played on two Super Bowl championship teams.

When the Quarterback Club invited Dave back to our annual affair to honor him with the Alumni Athlete Award, he gave one of the quickest and funniest opening lines I have ever heard as he accepted the award. At that time, Dave was a regional official with the Schlitz Brewing Company. Perhaps you remember the Schlitz advertising slogan, "If you're out of Schlitz, you're out of beer!" Dave began his acceptance speech with, "I understand that there is a rule that award recipients are not to use any commercial material to further their business associations. I understand why you have that rule, but I must tell you that, 'If you're out of Schlitz, I'm out of work.'"

When discussions about football begin, I am sometimes asked

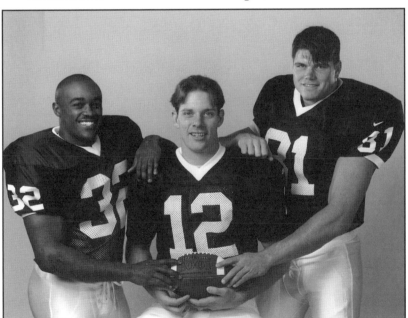

Penn State's 1994 team produced three first-round NFL draft picks: Ki-Jana Carter, Kerry Collins, and Kyle Brady.

my opinion of certain Penn State players I have seen play since I returned to campus in 1947. I am no expert on players or their skills and abilities. When I was in the radio business, our station subscribed to various news services, and we were often asked to vote on candidates for various All–America teams. I never voted because it seemed to me to be a little foolish to try and select the best 11 or 22 players in any given year, when so many hundreds of other players were probably just as outstanding.

After watching many, many Penn State games through the years, I have compiled a list, not necessarily of the best players, but of players I remember the most. These players stand out in my mind not only because of their outstanding play, but also because of their flair for the game or the way that they played.

I offer this list from my memories and with apologies to those fine players I may have missed:

Lenny Moore, Halfback
Dave Robinson, End*
Ted Kwalick, Tight End*
Dennis Onkotz, Linebacker*
Mike Reid, Tackle*
Charlie Pittman, Halfback*
Jack Ham, Linebacker*
Lydell Mitchell, Halfback*
Franco Harris, Fullback
John Cappelletti, Halfback*
Chris Bahr, Kicker*
Matt Bahr, Kicker*
Greg Buttle, Linebacker*
Bruce Clark, Tackle*
Matt Millen, Tackle*
Curt Warner, Halfback*

Kenny Jackson, Flanker*
Shane Conlan, Linebacker*
Steve Suhey, Guard*
Kyle Brady, End*
Lou Benfatti, Tackle*

Bobby Engram, Wide Receiver*
Ki–Jana Carter, Halfback*
Roosevelt Grier, Tackle
Richie Lucas, Quarterback*
Mike Munchack, Guard
Fran Rogel, Fullback
Mark Robinson, Safety*
Jeff Hartings, Guard*
Andre Johnson, Tackle
Bruce Bannon, Defensive End*
John Skorupan, Linebacker*
Randy Crowder, Tackle*
Tom Rafferty, Guard*
Chuck Fusina, Quarterback*
John Hufnagel, Quarterback*
Mike Hartenstine, Defensive End*
Keith Dorney, Tackle*
Andre Collins, Linebacker*
Bob Mitinger, End*
Roger Kochman, Halfback*
Steve Smear, Tackle

Glenn Ressler, Center/Guard
Dave Joyner, Tackle*
D.J. Dozier, Halfback*
Steve Wisniewski, Guard*
Blair Thomas, Halfback*
Darren Perry, Safety*

Kerry Collins, Quarterback*
O.J. McDuffie, Wide Receiver*
Todd Blackledge, Quarterback*
Sam Valentine, Guard*
Wally Triplett, Halfback
Matt Suhey, Halfback and Fullback
Andy Stynchula, Tackle
Neal Smith, Safety
Curtis Enis, Tailback*

Mike Zordich, Safety*
Sean Farrell, Guard*
John Bruno, Punter
Chuck Burkhart, Quarterback
Bob Campbell, Halfback
Chuck Drazenovich, Blocking Back
John Ebersole, Defensive End
Bill Lenkaitis, Center
Mark Markovich, Guard
Irv Pankey, Tackle
Charlie Zapiec, Linebacker*
Sam Tamburo, End*

Scott Radecic, Linebacker
Mickey Shuler, Tight End
*All–American ▪

2

Love at First Sight

I was orphaned when I was six years old. My mother and father died within six months of each other, leaving me with two brothers, ages 9 and 3.

The Orphan's Court judge refused to divide my brothers and me among various aunts and uncles, saying, "If there is someone who will take all three children, I will award them to you. If not, these boys will go to an orphanage."

My Uncle Morris, a fairly recent immigrant to this country, and Aunt Jenny had eight children already, seven of them living at home, but they stepped forward to take us in. This meant we would be part of a household of 12 people in a 3-1/2-bedroom house, with no car (Uncle Morris lived into his 80s and walked every inch of his life, never owning a car). The family income came from a small grocery store.

Although I didn't enroll as a freshman at Penn State until the fall of 1940, I had known that I belonged there for several years.

The high school I attended in Monessen, Pennsylvania, had fine athletic teams and, in addition, probably the best debating team in the state, year in and year out. I was a member of that team from 1936 to 1940, becoming a debater for an unusual reason. I was not especially interested in debating, but I definitely was interested in getting out of working 15 hours in Uncle Morris' butcher shop every Saturday. Beginning at 6 a.m., I scrubbed butcher blocks, hand delivered groceries, cleaned the inside of the meat cases, and cleaned chickens and ducks. I hated every minute of it.

Once I found out that the high school debating team traveled to other area schools for day–long tournaments practically every Saturday during the school year, I developed a sudden passion for debating. I tried out for the team and was selected. That meant, "So long, butcher shop!" I didn't know it at the time, but it also meant, "Hello, Penn State."

The state debating championships were held every spring at Penn State and in 1937 I saw that wonderful campus for the first time. Except for a trip in my cousin's car to visit relatives near Pittsburgh, I had hardly been out of Monessen. You can imagine the excitement of a trip to State College for a whole weekend. The president of the Phi Delta Theta fraternity was from Monessen and arranged for the boys on the team to stay at the fraternity house during the tournament. (Remember that 1937 was a De-pression year and the money saved on housing expenses undoubt-edly was important to the school budget.)

When I first saw the Phi Delta Theta house I was sure I was on a Hollywood movie set; the movies were the only place where I had seen such glamorous buildings with wonderful tall white columns. And that was only the beginning of our dream week-end.

Jack Economos, captain of the Penn State football team, and Stu Quailey, star of the baseball team, along with their girlfriends, took us to the Corner Room restaurant. Two things of note hap-pened that evening. First, I ate the first ham I had ever eaten in my life when all four of the "grown–ups" ordered a Ham à la Corner sandwich (a Corner Room tradition). There was no way I wasn't going to order what they ordered.

The second thing that happened was that every boy on our team fell in love with Jack Economos' girlfriend, including me. I can still recall her: a coed, at least a foot taller than me, her long blonde hair falling against her shoulders, wearing a yellow an-gora sweater (I had some on my sport jacket from sitting next to her in the booth and didn't brush it off for at least a week). You have to remember that she probably was 21 and I was only 15.

Our debating team returned to Penn State for the next three years and, while we didn't again stay in a fraternity house, I al-ready had fallen in love with the campus and each spring I re-solved that somehow I would be a Penn State student.

When I had been graduated from high school, the cashier of the bank that held the modest sum of money that my father had left me called me in and asked if I had any plans for further education. When I told him that I wanted to go to Penn State, he told me how much money was available and estimated it was only 50 or 60 percent of the funds that I would need.

I didn't hesitate for a minute, telling him that I would make up the difference somehow. He gave me the go–ahead to see if I could be accepted at Penn State. I did…I was…and that decision changed my life!

What's In a Name?

During a Quarterback Club banquet in 1981, I introduced Dr. John Oswald, the Penn State president at that time, to make his presentation.

"Thank you for the kind introduction, Milton," he said. And during his talk he referred to me as "Milton" several times. Now Milton is my given name, but I haven't been called anything but Mickey for the past 40 or 50 years.

When Dr. Oswald finished his comments, I said, "Dr. Oswald, I noticed that you used my Christian name, Milton, during your remarks." As I expected, this brought at least a smile from my friends, who know, of course, that I am Jewish. "I haven't used that name for many, many years. Would you like to know why I stopped using Milton?" Of course, he couldn't easily say no, and so I explained.

"Dr. Oswald," I said, "I was graduated from this university on a Thursday in May of 1943 and the next day I reported to the U.S. Marine Corps boot camp at Parris Island, South Carolina. When I had enlisted in the Marines in 1942, I entered a program that promised several things. First, they would allow us to graduate before we were called to active duty. Second, while officer candidates had always gone to Officer Candidate School in the Marines without going through boot camp, we would be the first group of potential officers to go through the course at Parris Island, just like the Marines who would be enlisted men under our command. Finally, unless we demonstrated a complete inability to deal with life in the Marines, we were promised that we would have a chance to go to Quantico and enter Officer Candidate School. They didn't promise us that we would be officers, but they did promise that we would get a chance to become Second Lieutenants in the United States Marine Corps. They did not indicate that we would enjoy Parris Island or Quantico, but they did keep their word that we would get our chance to be commissioned as officers.

"I boarded an old troop train in Pittsburgh, along with a couple of hundred other enlistees who also were headed for Parris Island. These were not college boys, like me, but were men who seemed to be from all sorts of backgrounds, including several young men wearing bib overalls. In light of what happened to me later, I wish I had been smart enough to wear bib overalls, too.

"We had a long, slow, and dirty trip south to Yamasee, South Carolina, where we stopped before boarding an old scow that would take us over to Parris Island. As soon as we piled out of the train, I saw my first real, live Marine Corps drill instructor, the famous D.I. Our drill instructor was a little man, perhaps 5'7", who looked like he carried about 165 pounds of muscle on his small frame. He wore one of the campaign hats that date way back in Marine Corps history. He had a sweat–stained khaki shirt, a whistle around his neck, and a Ka–Bar fighting knife attached to his belt.

"At this point, Dr. Oswald, I should tell you how I was dressed. Remember, I had left the fraternity house and campus just a couple of days ago and I must have forgotten where I was going. I wore a seersucker sport jacket, a blue button–down shirt, a black knit necktie, gray flannel trousers and, believe it or not, black–and–white saddle shoes. I looked perfectly dressed to entertain some sorority girls at a fraternity Sunday afternoon tea.

"Corporal Johnson, our D.I., lined us up in a single line alongside the train. The dust was so deep it almost reached to the top of my shoes and made my maroon brushed wool socks very dusty. Corporal Johnson bellowed, 'Alright you men, I am going to stand in front of each of you and I want you to sing out, in a loud voice, your name and where you are from and why you joined the Marines.'

"I was perhaps the 20th man in line. When Corporal Johnson reached me he stepped back and said, 'Well, well, well, look who's here—Mr. College Humor!' That's when I wished that I was wearing bib overalls. He then unstrapped his Ka–Bar fighting knife, reached out and cut off my black knit tie right below the knot. The two ends fell into the dust and I instinctively looked down. The drill instructor put the tip of the knife right against the end of my nose.

"He said, 'Boy, if you move your eyes one more time in this Marine Corps without my permission, I am going to cut your nose in half. Now tell me your name, where you are from, and why you joined the Marines.'"

I then turned to Dr. Oswald and asked, "Do you think I was going to say 'My name is Milton Bergstein, sir'? I said in what I thought was a loud and clear voice, but was probably more like a scared squeak, 'My name is Spike Bergstein, sir.' And, Dr. Oswald, I haven't used the name Milton since."

Sergeant Tommy Loughran

After I received my officer's commission in the Marine Corps, I was sent to the Philadelphia Navy Yard to join a large guard company. The big battleship USS Wisconsin was being built there and she was being closely guarded for fear that someone would try to sabotage the multi–million dollar battleship.

In addition to my duties with the guard company, I was the athletic officer and coached the baseball and basketball teams. The day I reported to duty, I was summoned by the commanding officer, who informed me of my coaching assignment and told me that Tommy Loughran, former world light heavyweight boxing champion, had been assigned to the barracks as a sergeant and would be my assistant coach and trainer.

A boxing fan all my life, I knew all about Tommy and his record and looked forward to introducing myself to him at the gym. My time with Tommy was one of the really enjoyable periods in my life.

First, Tommy taught me to box, or at least he tried to. Tommy was well over 200 pounds and stood 6'3" or maybe even taller. In boxing shoes, if I am up on my toes, I can probably stretch to 5'9" or 5'10". When they list the vital statistics for two fighters on the sports pages or on television, they give the difference in reach in inches. Between Tommy and me, they would probably list it in feet.

At any rate, while he did teach me some useful boxing moves, he also showed me how an old "pro" handles himself in the ring. For example, every afternoon we boxed for three or four rounds. These were the rules—I would throw all the punches; Tommy would not throw a single punch. If I could hit him anywhere but on his arms, he would owe me a Coke for every blow I landed any place on his body, not below the belt, of course.

We must have boxed 50 or 60 times and I never, I mean *never*, won a single Coke. I not only couldn't hit him on his arms, I almost never hit him above the elbows. I did hit him once. The last time we boxed I hit him right smack in the middle of the chest. He said, "I owe you a Coke!" Neither of us smiled and I did not take the free Coke. He knew and I knew that there was no way I could have hit him unless he wanted to give me a final send–off to my next post. He would never admit it, I know, but I took it as an act of extreme compassion and kindness.

Philadelphia always was a great fight town that produced many champions and highly–ranked fighters. When Tommy and I were stationed there, we used to go to the Arena, a boxing hall in West Philadelphia. Everyone, of course, recognized Tommy, because he was a Philadelphian and had fought many important fights in his hometown. As a matter of fact, Tommy fought the semi–final on the famous Dempsey–Tunney fight that was held in Municipal (now Kennedy) Stadium in South Philadelphia. His opponent that night was Georges Carpentier, known as The Orchid Man, from France.

Whenever we went to the Arena, Tommy would get about $10 in quarters. As we walked up to the Arena, every ex–pro in Philadelphia stopped him, and there always seemed to be dozens. Almost all of them looked the same—cauliflowered ears, a nose obviously broken many times, scar tissues over the eyes, etc. They all called Tommy "Champ."

"Hey, Champ, can you spare a little change?" Or, "Hey, Champ, you look great. When's your next fight?" Some told him that they were back in training and thought they would get another shot soon. It was pathetic to see and hear. Tommy would always say something like, "Keep punching" or "One of these days your luck will turn." And, with that, he would hand them a couple of quarters. As we walked away, Tommy sort of apologized to me by saying he wished he could give them more. From then on, when Tommy stopped to pick up his supply of quarters, I also cashed a $10 bill and the ex–pros had two sources of income. I kind of got to like the routine because they soon began calling me "Champ," too.

Tommy had a famous trademark that was in evidence every time he climbed through the ropes. Every time the bell sounded ending a round, both fighters were <u>always</u> in Tommy's corner. That meant he simply sat down on his stool, while his opponent had to walk all the way across the canvas to sit on his stool.

Tommy was a masterful boxer. Some old boxing fans will tell you that while Tommy was not a heavy hitter, there never has been a big man who could box as well or maneuver his opponent around the ring as well. Tommy told me how he managed to always end the rounds in his own corner. Everything he did in training he did with a phonograph record playing in the background, and he had his manager find a supply of records that lasted exactly three minutes. So, whether he was sparring or shadow boxing or skipping rope, he always did it with a three–minute record playing. It was amazing. We could be having a conversation and Tommy would say, "I'll stop this conversation in exactly three minutes and I won't look at my watch." He would say "stop!" and never was more than two or three seconds off the three–minute mark.

He told me he adopted this as a gimmick initially, but then began to notice that it got under his opponents' skin. Some of them, while the referee was giving his instructions before the bout, would say, "You're not going to make me walk across the ring the way you do everyone else." Tommy told me that was the little edge he was looking for. The last 30 seconds or so the other guy seemed to have his mind more on where they were in the ring than on Tommy. Tommy told me that this little break in concentration gave him openings he never would have gotten without the three–minute gimmick, and he used it until he hung up his gloves.

Tommy taught me another interesting lesson. When we were at the fights, especially the amateur bouts when neither he nor I knew one fighter from the other, we used to bet a quarter on each bout. We waited until the fighters took off their robes and then took turns picking the fighter we thought would win the bout. I would win an occasional bet, but it was uncanny how many more fights Tommy picked correctly without seeing the boxers throw a single punch or even dance around the ring.

After beating me fight card after fight card, Tommy finally let me in on his secret. He said, "There are three rules you want to follow when you know nothing about a fighter or his record. First, never bet on a fighter with square shoulders. Those guys can never punch. They might be able to box well, but because of the position of their shoulders and the absence of muscle from the shoulder to the neck, they can never punch hard. So don't bet on them. Second, always bet against a guy with a narrow chin. Those guys usually have a narrow face. You almost never see a guy with a narrow jaw who has a heavy neck. Skinny–necked guys can't take a punch and if they are in there with a puncher, they almost never finish the fight. The first real shot they take, their legs turn to spaghetti. Third rule, always bet on a bowlegged fighter. Because of their legs, they usually fight with their feet well apart. Bowlegged guys never fight up on their toes, they have a good solid base, and they usually fight flatfooted. That means they can't move very well because they shuffle instead of dance, but they fight from a good solid base and they can always hit hard. Once a strong, bowlegged guy hits you, it usually means you're gone."

When I returned to State College and went into radio, college boxing was a major sport and I broadcast all of Penn State's dual meets as well as the Eastern Intercollegiate Tournament each year. If Penn State had any entrants in the tournament, and they usually did, we did blow–by–blow broadcasts of the NCAA national championships.

Other than the eastern fighters whom I saw year after year, I had never seen the fighters whose bouts I broadcast. So I would play the same game with the other announcer that Tommy played with me. But the other guy didn't know about the square shoulders, the narrow jaw, and the bow legs. The result: I won lots of quarters and developed an undeserved reputation for knowing a lot about boxing because I called so many winners before the first bell sounded.

I Wish I Knew Their Names

One thing I know for certain: If I ever have to go into combat again, I want to do it as a United States Marine. Unless you have been through Marine Corps training, you can't appreciate the thoroughness of the preparation you receive. You can't appreciate the quality of the officers and you can't imagine the length to which the leaders go to make sure that you are personally prepared to lead your men and are ready to do your job, whatever it may be.

As thorough as the preparation for combat is, however, you cannot be prepared for the awful noise of combat, the smoke and fire, the sound of shells rocketing overhead, the explosion of artillery and mortars, the closeness of air support and, above all else, the confusion of troops and materiel being dumped on a beach. Most of all, how can you prepare young men for the fear that they feel and the numbing shock of seeing body parts and dead bodies?

When you are in such a situation, you realize that, because of your training, you are able to perform your job, whatever it is, regardless of your fear. I suspect that men in combat, especially for the first time, are in some sort of a state of shock. It isn't until much later, after you have been wounded and evacuated or the fighting is all over, that you realize where you have been and what you have seen. I think this kind of shock insulates you from the sight of the dead and wounded—a sight that you never saw before and hope you never see again. And when the shock wears off much later, you know and understand what it means to shoot and be shot at, to see the dead and dying, and to know, probably for the first time, what war is all about and how awful it is.

I wasn't on Green Beach at Iwo Jima very long, but during the few hours I spent there after I was wounded by mortar shell fragments in my arms and legs, two men earned my respect for their bravery and courage. I had never seen either of them before, and to my knowledge I never have seen them since. I wish I knew their names so I could find them and thank them.

There were dozens of men who had been wounded and were lying on the sand until the fighting and firing let up and someone, we hoped, would come and help evacuate us to one of the ships lying offshore. We were near the foot of Mt. Suribachi and the artillery and mortar fire were very heavy. Because the Japanese had control of the high ground, they continued to fire onto the beach where, because there were so many men and so much equipment that had arrived with them, every time they fired they were sure to hit one or more men or damage one or more pieces of equipment.

We were under fire for several hours before a man came crawling down the beach to us. I have no idea who he was, but I can still see his long red mustache and his wild red beard. I don't know why, but I have the impression, probably because of his age, that he was a Seabee rather than a Marine. He began to drag

Mickey Bergstein and other veterans of the 28th Regiment, Fifth Marines, who were involved in the raising of the U.S. flag at Iwo Jima, attended the 10th reunion commemorating that event.

the wounded one–by–one toward the shoreline a couple of hundred yards away (although it seemed like a couple of miles). During most of the time that we lay on the beach, several of our landing craft attempted to land to evacuate the wounded.

Each of these small landing craft flew the international Red Cross flag that, under the rules of war, was supposed to declare them off–limits for firing. I say "supposed to" because I saw craft after craft take a hit from the Japanese gun positions, and I only saw one landing craft successfully load wounded aboard and get off the beach without being destroyed by enemy fire.

The man with the red beard seemed oblivious to the explosions landing all around him. He seemed determined to get as many wounded as possible off the beach, and he methodically continued to gather the wounded. When he came to me, he grabbed my dungaree pant leg in his big fist and literally dragged me down the sand and sort of rolled me onto a pile of men he had already loaded on board.

I don't know how many men he helped get off the beach, and I don't know if he survived all the fire around him, but I do know that I would never have believed that a man could carry out his assignment under fire with such single–minded purpose and bravery. Perhaps it wasn't even an assignment. Perhaps it was simply that he saw something that needed to be done and went about doing it. I wish that I knew who he was and where I could find him. I would like to thank him for all of us he saved on Green Beach at Iwo Jima.

The second "man" I want to tell you about was probably only 18 or 19 years old. He was the coxswain of the landing craft and his job was to get us to one of the vessels anchored offshore where we could receive medical attention. After we were loaded into the boat, someone on the beach with a battery–powered bullhorn yelled to the young coxswain, "Get this craft off the beach!"

The young sailor stood up and yelled back, "I'm not leaving until this craft is full to the top. There are wounded men lying up there on the beach and if I don't get them out of here, they're going to die."

I must admit that this was not good news for those of us already in the boat although when I thought about it later, I realized he was taking as much of a chance with his own life as he was with ours. While we were on the shore, the shells continued to fall all around the landing craft. We could hear them splashing uncomfortably close to our boat and a couple of others that were being loaded with wounded.

At any moment, a shell might have landed in our small craft. And if it had, everyone would have been blown away, including the young coxswain. So, while we kept our fingers crossed and, I suspect, did lots of praying, he didn't put the craft in reverse to back it off the beach until another dozen or so men had been thrown on board.

Late each afternoon, when darkness wasn't too far away, all of our ships hoisted anchor and went further out to sea to what was called the "outer anchorage." The reason for this was that Japanese swimmers would swim out after dark and place a magnetic mine at the water line of any craft they could reach. The exploding mine blew a hole right at the water line that, if serious enough, disabled the vessel for further use. So they took all the boats far enough off-shore that the swimmers could not reach them to attach their mines.

Our young coxswain went in search of a ship to take our wounded from his small landing craft. He went alongside an LST that was getting ready to pull up its anchor and head for the outer anchorage. An officer with a bullhorn called down, "Stand away with your boat. We are ready to get under way to move to the outer anchorage."

Our pilot called back, "I have severely wounded men on board and if you have a doctor aboard, can't he come down the ladder and look at them?" The officer on the LST called back, "Repeat. Stand away. We must get under way and have no time to offer medical attention." As I've said, our "boat driver" was a very young man and could not have had any meaningful rank. Almost any other low–ranking enlisted man would have replied, "Aye, aye, sir. We will stand away immediately." But not our driver. He yelled back to the officer at the rail of the LST, "Sir, no disrespect intended, but I have men here who are going to die if they don't get medical attention."

Back from the officer at the rail, "I repeat, stand away immediately."

"Sir, I have the number of the LST. What is your name? If any of these men die during the night, I am going to report you to proper authorities." Long silence from the officer on the LST. Then, "Hold fast. We are sending down a doctor who wants to examine all stomach and head wounds." They lowered a chain Jacob's ladder and a Navy doctor came down and looked through our casualties. He managed to transfer the most severely wounded to the LST and told us that while the rest of us certainly needed medical attention, our wounds were not so severe that we would not survive the night.

After the transfer of the wounded, we began the longest night of my life. I have no idea what time it was, but it was just beginning to get dark. All the bigger craft had moved or were in the process of moving to the outer anchorage. The only ones left were several landing craft carrying wounded men that had no place to go. So we began long, slow circles that kept up all night. We were lying on top of each other almost like a cord of wood that had been dumped off the back of someone's pickup truck in a driveway.

The shock of our wounds and the rolling motion of the landing craft began to take their toll. The longer we circled, the sicker most of us became. It wasn't a matter of leaning over the side to relieve yourself. As one of those aboard said later in making his report to an officer of the ship that eventually took us, "You threw up where you lay. And if it happened to be on one of your buddies, he understood because he probably had just finished throwing up on someone else."

With the morning, the bigger ships moved back toward the beach and after inquiring stops at a couple of troop ships, our coxswain found a troop carrier with two doctors aboard who agreed to take us. They sent down a flat board, placed us one at a time in a wire basket, and hauled us aboard. If you wonder why we didn't end up on a hospital ship with the personnel and equipment and space to take care of the wounded, there is a simple answer. Our higher–ups had indicated to us that Iwo Jima didn't appear to be a particularly difficult landing or battle.

The U.S. Air Force apparently had bombed the island for about

72 days and U.S. Navy forces had blasted it for 72 hours. This information had been given to us in various briefings. As a result, it did not appear that there would be a large number of casualties and so only a small number of hospital ships would be needed.

When it turned out that all of the intelligence estimates of the strength of the defending Japanese were way off the mark, a great number of ships that had been used to bring the troops to the island had to be turned into mini–hospitals to take care of the large number of casualties. Our particular ship carried only two doctors, and one of them told me that there were some 550 patients who needed some sort of attention on the ship. The doctors appeared to work night and day and, while I don't know if they received any special recognition, I think that they deserved the highest commendation for their work.

Time Stands Still on the Troop Ship

It's hard for me to explain where and how we were quartered on the troop ships. Below decks there were several holds that contained the simplest of cots hung from upright supports stacked five or six deep. The cots were simply pieces of canvas stretched between pipes. Even though it was not the most luxurious way to take an ocean voyage, it was manageable on the way to our landing at Iwo Jima. The men were all fit and could leave the dark holds where they slept on the cots and spend their days on deck in the fresh air and sunshine.

But being confined in a dark hold on a canvas bunk all day and night for a couple of weeks was a different matter. Our area was about four levels below the main deck and was far forward, almost in the ship's bow. There was practically no light since we were below the water line and there were no portholes to open for light or air. There were a few very small blue bulbs that gave enough light for those who were ambulatory and not depending on a bedpan to make their way to the bathroom.

The entire time I was confined to the cot in the hold, time stood still. I could not tell daytime from nighttime. I couldn't even read the face on my watch, so I had no idea what time it was or whether it was daylight or darkness. Further, since it made absolutely no difference, I had no idea what day it was. Why should it matter? I can tell you, without exaggeration, that time literally stood still.

If you were to offer me $1 million or more, I could not tell you how many days we were on the troop ship. But I *can* tell you of three Marines on that ship—one to whom I shall be eternally grateful, one who made me laugh the only time I laughed during that entire voyage, and one who made me so disgusted that I had to fight nausea in my narrow bunk.

First, let me tell you about my Good Samaritan. Anyone who has been in combat and been wounded and loaded onto a ship with other wounded will tell you that there is one very important thing that every wounded man does—cover the entire ship if you are ambulatory, all decks from bow to stern, to ask everyone if they know what happened to your friends once the landing had been made. I can't tell you how isolated you feel not knowing if your men and fellow officers and friends are alive, wounded, or dead.

In the dark of the hold one day, I heard someone ask, "Is there anyone here from the 2nd Battalion, 28th Marines?" That was my battalion and I called out, "Over here. I'm from Fox Company of the 2nd Battalion."

The young Marine who emerged from the darkness was from E Company. I recognized him, but his name wasn't familiar to me. He had suffered a shoulder wound and his arm was elevated in a cast, but he was able to walk around. "Lieutenant," he said, "I don't know where you are wounded or if you can move around, but if I help you can you manage to get up on deck and sit in the fresh air instead of here in the hold?" I sure was going to try so I said, "My left leg has a hole in it and my right shoulder has some shrapnel in it. But if you are able to get me up the ladders to the deck with your bad arm, I sure would be grateful."

We decided to give it a try and must have been quite a sight. I went up three steep ladders one step at a time sitting on my rear, while the Marine from Company E pulled me from under my good arm.

When we got to the deck, we both were drenched in sweat and exhausted. But what a wonderful feeling to breathe air instead of the stench of blood–soaked casts, dried bloody bandages, and all of the other smells of unwashed men who lay in their bunks day and night and perspired.

Every morning after that my friend came down and dragged me up the steps to the deck.

He somehow found a pillow for me to put between my rear end and the hard metal deck. We sat there all day, every day. He found a couple of paperback books for us to read and managed to get some mess gear and stood in line to get us something to eat. I use the word "eat" in a different sense. I really mean that he got us something to force down our throats because I knew that it would be dangerous to go a long time with no food, although I rarely was hungry during the entire trip. I have forgotten what he and I talked about all day, except when we talked about his major concern.

When we were in Hawaii on our way to Iwo Jima, he and some of his buddies had gotten tattoos. His was a Marine English bulldog wearing a steel helmet, and it was a big one. It turned out that his family members were people of some social standing, and all that he was concerned about was what his mother would say when he showed up at the country club with his tattoo. In some circles, tattoos have become more acceptable in recent years, but 45 years ago they were almost confined to soldiers of fortune and roughnecks.

He told me that even if his mother threatened to disown him or tried to have the tattoo removed by plastic surgery, he would never give it up. He said he would always keep it in memory of his Marine Corps friendships or, in the event that one of his tattoo partners hadn't made it through the battle for Iwo Jima, as a memorial. I haven't heard of or seen him for more than 50 years, but I sure would like to see him to thank him for dragging me out of the hell–hole every day. If I see him and he still has his tattoo, I think I'll get one to help me remember what he did for me.

The food on the ship was indescribably bad, and although I wasn't hungry, I found myself dreaming about things that I wanted to eat after I got home. I dreamed about everything from a corned beef sandwich to donuts to apple pie to chicken soup to every other delicious food I had ever enjoyed.

One day (or night, since I couldn't tell the difference in the dark hold), I heard a voice call out, "Anyone here from western Pennsylvania?" I said, "I'm from Monessen, right near Pittsburgh." It was a sailor from the ship's company who had asked for someone from my home area. He said that he had a small ice cream freezer and from time to time, when he could get the ingredients, he would make a small batch of ice cream. He said that he wished he could give some to everyone, but didn't have enough for that. "Since I'm from near Pittsburgh, too, I thought I would give some to someone who lives near where I do."

With that he scooped out some chocolate ice cream and put it into a big tin cup. What ecstasy! I just nibbled at it because I wanted the ice cream to last forever. The sailor asked me for a favor. He said that his older sister, who lived in Pittsburgh, had raised him, and he gave me her name and telephone number and asked if I would call her when I got ashore and could find a phone. All he wanted me to tell her was that he was okay and that he would write to her when the mail boat came by again.

When I had been lying on the beach, a wounded young man had been right next to me. While his wound wasn't life threatening, he was in agony. It seemed that a piece of shrapnel had hit him in the rear end while he was lying face down on the beach and had sliced one of the cheeks of his buttocks almost in half. The wound ran the length of the cheek and must have dug a furrow almost three or four inches deep.

I don't know how it happened, but that young man ended up on the cot right next to mine. He watched me eating the ice cream and I knew that it would taste at least as good to him as it did to me. I offered him part of my ice cream and he said he was going to hold it in his mouth as long as he could.

Because there were so many wounded men aboard and so few medical corpsmen, they had recruited motor machinists, cooks, electricians, and anyone else they could spare to perform simple medical duties. One of their jobs was to go through all the holds with a clipboard and record everyone's temperature. I assume they wanted to know our temperatures because a high one might give a clue to a serious infection.

When the motor machinist came to the man next to me, he

stuck the thermometer in his mouth. What he didn't know, of course, was that the man was holding a mouthful of ice cream. I stuck my head under the pillow to keep from laughing. After a short time, the machinist took out the thermometer, turned his flashlight on it and told his partner who was recording the temperatures that the man's temperature was 56 degrees. His partner dutifully wrote it down. All I could think of was when the doctor finally got around to reviewing the temperatures he would ask, "Have you buried him at sea already or are you going to wait until later this afternoon?"

About two or three hours later, there was lots of commotion as both doctors, three or more corpsmen, and assorted other people came into our hold with their flashlights on. One doctor asked, "Which is his bunk? Where is he?" They came to the man next to me and started looking in his eyes, putting another thermometer in his mouth, feeling for lumps in his neck and all sorts of other medical procedures. I couldn't stop laughing.

The doctor asked me, "What are you laughing at?" I said, "Tell the doctor what you had in your mouth when they took your temperature the last time." "I had a mouthful of ice cream," he said. Everyone burst out laughing. "Damn you," they said to me, "that's very funny but we don't have time to be funny. If it weren't so funny, we'd bury *you* at sea."

The Marine who disgusted me so much was a member of my own platoon. As I recall, he was 18 years old. He, among others who were ambulatory, roamed the ship looking for a familiar face who could fill him in on the fate of his buddies. While he was walking between the bunks looking for a friendly face, he found me.

After telling me about the platoon casualties he had heard about, he said, "Look what I got, Lieutenant." He took out a small pouch that had held tobacco and shook out about a dozen objects that looked like stones. "Look at these gold teeth, Lieutenant." "Where did you get them?" "From the Jap corpses; I knocked them out with my rifle butt."

I don't know whether I was more stunned or more revolted. I do know that I was very, very angry and I really laid him out. "Did you grow up in America?" I said. "Where did you go to school? Did you ever go to church? Who told you that this is reasonable or appropriate behavior? I am disgusted and damn mad at you. If you had grown up in Germany, you probably would have been one of the soldiers who could have turned on the furnaces in the concentration camps. Now I want you to take those things off my bed, put them in your bag, and get out of my sight. I never want to see you or hear about you again!" We'll hear more about this Marine and the unusual ending to his story later.

In the Naval Hospitals Stateside

Following a long stay on the troop ship, we were taken ashore at Guam to have our bandages changed, casts replaced, wounds checked for infection, etc. In my case, it was simply a matter of changing dressings and bandages and getting a couple nights of good sleep.

Our "hospital" on Guam was simply a large Quonset hut with long lines of simple beds. As soon as everyone had been checked, we were carried back aboard the troop ship and started another long voyage, this time to Hawaii. When we got there, a decision was made concerning the final destination of all the wounded. As I recall, those whose wounds looked like they were likely to heal satisfactorily within three months were transferred to a hospital on Hawaii for their recuperation. Those who faced a longer recovery period were put aboard a ship that would bring them to San Francisco for transportation to various naval hospitals around the country.

At the Oakland Naval Hospital, where I first was sent, there was a Navy commander who was in the bed next to me. He had been the executive officer aboard one of the cruisers in a naval engagement and was heavily wrapped to protect the burns on his shoulders, neck and face; his face was completely bandaged except for the area around one eye. We didn't talk much about our experiences, although he did tell me what happened to him and his ship.

I have forgotten the naval engagement in which his ship was involved, but it was at the time when the Japanese had started to use their kamikaze strategy. This strategy involved a Japanese pilot picking out a target of opportunity, usually one of the larger U.S. ships, and then diving his plane into the ship on a suicide mission designed to sink or at least seriously damage the ship at the expense of one airplane and one Japanese pilot sworn to commit suicide for his emperor.

My roommate told me he had been standing on the bridge of his cruiser scanning the skies for Japanese airplanes. He focused his field glasses on a Japanese Zero that was heading directly for the bridge. He told me, "I said to myself that there was no way that this guy was going to kill himself. I'm sure he'll fire his weapons and then pull up. The next thing I knew I was in the water and on fire." He then looked at me through the one eye that was showing and said, "I learned a very valuable lesson that day. If the guy you're fighting doesn't mind dying, you've got a helluva problem."

One of the courtesies extended to us at Oakland was from AT&T. Each of the wounded was given a free call to any place in the country to inform our families or friends that we were back in the country and recovering in the hospital. We were taken to the phone room in wheelchairs and lined up outside various phone booths. I heard the officer in the chair behind mine, in answer to a question from another Marine about which outfit he had been with on the island, say that he was the mortar officer of F Company, 2nd Battalion, 28th Marines. I was taken aback when I heard this because of my role in that company, battalion, and regiment. I turned to him and said, "I don't know how you could have been in charge of that mortar platoon since that was my platoon."

He said, "Well, you're the guy I've been looking for. I was in the replacement officer pool, and on the third day of the fighting I was sent ashore with orders to find F Company in the 2nd Battalion of the 28th Regiment, and I was instructed to take over as the officer–in–charge. That was some platoon you left me! There were only 12 or 15 guys left, and because their 60mm mortars were useless in that kind of fighting, they had been turned into riflemen. By the way, were you the original officer in that platoon or the second? When I got there I was told I was the third officer they had had in three days."

I then found out that after I was knocked out of action the first day, I had been replaced by another officer on the second day, that he was wounded on that day, and that the officer I was talking to now had taken over on the third day, and had been wounded on the fourth.

These memories of my war experiences have a fascinating coda. In 1992, some 47 years after Iwo Jima, my wife answered the phone on a Sunday night. She told me it was for me and when I answered the phone I realized that it was one of my platoon guys, the one who had spread those gold teeth on my bunk.

He said, "Lieutenant, you told me something once that I have thought about off and on for many years. I am calling to apologize to you and to ask you to forgive me and to tell you that I am in your debt for what you told me."

He went on to tell me that he was living in the west, was retiring in Oregon, and that he was going to write and send me his phone number when he was settled. He went on to say that if I ever needed him, or if he could ever do anything for me, all I had to do was call and he would come to me. I thanked him for calling and complimented him for his willingness and ability to reexamine his priorities and review his actions of 47 years ago.

I couldn't believe he had called me after all that time. It was very encouraging to me since I had been teaching at a university for more than 45 years and often have wondered how much of an impact I have when I try to say something important to my students and they give me a blank look that makes me want to say, "If you understand what I'm saying, please blink your eyes."

On February 19, 1995, my wife and I joined some 1,600 others, survivors of Iwo Jima, many with family members with them, in Washington, D.C., to commemorate the landing 50 years earlier. In the group were Marines, Coast Guard personnel, U.S. Navy personnel, Navy nurses, and others who were involved in the battle for the island. It was a moving experience we will remember for a long time.

When we returned to State College, I noticed what appeared to be a purple bruise on my hip. I showed it to my doctor and he said that it was some sort of cyst, opened it, didn't stitch it, and told me to allow it to drain. About a week later it reopened and I rebandaged it. Another week later it stopped draining and then reopened for the second time.

I returned to the doctor and after some probing he reached in with a narrow instrument, removed something, washed it, and then showed me a piece of mortar shrapnel that had finally emerged 50 years after I was hit. Where had it been all this time? God only knows. Someone said that it showed up to remind me of Iwo Jima. As if I could forget!

At Last, Back in Pennsylvania

In 1946, my Marine Corps career ended at the Philadelphia Naval Hospital. I had spent the last 15 months of my days in the Marine Corps as a patient in that hospital, and there is no place more poorly equipped to prepare a young man for the challenges of the rest of his life than that length of service as a hospital patient.

I have tried to talk and write about spending weeks and months in a hospital, especially at a fairly young age, and I have found it impossible to describe the state of near suspended animation that your brain goes through when you spend that much time without making a single meaningful decision. Everything is decided for you. You have no input into when and what you eat, when the wake–up lights tell you that it is time to get out of bed and when the lights are lowered, meaning it is time to try to sleep. You make no decisions about what to wear because you wear only a Marine Corps uniform outside the hospital and probably a bathrobe when you are inside. You find it impossible to think of the future because you don't know when the future will begin. You are just there.

After a while, a kind of dullness sets in and you probably are lucky that it does. I mention this state of mind, or lack of a state of mind, only to point out how unprepared you are when you are told that your physical condition is as good as it is going to get, and then you are told that it's time to go home because the war, at least for you, is over.

All of us have had periods of indecision when we struggle to make one decision or another. Like most of you, I, too, had many of those times in which I mulled over a series of decisions. But

May 23, 1946, was the day of the greatest indecision of my life. That was the day of my military discharge. That was the day when I had to answer the question, "What's next?" I had made only one decision, and that was not to return to Monessen. I had no reason to go there. My aunt and uncle who raised me were aging. There was no family business beckoning. Monessen was a town of wonderful people, but it was not a town of wonderful job opportunities.

I received my discharge at the Marine Barracks at the Philadelphia Navy Yard. Everything I owned was in the trunk of the green 1940 Chevrolet convertible that I had purchased from my older brother. I had built a square wooden box that matched the trunk's dimensions, and the few clothes and mementos I owned were inside that box.

Those who know Philadelphia know that Broad Street runs the length of the city from north to south. It begins somewhere in the northern suburbs and dead–ends in the Philadelphia Navy Yard, which is on the Delaware River and subsequently the Atlantic Ocean.

I began to drive up Broad Street and when I stopped at the red light at Broad and Chestnut Streets, I realized I also was at a crossroads in my life. There I was, right in the middle of the city, with a major decision to make.

If I continued driving north on Broad Street, I would end up at some "up north" city. If I turned east on Chestnut Street, I would be heading toward some New Jersey city or even New York City. If I wanted to head west, perhaps to Pittsburgh, I'd have to drive around City Hall and head west on Walnut Street. I didn't want to head south because I had just come from there and Broad Street dead–ended at the Navy Yard.

Where did I want to go? It had been so long since my mind was really active that I felt panicky. I pulled into a No Parking space, turned off the engine, and began to think, but I couldn't seem to get myself to think logically and clearly. Because I couldn't park there too long, I made one decision—to drive around City Hall until I reached Chestnut Street again. I drove east on Chestnut, parked my car in an indoor garage, and checked into the Ben Franklin Hotel, where I stayed for four or five days while I tried to sort out my options. It was a very scary period in my life.

The next few months I refer to as my gypsy period. I went to New York to live with a friend and, while there, another friend found me a job as an executive trainee for a drug company. I was ready to work anywhere and do anything. I was living in Brooklyn and my job was in Jersey City. This meant a long subway ride, a train through the tubes under the river, and then a half–hour bus ride. This kind of daily commute for a guy who had never lived anywhere but Monessen and State College, neither of which had or needed public transportation! The job didn't last long. I woke up eight straight mornings with a bloody nose and decided that I had better quit before they found a dead commuter on the subway, train, or bus heading toward Jersey City.

During this period I was not alone. Most of my friends also were on a treadmill, going nowhere! I went back to Monessen to see if I had missed something. I hadn't, and stayed for only two days.

I went to Boston with my closest friend. In retrospect, I might have made an intelligent choice if I had put down roots there. But apparently I wasn't yet able to end my drifting. A friend and I arranged for a summer job as lifeguards at The Balsams, an expensive New Hampshire resort hotel. But, of course, the summer came to an end.

Finally, the father of one of my friends gave me what was life-saving advice. "Son," he said, "you and your friends are making a terrible mistake. You are looking for the perfect city and the perfect job with the perfect company in the perfect industry working for the perfect boss. There may be such a situation, but if there is, why would they hire one of you guys who have done nothing but drift around waiting for the world to discover you? If I were you, I would take the first job to come along. What it pays doesn't matter. What you will be doing doesn't matter. You will be working and you will have started to build a career. You will have grown up." Of course, he was right.

I drove to State College and slept on the floor at my fraternity house for the next two weeks. Ridge Riley, Penn State's Alumni Director, told me that a brand new radio station had gone on the air within the last few months, making State College the smallest town in Pennsylvania with its own radio station. He called the station manager, Bob Wilson, and asked if he would talk with me.

As it turned out, Bob Wilson had been my Sea Scout counselor at camp many years before. Bob auditioned me. I'm not sure I had spoken over a microphone more than once or twice in my life. But I had been the high school dramatic reading champion in Pennsylvania in 1938, and I thought that I might try to "act" like the radio announcers I had heard.

Bob apparently thought I was good enough and he hired me at $35 a week. It wasn't much, but it was a start.

I had no place to go; State College took me in and I have been here ever since. ▪

3

Penn State Hoops

Penn State was fortunate to have an outstanding basketball coach in Dr. John Lawther, credited with inventing and perfecting the sliding zone defense. During the 1930s and '40s, he was able to accomplish a lot with little or no scholarship help.

John Lawther and his zone defense teams were teams the big basketball schools wanted to avoid if at all possible.

John was personally tough and his teams were just as tough. As one newspaper reporter wrote following one of Penn State's games at the old Convention Hall in Philadelphia, "Penn State's basketball team made its annual visit to Convention Hall last night and, as far as Philadelphia rooters are concerned, they would like that visit to be the last." We had upset an outstanding Temple University team that night.

People who watched John coaching from the bench and during timeouts could sense that this was a guy who demanded the very best, all the time, from his players; a player who didn't produce ran the risk of having his hide stripped off in front of all the fans who had come to the game. During timeouts, there were many referees who stood as far away from the Penn State bench as possible, in hopes of not having to face Coach Lawther.

Penn State always played a zone defense and, for example, if an opposing player ever tried to drive along the baseline from the corner to the basket, he either ended up in the bleachers or probably sprawled somewhere between the end line and the far wall of the gymnasium. If he got in close to the basket, the Penn State player he had driven past immediately came out of the game. Penn State's backline always was positioned with one foot on the baseline, and if someone was able to drive through the zone, John knew that his player was either out of position or careless. Either way, he was headed to the bench.

John was the first athletic coach I knew who had earned a Ph.D. There have been others, I'm sure, but how many had earned their doctorate in psychology and had written a best–selling textbook? But you wouldn't believe John's academic background if you heard the language he used on the court, where he often sounded like a hardened stevedore.

John either invented the zone defense or received credit for turning the basic zone into the sliding zone that became his trademark. If you were a basketball fan, it was a revelation to see John coach, either in practice or in a game. From the day I joined approximately 30 other sophomores competing to become the head basketball manager until the last game of my senior year as team manager, I never missed a practice. It was a privilege to see a master teacher at work.

In a practice scrimmage, John often played six offensive players against five on defense. He wanted to see as many passes as possible to see if his team was able to make slides in the zone to cover any possible spacing or situation that could occur in a game.

If an offensive player worked free for a fairly short shot or lay–up, John would blow his whistle and tell each player to stand on the exact spot where they were when the opponent scored. He then would have the offense recreate the last three of four passes that had led to the score. He then would walk through the passing lanes and say something like, "I don't think we can stop that shot using the slides we are using." On the spot he would create a new series of slides where his players took up a new position, depending on where the ball was, so that if that passing sequence were to be recreated in a game, the open shot wouldn't be there any longer.

One of the junior manager's jobs during games was to sit in the front row of the balcony with a clipboard containing a sheet that depicted the court, complete with sidelines and baselines, the foul line, the baskets, etc. His job was to mark the exact spot from which an opposing player took a shot. At the end of the first half, he would hustle the sheet down to Coach Lawther in the locker room. At a glance, John could tell where his defense was breaking down—the slide they had to make was too long, the player was sliding too slowly, or there was some other sort of breakdown. On the spot he would create a new slide or two to plug the weakness. I saw Penn State win game after game in the second half by shutting down the opponent's offense to the point that they scored fewer points in the second half than they had in the first.

I could never figure out if John was a tough guy or a softie. Finally I understood that he was both. John played tennis and handball and, when squash courts were installed, he became a tough squash player. He played all the games the same way—flat out and as hard as he could.

Often before basketball practice began, John and I would play a two–on–two competition with the first two players to arrive for practice. One evening, John and I were partners against his son, Jim, a starter on the team, and another player. John told me, "Jim is my man; you take the other guy." John and his son really went at it. Neither would give an inch and, without a referee, any foul was okay. John went up for a rebound and, after having been fouled repeatedly for the past 15 minutes, Jim took out all of his frustrations by hitting his Dad with a hard elbow in the ribs while John was still up in the air. When John came down with the ball, he passed it to me and said to his son, "Don't screw around with me, Junior, or I'll knock you right on your ass." I'm sure that John loved Jim, but he also loved to win any game he played.

After John Lawther retired from coaching, he moved to North Carolina. But he often returned to campus to continue working with graduate students whose dissertations he was supervising. On one visit, he asked if I was available for a squash game later in the afternoon. John was probably about 20 years older than me, but he still played the game flat out. After two tough games, John sat on the floor of the court with his back against the wall. I was tired, but John seemed more worn-out than I did. Because I was afraid that he was overdoing it for a man of his age, I said, "John, those were two very hard games. Shall we call it a draw since we each won one?" I should have known better. John looked at me and said, "Don't patronize me. Do you want to play the best out of five, seven, or nine games?"

Tough…and Tender

One of our bitter basketball rivals in the Lawther era was Syracuse University, coached by Lew Andreas. He and John coached against each other for years and the games were always tough.

In 1947, Syracuse had an outstanding player in Billy Gabor, who made almost all of the All-America teams that year and went on to a long and successful career in pro ball. Gabor played in pain during the early season games because of a knee injury that, during most games, forced him to sit on the bench by the time the second half came around. Syracuse came to Rec Hall, Penn State's venerable field house that was home for all winter sports teams, for a mid–season game that year and the press had reported that Billy Gabor probably wouldn't be able to play, making it look good for a Penn State victory.

John had called Coach Andreas and had found out that Gabor would be with the team, but probably wouldn't be able to play and if he did, it would be practically on one leg. John talked Gabor's situation over with his good friend Jack Hulme, the Penn State trainer, and they suggested that Coach Andreas bring Gabor to the Penn State locker room before the game so Hulme could take a look at his knee.

Jack was a self–taught trainer who had been in the business for a long, long time. He carried an old metal trainer's kit that contained things you wouldn't find in the kit of a traditional trainer, including various size pieces of an automobile inner tube. He examined Gabor's knee and then wrapped it in a very unusual fashion, using pieces of the inner tube. Jack then wrapped the knee in an Ace bandage and sent Gabor back to the Syracuse locker room.

Did Billy beat us that night using Jack Hulme's brace? No, he didn't. But he did play the entire game and was their leading scorer!

One final personal experience helped me understand the paradox of John Lawther as tough guy and softie. As I described in Chapter Two, after I was wounded on the beach at Iwo Jima, I eventually ended up as a patient at Philadelphia Naval Hospital. John and his wife, Bess, had kept in touch with many of his players and managers during the war and they knew that I was hospitalized in Philadelphia.

Early one afternoon, John showed up in my hospital room. If you know John Lawther as I do, you'd understand that he seemed embarrassed to be there. John always tried to avoid any signs of emotion and never seemed comfortable making a kind or caring gesture. He explained his presence by saying, "After I received your letter that you were here, I realized I would be in Philadelphia for a meeting. So I left a little early this morning so I would have time to drop by and see you before going to my meeting." He asked me to tell him about some of my experiences and went to some lengths to assure himself that I was okay and would certainly recover. I don't think he was there more than 20 minutes.

After my discharge, when I had returned to State College and begun working for WMAJ, I attended a reception for someone in the Athletics Department. John's wife Bess was there and after I greeted her she told me, in her very soft voice, that there was something she thought I should know. She said, "Mickey, promise me that you will never, never tell John what I am going to tell you. Do you remember the day he came to see you at the hospital in Philadelphia?" I told her that I remembered it very well and that I had been so touched that he would come to see me. She continued, "I know that John told you that he was in Philadelphia for a meeting, but that wasn't true. He took that trip to Philadelphia (about 400 miles round–trip) for only one reason—to see you. That morning he drove to Lewistown (the nearest train stop), took the train to Philadelphia (about four or five hours), took a taxi to the Naval Hospital and, after he had visited with you, turned around and came back to State College. Promise me you'll never tell him I told you. If he finds out that I did, he'll be awfully mad at me."

That's just one reason why I think of John Lawther as both tough and tender.

The Lawther Zone Meets the Carlson Figure 8

The Lions played many memorable games at Rec Hall over the years, but one was especially unforgettable, a game against Pitt on February 20, 1943. It is a game that will never be repeated here or anywhere else as long as there is a shot clock.

The Pitt coach was Dr. "Red" Carlson, who was also on the faculty of the Pitt dental school. Carlson had invented the Figure 8 offense, which was quite an innovation at the time. He was widely known for that offense and for his hatred for John Lawther's zone defense. He hated the zone because of the old basketball maxim, "Against a man–for–man defense, you move your players; against a zone, you move the ball." Carlson's trouble with the zone was that the Figure 8 offense featured constant player movement, while Lawther's zone didn't chase the players in the Figure 8. Against that defense, Pitt could hardly manage an open shot.

On that particular night in 1943, Coach Carlson walked into the gym with his players and threw handfuls of unshelled peanuts into the student sections saying, "Okay, clowns, get ready to see a circus!" And he wasn't kidding. Helping Carlson's strategy was the lack of a shot clock and a rule that a team that had been fouled could elect to take the ball out of bounds at mid–court rather than shooting the foul shot.

Pitt controlled the center jump at the start of the game and immediately began freezing the ball, while taunting the Lions to come out of their zone and "play basketball." Neither team would change its strategy. Pitt continued to freeze the ball, even sitting on it at mid–court. Meanwhile, Penn State remained in its zone.

The students threw the peanuts back at Coach Carlson and eventually began throwing them onto the court. One coed came onto the floor and handed her knitting to one of the Pitt players. Carlson, I'm sure, began dreaming of the first scoreless ball game, but it didn't quite work out that way. Pitt made a couple of ball–handling errors while passing it around and was called for traveling violations once or twice. Penn State took advantage of the

Pitt mistakes and scored a couple of times. At the half, the Lions led 5-2 and the Panthers had not attempted a field goal. They had scored only by sinking two foul shots right at the end of the half.

The second half was a copy of the first until Pitt was behind enough points that it seemed futile to continue the freeze and they began to shoot, without much success against the zone, I might add. The final score was Penn State, 32, Pitt, 13. Pitt tried that strategy again in the 1952 season, with no more success than the first time.

After the game, a reporter asked Coach Carlson why he used his freeze strategy and Carlson said he wanted to show how ridiculous the zone defense was by keeping the score so low. He further explained that he had intended to wait until the final two minutes and then have his players shoot as quickly and often as they could. He had hoped that his team could outscore the Lions in a two–minute period, knowing that he did not have enough good players to outscore Penn State over the course of an entire game, especially against the hated zone. Dr. Carlson coached for many more years after his bizarre effort to humiliate John Lawther. He continued to use the Figure 8 offense with some impressive success. Every time I saw the score of a game in which Pitt won, I always felt like saying, "I'll bet the other team didn't play a zone."

The Big Fake

We did two basketball broadcasts that I suspect are unique.

At the conclusion of the 1953–54 season, Penn State was rewarded with an invitation to the NCAA national basketball tournament. Penn State had a fine team, led by Jesse Arnelle, who went on to a successful law career in San Francisco and was elected president of the university board of trustees in 1995, after serving many years on the board. Other players on that team included Jack Sherry, who also played end on the Lions' football team; Jim Blocker, an outstanding rebounder; Ron Weidenhammer, scoring guard; Jim Brewer, Earl Fields, Bob Rohland, and others.

Penn State was to play Toledo in a first round game, which served as a qualifying game to move on to the rest of the tournament. The Lions defeated Toledo on the road and moved on to the regional qualifying round, defeating both Louisiana State University (with their all–time, All–American Bob Pettit) and Notre Dame (with their star Dick Rosenthal, who served as Irish athletic director from 1987 to 1994), despite being a heavy under-dog.

After beating those two opponents, Penn State lost in the semi–finals to Tom Gola's LaSalle team and then came back to defeat California and win third place in the tournament.

The broadcasts that were so unusual were of the LSU and Notre Dame games.

There was great interest in the team and our radio station wanted very much to travel with the team and broadcast the games back to State College and the campus. We knew, of course, that if we won the first game we would have to broadcast the second. But when we checked the cost of installing and using long dis-tance phone lines for the broadcasts, we found it was not within our budget, and it became very clear that we would not be able to sell the games to local sponsors and meet our costs.

I knew we could have a large audience because these games would not be covered on any radio network and television was in its infancy. I came up with what sounded like a ridiculous idea based on experiences I had had visiting the origination studios for network broadcast of Pittsburgh Pirate baseball games that our station in State College carried. You may remember that there was no live broadcast of Pirates road games because it was far too expensive to travel with the team and lease broadcast phone lines for the 77 road games that each major league team played in those days. So the games were recreated from description of the action that was sent by telegraph lines to the studio, where a Western Union telegrapher deciphered the dots and dashes and typed them on a page, from which an announcer created his description. That was fairly easy to do.

The operator at the game site transmitted a simple code—cer-tain letters for balls and strikes—and then something like, "Vaughn single to center, Walker scores from second." Or, "Vaughn bounces to short, out at first." From such a bare bones description, the announcer recreated the game. I had had a chance to sit and watch Rosey Rosewell, the long–time Pirate announcer, recreate two or

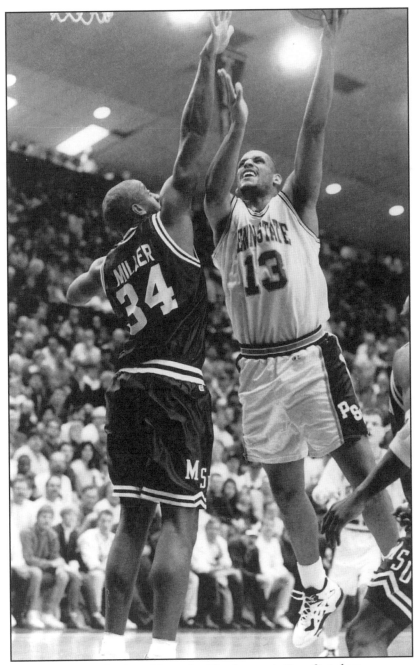

Penn State center John Amaechi, number 13, who came to Penn State from Manchester, England, scoring against Michigan State University in a 1993 game. Amaechi is 6th on Penn State's all-time scoring list.

three games. Rosewell, as old–time Pirates fans will recall, made famous his call of a Pirate home run. Knowing from the wire that a home run had been hit, he had the engineer ready the sound effect and then would say, "Well, you can open the window, Aunt Minnie, here comes a two–run homer and the score is now 4-2 in favor of the Pirates."

I had never heard of anyone trying to broadcast anything but baseball using the Western Union ticker. I wasn't sure it could be done, and if I had really thought it through, I'm not sure we would have tried it.

It was my decision to make since I was the announcer who could make a damn fool of himself stumbling around trying to recreate the fast action of a basketball game with only a few words on the ticker to give me an idea of what actually was happening. The more we thought about it, the more fascinating the prospect became. If I could get some help from someone who would be at the game, I decided I'd give it a try.

We told our listeners that we would broadcast the games and then tried to figure out just how we were going to do it. The Western Union part of the operation would be no trouble. Bill Meredith, father of Bud Meredith, current Penn State ticket manager, was the manager of the local Western Union office and an outstanding ticker tape operator. In those days, the writers who covered Penn State football games would type their stories and give them to Bill Meredith to send to their home newspapers via ticker tape. Watching Bill Meredith send thousands of words in dots and dashes while conversations were going on all around him in the press box, often answering questions while still transmitting, was something to see. When I asked Bill if he would be willing to set up his receiving equipment next to me in the studio, he was very enthusiastic. "If someone will send it, I'll read it and type it and do my best to stay up with you," he said.

The next problem was to get someone at the game site who would be willing to send the information to me in a code that would make it sound as though I was actually at the game. Jim Coogan was the Penn State Director of Sports Publicity and was very enthusiastic about the idea. He said he would be willing to feed me the information I would need and work with me as we put together our code words so I could understand what he was sending.

It was then that Carl Volz, our station engineer, came up with an idea that helped make the broadcast. He thought we should have some game sounds and thought he knew how he could do it with one regular season home game remaining. Carl took two tape recorders to the game at Rec Hall and recorded through the entire game. That meant we had two fairly long tapes that carried only background sounds of a game.

You know, of course, that there is a steady hum of crowd noise during an entire game and when a basket is scored or someone converts a free throw, there is a loud crowd cheer. So Carl took one tape and cut out all of the cheers. That left him with a tape containing only background crowd noise. Then he took the second tape and cut out all the background noise, ending up with a tape that had one loud cheer after another on it. He then made a large loop out of each tape so it would play continuously.

During my broadcast, the engineer ran the crowd noise tape the entire time. During my description of the action, most of which I was making up, I would raise my hand to signal that one of the teams was going to score. When I said, "The ball is in," or something like that, he would start the loop that had the cheers on it and run the cheer over the background sounds. If you were listening on the radio, you would swear that you were at a "live" game with a large crowd.

The only other preparation was for Jim and me to decide what he would send, using as few words as possible. Now 1954 is a long, long time ago, and I have to rely on my memory to give you an idea of what Jim transmitted to me. We decided on code letters to describe a shot from outside, a shot from the corner, or a mid–range shot from 10–12 feet. As I remember it, the information that Jim sent over the ticker for Bill Meredith to decode and type looked something like this: Arnelle X good. Sherry Y miss. Brewer RB (rebound), Brewer Y good. 14-12.

As I broadcast the game, I would have the team moving the ball around. I would have someone dribbling from left to right. I might have him almost lose the dribble (all of this I was making up, of course), and then I would say, "Sherry from the sideline in front of the Penn State bench…No good…Rebound in the corner captured by Brewer…He feeds Blocker further outside…To Weidenhammer at the top of the key…To Arnelle right of the lane…To Brewer on the sideline…Brewer puts it up…Good! Penn State now leads 14-12."

We had other signals, of course, to tell fouls that were committed and who was fouled, turnovers, timeouts, etc. I had decided that the pace of the game was important. We couldn't very well have the game end in an hour, and if I said too much to describe the "action," we would have a three–hour game. So I decided that the game would last about an hour and 40 minutes, including the half–time, when we played recorded Blue Band music, reviewed the action, and ran down the scoring statistics. The first game I described was the LSU contest. Their star was Bob Pettit, the all–time great, who scored a lot of points in that game. Arnelle and Sherry scored well, the others shot about their season average, and we upset the LSU Tigers.

The response from the audience was very rewarding. The phone in the control room rang almost constantly and the question was always the same, "Is Mickey Bergstein at the game? We're having an argument at the fraternity house because someone said he taught his class this afternoon." We had literally dozens of calls asking us to settle bets as to whether the game was live or recreated.

The next morning, I sat in the studio and listened to a tape we had made of the complete broadcast the night before. I wanted to hear how it had sounded so we could improve our technique for the next night's game with Notre Dame. I was pleased with how it had worked out, but must admit I made some stupid mistakes. I got so caught up in following the information that Jim Coogan had sent, and in trying for an even description of the game, that I forgot to include something that happens at every game—I didn't describe a single time when the ball was lost out of bounds. What an oversight! The funny thing was that no one listening seemed to notice. At least, no one mentioned it.

The next night we recreated the game with Notre Dame. The Irish also came into the game with an outstanding record and an outstanding center in Dick Rosenthal. As I remember it, Arnelle had a big night and did a good job of holding Rosenthal in check. The game ended with Penn State on the long end of the score, moving into the Final Four, where they lost to LaSalle and then beat the University of Southern California to take third place.

NCAA Tournament Memories

One of the post–World War II arenas that attracted large on–campus crowds was Reynolds Coliseum at North Carolina State in Raleigh. In 1951, Penn State's basketball team was invited to regional NCAA playoffs, with the first round being played at Reynolds Coliseum. The field included Kentucky, St. John's, and N.C. State. While all four teams brought outstanding records into the tournament, the heavy favorite was the Kentucky Wildcats, which was one of that state's really great teams.

The two stars of the Kentucky team were Cliff Hagan, later a professional star with the St. Louis Bombers and still later Kentucky Athletic Director, and Frank Ramsey, who starred for many years with Bill Russell, K.C. Jones, Sam Jones, John Havlicek and others with the Boston Celtics. Frank Ramsey was the first professional player to establish the worth of a team's sixth man who, although he didn't start, came off the bench to spark his team when needed. Ramsey won the NBA's coveted Sixth Man Award many times while he was playing in the National Basketball Association.

Penn State came into the tournament with an outstanding defensive team but only one offensive star, freshman Jesse Arnelle whose Penn State basketball records include highest point total of any Penn State player (2,138 points), highest scoring average per game (21 points), and season scoring leader (731 points). Remember, too, he earned these records when there wasn't a three–point goal. Two other starters were Hardy Williams and Jack Sherry. Williams went on to earn a law degree at the University of Pennsylvania and to have a long and rewarding career as a senior member of the Pennsylvania Senate. Sherry now heads his own office equipment and seating company in Philadelphia. Penn State, coached by Elmer Gross, was no match for Kentucky, ranked number one in the Associated Press poll, and lost 82-54. The highlight for Penn State was Jesse Arnelle's performance in scoring 22 points against All–American Cliff Hagan.

The second game that night matched St. John's and North Carolina State and stayed very close to the end. As the clock wound down, the coliseum organist and crowd tried to inspire the home team as the organist boomed out the traditional fight song, "Dixie," and the crowd waved their Confederate flags. The St. John's fans were amused to find, after consulting their programs, that the team from Dixie was then playing two players from New York City and another two from New Jersey!

While in Raleigh, Penn State fans heard a story about Adolph Rupp, the legendary coach of the Kentucky Wildcats. The widespread use of credit cards today (in 1995, 100 million Americans used 917 million credit cards) makes it hard to remember a time when a person either carried cash or depended on finding someone willing to cash a personal check.

Kentucky basketball at that time assumed the proportion and fervor of a religion. The man responsible for the sport's popularity was Rupp, the long–time coach of the Wildcats. Not only was he a highly successful coach with a national reputation, he was undoubtedly the most widely–known and recognized figure in the entire state. Known as "The Baron of Bluegrass Country," he was never seen not wearing his trademark brown suit.

Kentucky basketball fans tell the story of a game that the Wildcats had scheduled to be played in the Coliseum in Louisville. Coach Rupp decided he would use the evening before the game to scout a high school team whose star he wanted to recruit. He turned the Wildcats over to his long–time assistant, Harry Lancaster, to take to Louisville, oversee their practice, and get them registered at their hotel. In the meantime, Rupp would drive to the small town where the high school team played, scout the prospect, and then drive to Louisville and take charge of the team.

Rupp drove a top–of–the–line Cadillac that was almost as much of a trademark as his brown suit. While driving on a rural road, he noticed he was low on fuel and thought he'd better fill up at a gas station along the road. He drove his Cadillac up to the single pump and told the older man in bib overalls who came out of the station to fill the tank. When the tank was almost full, Rupp suddenly realized he had no cash with him, just a checkbook. When the man finished filling the tank, Rupp got out of the car and sheepishly told him, "I'm sorry, but I don't seem to have any money. I was in a hurry and evidently forgot to put any cash in my pocket. I'm afraid I'm going to have to ask you to take my check."

Rupp was surprised that the man didn't seem to know him; he thought that everyone in Kentucky knew who he was and would certainly recognize him. The attendant informed Rupp that he didn't take checks, especially from strangers. Rupp then tore a check out of his checkbook, pointed to his name printed on it, and confidently asked the man, "Do you know who this is?" The man studied the name very carefully and then said, "I sure hope it's you."

The 1942 NCAA Basketball Tournament

Penn State lost to Dartmouth on their way through the early rounds of the 1942 post–season NCAA tournament. Dartmouth's star, Gus Broberg, had led the team all season and continued his excellent play in the win over Penn State. He was a tall and very smooth player, with a blonde crew cut that helped him stay in my memory.

While I was a patient at the Philadelphia Naval Hospital during the latter part of 1945, time weighed heavily on my hands and I spent some time, as other patients did, wandering around the hospital hoping to see someone who served in my company or battalion. One day I stopped in the gymnasium to see if there was any equipment that I could use in my rehabilitation. The gym was empty except for a tall man in a hospital bathrobe shooting one–handed set shots at one of the baskets.

I especially noted his shooting style because the one–handed shot had recently come into vogue and it was almost always a jump shot, except at the foul line. But this man was standing flat on the floor, just beyond the circle, shooting with one hand. He was a tall blonde man with a crew cut, and all of a sudden I recognized him as Gus Broberg, who had helped defeat Penn State in the 1942 basketball tournament.

His bathrobe, which identified him as a hospital patient, was tied tightly around his waist and, when I looked more closely, I saw that one sleeve was tucked into the pocket. Since the robe obviously did not cover a cast, I realized that Captain Gus Broberg of the U.S. Marine Corps (I looked up his rank in the records office) had lost an arm in combat and the only shot he could manage, other than a lay–up, was a one–handed push shot.

Did I walk up to him and tell him that I remembered his role in defeating Penn State in the 1942 tournament? I did not. If I had reminded him of his outstanding play, what would have been accomplished other than yet another reminder that he would not play basketball again?

Before telling you this story, I thought I should verify that the Gus Broberg I saw in the hospital gymnasium was indeed the Dartmouth player and that he had lost an arm serving in the Marines. I called the Dartmouth alumni office and they confirmed that their former basketball star had served as an officer in the Marines and had lost an arm in World War II. I didn't ask if anyone there could tell me if Gus had had aspirations to play professionally. I was afraid to hear the likely answer.

Senator Bradley, You Owe Me

Basketball fans undoubtedly will remember that the recently–retired U.S. Sen. Bill Bradley of New Jersey was an outstanding All–America basketball player at Princeton in the mid–1960s. He was named a Rhodes Scholar and, after his studies at Oxford, began an outstanding career with the New York Knicks of the National Basketball Association. When he retired from basketball, he entered politics and had a distinguished tenure in the U.S. Senate.

Several years ago, I had a legislative proposal that I hoped someone in government would be willing to read and consider. My idea was to propose an updated version of the G.I. Bill of Rights that had been such a successful piece of social legislation after World War II. That bill provided educational costs and a modest monthly living allowance to veterans who wanted to pursue a college education or enroll in an approved training program in designated careers.

Since I was concerned, and continue to be concerned, about the lack of education and job skills of disadvantaged inner–city men and women, my idea was to offer something similar to the G.I. Bill to deprived men and women who wanted to pursue a college education or a job training program. I suggested that young men or women from economically depressed families who had earned a high school diploma could qualify for a government–funded education or job training program. Rather than telling people they qualified for such benefits because they were veterans, we would say, "You qualify for this new program because you are an American."

Because I wanted an inventive way to call attention to my proposal, in hopes that it would stand out in all the mail senators receive, I attached this note.

> Senator Bradley:
>
> I hope you will be willing to read and consider the attached legislative proposal. Although the proposal is in outline form, I am certain that you will quickly sense the idea that I am advancing. If this proposal seems to merit further attention, I will be happy to submit additional data to support this idea I am proposing.
>
> On the chance that you will give this your attention, I suggest that you may agree that you might "owe me one." If you do, I would consider your reading and considering this idea as payment in full.
>
> Please turn your memory back to the spring of 1965 when your Princeton basketball team defeated Penn State in an early NCAA tournament game at the Palestra in Philadelphia. The game score was 60-58.
>
> With the score tied at 58, Penn State had the ball

Carver Clinton, number 20, 9th on Penn State's all-time scoring list, goes up for a layup against Navy in a 1964 game. This Penn State team lost to Princeton 60-58 in the NCAA championship tournament. The star of the Princeton team was former U.S. Sen. Bill Bradley.

at mid–court and was looking to set up their final play of the game. Our player with the ball was fronted by you as he crossed the 10–second line. As I saw it, you reached for the ball, made contact with the Penn State player, took the ball away with a physical move, and knocked down the Penn State player. When the referee blew the whistle, he called the foul on the Penn State player, awarded you two foul shots, which you converted, and your team won the game by two points. You later went on to the Final Four where you lost, as I recall, to Michigan of the Big Ten.

I'm not sure that you believe the foul called in your favor was justified. Most of the crowd did not, but since they didn't have the whistle, their opinion didn't matter. I gave you credit for pulling off a risky play. The reason I say you "owe me one" is that I was slated to go on with the Penn State team to broadcast their games as long as they kept winning in the tournament. So, your stealing the ball not only cost me further broadcast fees, but it also cut short a vacation traveling with our team to the next game or games. Instead, your play, which I really be-lieved should have been called on you (probably giving us the game), sent me back to my regular workday the very next morning. I never have forgiven you, but your consideration of my legislative idea will wipe the slate clean.

Thanks for your consideration and, as the song goes, "Thanks for the Memory."

One final note. Despite what I thought was a sure way to get the senator's attention, I never had an answer to my letter or my proposal. Incidentally, I still think that I had submitted a helluva good idea! ▪

4

Third and Long

During the football season ever since 1928, about 300 football fans gather every Wednesday at noon at the Nittany Lion Inn to review the previous Saturday's game and talk about the next game on the schedule. The main feature of the weekly program now is Penn State coach Joe Paterno and I host the program, a role I have filled for the past 40 years.

Joe brings two of his players to the session and I interview them to begin the after–lunch program. The interview, while it talks about the team and last week's game, tries to focus most of the attention on the player himself, his family, his studies, his future plans, etc. The purpose is for the fans to get to know more about each player as they watch him play, to know more than his size, weight, and jersey number, to know him as a person.

Next it's Joe's turn, and for 30 to 40 minutes I ask him about last week's game and next week's opponent. I try to make these interviews different than the typical sports interview. We have a tradition that makes a different type of interview possible—the interview is "off the record." Although members of the media who cover Penn State games are always present, and often there are reporters from metropolitan newspapers there as well, we ask them to honor our tradition that nothing that is said there can leave the room. We do this so that we can have a free and open discussion and that Joe will feel free to share with us some "inside" or personal information that we will find very interesting, comfortable in the knowledge that he will not be quoted in print or on radio or television. The result is that these luncheons are always interesting and have become a football tradition in the community and on the campus.

The lunch programs began long before Joe Paterno became head coach. In the late 1920s, a group of State College business-men decided to ask Bob Higgins, the head coach at the time, to come to a luncheon or send one of his assistants, and offer com-ments about the games along with films of the previous game. There was no television at the time and this provided a rare op-portunity to see all the games, both home and away, along with appropriate expert comments and observations.

Coach Higgins agreed and the State College Quarterback Club was born. It was a really interesting way to watch a game if you were a serious football fan. The coach would stop the projector many times and ask the audience to watch for certain things dur-ing the upcoming play, things all of us probably had missed if we saw the game live. He would point out a certain well–executed block or would note when a player totally missed an assignment and what happened as a result.

On one occasion, after a couple of remarks from Coach Higgins, we settled back to watch the film with the usual stops for a particular play, a missed assignment, a blown call by an offi-cial, etc. Sometime in the second quarter, as I recall, our tailback broke over tackle, swung to the sideline, turned the corner, and outran the opposition's safety for a 55–yard touchdown.

As soon as the play was over on the film, Coach Higgins jumped to his feet and asked, "Did you all see that?" We hadn't the faintest idea what he was referring to. Somebody asked, "See what?" Higgins turned to the assistant coach who was running the projector and said, "Run that back again and you guys watch closely."

They ran the play again and Higgins again asked," Did you see it this time?" Not a word from the audience; no one had seen anything unusual. Higgins had the projectionist run it a third time. Again, "See that?" Again, nobody had seen anything unusual. So Higgins gave us a hint, "This time don't watch the tailback, watch the referee."

At this point I should tell you about the tailback. Sparky Brown, the Number 1 tailback that season, was a short, rather thickly built runner from upstate New York. He was a workman-like player who possessed no outstanding skills but was a hard–

nosed guy who went all out on every play, not your typical multi–talented player who was the key man in the single–wing offense that we and most teams ran in those days. Also, because he was prematurely bald, Sparky appeared to be much older than his teammates.

When they ran the film back yet another time, we watched Sparky cut over the left tackle, cut to the sidelines, turn the corner, and outrun the safety for a touchdown. The only difference was that we followed Coach Higgins' directions and, as Sparky opened up the throttle to top speed, we saw our tailback running as fast as he could go and saw the referee holding his cap on his head with one hand and running right past Sparky into the end zone before Sparky got there.

Mickey Bergstein interviews Penn State football coach Bob Higgins as the team returns from a 13-13 tie in the 1948 Cotton Bowl.

Coach Higgins had a rather high–pitched voice and he almost yelled, "Did you see that? The referee? How do you expect me to win football games when the referee runs faster than my tailback?"

What the coach didn't tell us was that the referee that day was a former Syracuse University athlete named Ray Barbutti. He didn't tell us that Ray Babutti had been a track star for the Orange and had won two gold medals in the preceding Olympics, including one for the 400 meters!

The scope and purpose of the Quarterback Club changed drastically when Penn State's games started to be televised. If the game had been televised live, we had already seen it. Even if it wasn't televised live, it usually was shown on a delayed basis on Sunday or Monday and you could see it then. And Joe had a Wednesday evening television program that featured key replays. As a result of all this exposure, it didn't make sense to get together just to watch game films for another time.

Joe agreed that we wouldn't show a film or video at Quarterback Club lunches, but would use the time to get to know some of the players and then have his comments on the previous and upcoming games. Joe has been meticulously faithful about his commitment. In more than 30 years as head coach, he has missed just two luncheons. One was the week that one of his sons suffered severe injuries after falling off a school trampoline, and Joe and his wife, Sue, were at their son's bedside. And the other was in 1997,when he was ill with the flu.

Joe Garagiola, Don Meredith, and the Quarterback Club Banquet

On the second Sunday after our final football game each year, the State College Quarterback Club hosts a banquet to honor the team and thank the players and staff for their achievements and the entertainment they provided their followers that season. Many years ago, because of my association with the radio broadcasts of the games, I was asked to be toastmaster for the banquet. I would guess that I have now filled that role for 40 seasons or more. Thinking back over all the Quarterback Club banquets I've attended, there are two that particularly stand out in my mind.

When Joe Garagiola was still a member of the NBC "Today" show crew, he also was active in network baseball broadcasts and obviously was a widely recognized and respected sports figure. As it turned out he also was a great fan of Joe Paterno. In the early 1970s, the Quarterback Club speaker committee had invited Garagiola to be our banquet speaker. He accepted the invitation immediately and told us how much he admired Joe Paterno and his program and the high regard in which he held Penn State. Further, he offered to waive his regular speaking fee. Because he was involved in taping a television show, we had to charter a plane to get him to the banquet on time and gave him a set of golf clubs as a gift. So while his appearance was not necessarily inexpensive, we were pleased to know of his high regard for Joe, our team, and Penn State.

We never try to combine a reception at which beer or other liquor is served with our banquet. In addition to recognizing the age of our younger players, we don't think that kind of reception is appropriate for a sports banquet. However, an hour or so before the banquet we do have a small reception for our invited guests, the speaker, any members of the university Board of Trustees in attendance, and some of the university officers.

In this case, we met at the Nittany Lion Inn, while the banquet was held in the ballroom of the Hetzel Union Building. I introduced myself to Joe Garagiola and offered to get him a drink. I've never forgotten his response. He thanked me for the offer and then said, "I do drink socially on occasion, and I would be glad to join you under other circumstances. But someone told me there would be 500 or more people at the banquet, including children, and I know that they have seen me on the "Today" show and on other sports telecasts. I'm sure they've paid to attend the banquet and even if they haven't, they are entitled to my best efforts. My best efforts are not possible if I've had a drink or two before I speak. So, I'll be glad to join you for a drink after the banquet, but I never, never take a drink before I speak."

I told him that I admired and respected him for his attitude, and that I had attended some banquets and had heard some sports figures speak who quite obviously did not follow his no–drinking rule. He then reached into an inside jacket pocket and took out a number of typed 3x5 cards.

"There is something else I would like to tell you," he said. "When I show up at a function where I am going to speak, I always am ready and I never simply get up and wing it, although it may seem that way sometimes. You probably are going to have me speak last. But even if you put me first, I am ready to do about 40 minutes of fresh material that I have planned and thought through. During dinner, you will see me doing lots of writing on these cards. I don't want you to think that I am preparing my speech. I am making notes based on what has happened or been said by the speakers who precede me and I will weave all that into my intended speech.

"If you introduce me first, and no one has said a word before me, I am ready to go." And then he handed me the cards on which he had outlined and underlined things he intended to say and the order in which he would say them.

When he spoke later on, you would have sworn that everything he said was a fresh ad lib and that he was speaking off the cuff. Because of the business I am in, I have heard literally hundreds of speakers and I never heard a better-prepared speaker. I should also tell you that, unlike many speakers who can hardly wait to get out of the room, Joe stayed and signed autographs until there wasn't a single autograph seeker left in the hall. In fact, he didn't eat a mouthful of his dinner because from the moment he sat down, a long line of children and some adults formed and filed past where he was sitting. He not only signed his name but, especially for the kids, he included a short note. He would ask what position they played and then would add some appropriate advice above his autograph.

For example, one very small kid, probably 7 or 8 years old, approached Joe. When the boy told Joe he was an outfielder, Joe wrote, "Remember, when you catch a fly ball, make sure you have it in the pocket of your glove before you throw it back to the infield. On a ground ball, be sure you get down on one knee so the ball doesn't roll between your legs and go for extra bases."

Some famous athletes don't seem to know the meaning of public relations or in some cases, I'm afraid, even how to spell it. They could take a lesson from Joe Garagiola.

The other banquet I will always remember was held in 1978. By this time the banquets had grown in popularity and were being held in Rec Hall with an audience of approximately 1,100 people. Our speaker that year was Dandy Don Meredith, the star of the ABC Monday Night Football telecasts. Meredith was a friend of a well-known Penn State alumnus, Walter Conti, and Walter made all the arrangements involved in having Meredith appear at the banquet.

Don had spent the two weeks before the banquet skiing in Utah and arrived at Rec Hall wearing a cowboy hat and a two-week growth of beard. He looked like someone about to go round up the cows and head them to slaughter. Don Meredith can be a very funny man and at the reception before the banquet he told story after story and received laugh after laugh. He impressed me as a loose and relaxed guy who never worried about anything. This impression turned out not to be true, and that's the reason why I tell you this story.

One of the banquet traditions is to award an appropriate memento to a former football player who has gone on to achieve high marks in whatever field he has chosen. We call the award the Alumni–Athlete award and much thought goes into choosing the recipient. A few of the recipients have achieved greatness in football, while others have made their marks in other fields, medicine, finance, education, and various elements of the corporate world.

One of the outstanding members of our 1948 Cotton Bowl team was the late Steve Suhey, who was named an All–American at Penn State and became a recognized star with the Pittsburgh Steelers in the NFL. Not only was Steve a Penn State star, but three of his sons also were members of Nittany Lions football teams. Larry was a fine fullback, Matt went on to play 10 seasons in the NFL with the Chicago Bears, and Paul went on to become an orthopedic surgeon. Additionally, Steve's widow was the daughter of Penn State football coach Bob Higgins. We realized that there would be only one year when two of the Suhey boys would be on the same Penn State team. Larry had graduated before Matt became a member of the team and Paul would graduate after this season, while Matt would play for another year. We had never presented a posthumous award before, but decided to do so this year since Steve had died earlier in the year after suffering a heart attack.

We voted to honor Steve and asked his wife, Ginger, to accept the award on his behalf. Ginger thanked us for the award but expressed the thought that accepting it on behalf of Steve could be too sad and emotional for her and asked if her son Paul could accept on behalf of the Suhey family. We, of course, agreed and decided that we would make the award presentation next to last on the program, and that Dandy Don Meredith would follow the presentation as the main speaker.

No one can recall who made the presentation to the family; most likely it was one of Steve's former teammates. I am absolutely certain that not one person in the 1,100 present, with the exception of the Suhey family, had any idea of the emotional experience that lay ahead as Paul Suhey, in his senior year at Penn State before entering medical school, came forward to respond on behalf of his family. I will not attempt to recall everything Paul said or his exact words, but will give you his closing statements as I remember them.

Paul was very gracious in thanking the Quarterback Club for honoring his father. Then he said, "Ladies and gentlemen, I hope you will allow me to address my teammates for just a few moments." Facing the team tables he said, "I would like to ask all of you to think about doing something very important. When you see your mother the next time, be sure and give her a warm hug. And when you see your father, give him the same kind of hug. I think you ought to hug both of them as often as you can. I'm not sure I ever hugged my dad. If I did, I never hugged him very often. There's nothing that I would like to do more right now than hug my dad, but I can't because he's gone. Please remember what I just said." And with that, he took the award and returned to his seat.

Remember, I was the toastmaster. It was now my job to go to the microphone and introduce the main speaker, Dandy Don Meredith. I looked out over the audience, which filled the floor of Rec Hall, and couldn't see anyone who wasn't in tears. It was as if we were in the middle of a funeral, and now I was supposed to introduce a funny speaker.

I looked next to me where Don had been sitting and his chair was empty. He was gone, and I didn't know where he was. There was only one thing for me to do. I said to the crowd, "Ladies and gentlemen, I think it might be a good time and place in the program for us to take a short break." Then I went looking for Don Meredith. I walked behind the curtain where there was a men's room and there he was. He was leaning over the sink sobbing, his beard wet with tears.

After a while he washed his face, turned to me and said, "Mickey, please don't ever do that to me again." I apologized, of course, and said, "Don, I had no idea what Paul Suhey was going to say, and I certainly had no idea how the crowd was going to react. If it makes you feel any better, there are about 1,100 people on the other side of that curtain feeling about as emotional as you are." I then told Don I had called a recess and, if he felt ready, perhaps we could go back inside and resume the program. He agreed and we returned to the speaker's table.

How could he begin? What could he say to explain his disappearance? Perhaps you remember that Don was the television spokesman at that time for Lipton tea. After I introduced him he said, "Sorry to have held up the banquet—but that Lipton tea follows me wherever I go." He paused and then continued, "You know, Steve Suhey was a wonderful guy and a helluva football player. I know that he would be very proud of his sons and their mother. I am honored to be part of a program that honors the Suhey family."

He had brought everything to a proper close. The ice was broken, and he went on to say what he had originally planned to say. A friend later asked me how Meredith was able to handle the difficult situation and move on to the next thing. I had only one answer. "He's a professional, and a professional is always ready."

Of Hot Dogs and Two Coaches from UCLA

Many Penn State football fans remember the 1970 season as the year that a long Penn State winning streak came to an end when, in the second game of the season, Colorado defeated the Lions 27–3 in a nationally televised game. That was the year when Joe Paterno moved defensive safety John Hufnagel to quarterback for the Army game after alternating Mike Cooper and Bob Parsons at quarterback through the first six games. John led the team to five wins the rest of the season and 21 wins in the next two seasons.

We traveled to Madison, Wisconsin, to play the Badgers for the third game of the season. We were in the press box getting ready for our broadcast when a young man came into the booth and presented a large box to each person connected with the broadcast—announcers, engineers, statistician. The box was a gift from a Wisconsin meat packing company and included a substantial collection of hot dogs, sausages, salami, and other processed meat products. Shortly after that, the sports publicity man for Wisconsin brought to the booth a rather impressive and well–dressed man who was wearing a handsome blue blazer with a fancy crest on the breast pocket. The crest was woven of very thick gold–colored thread that surrounded a rather intricate design. I was sure the man was the skipper of a yacht club or a member of an exclusive golf club, and I wondered about his presence in the press box.

When I looked closely at the design of his blazer patch, however, I discovered that rather than being the crest of some exclusive organization, it was a platter of intertwined hot dogs, sausages, salamis, and other meat products. Just about the time I decided the man had something to do with the free gift boxes, the publicity man introduced him as the director of public relations for a Wisconsin meat packing company that was one of the sponsors of the Wisconsin radio broadcasts. The publicity man asked me if I would be willing to interview the meat packing executive during the half–time break. Since we usually interviewed someone in the press box who was either a football scout or coach or a newspaper man or had some other connection with one of the universities involved in the game, I couldn't figure out the rationale for asking us to interview a meat packing company official.

I thought he might have been a former football great who could turn out to be an interesting guest. When I asked why they thought I should interview this particular man, the answer was, "This meat packing company also has a plant in Pennsylvania, and they em-

ploy a considerable work force in your home state." Without of-
fending the executive, I was forced to point out that we were not in
the meat packing publicity business, and unless we could make a
direct connection between the company and the game, I didn't believe that he would be an appropriate guest. I apologized to the
two men and they left the broadcast booth. Shortly after that, the
young man who had given us the gift boxes of meat products
showed up again and took back our gifts. The joke was on them,
however, since I had thrown my coat over one gift box and when
they took the boxes they ended up one short because they didn't
see the box under the coat.

Even though we had a lot of fun with that incident, we still had
a problem of finding an appropriate halftime guest. I walked around
the press box and recognized one of the greatest coaches of all time
sitting in one of the guest sections. It was John Wooden, the great
UCLA basketball coach whose records, especially his number of
national championships, probably will never be matched by any
other coach or any other school. I introduced myself to him and
invited him to go on the air with me during the halftime break. He
graciously accepted and presented himself at our booth just before
halftime.

He was a very interesting and knowledgeable guest who, as it
turned out, not only knew everything there was to know about
basketball, but was very knowledgeable about football as well. He
was a very courteous gentleman and thanked me for offering him
the opportunity to talk about his team, his program, and the Penn
State–Wisconsin game. I thanked him for giving us a wonderful
interview and, as a gift from our broadcast crew, I gave him the
meat packing gift box.

Four years earlier, I had occasion to interview another UCLA
coach and, in contrast to the interview with John Wooden, it turned
out to be a most unpleasant experience. During 1966, Joe Paterno's
first year as head coach, we played UCLA at the Los Angeles Coliseum.

As the color announcer on the Penn State Football Network,
one of my jobs each week was to tape record a five-minute interview with both coaches; when we went on the air, these interviews opened our broadcast. I always interviewed Joe Paterno

early in the week before the game and made arrangements to interview the other team's coach some time on Friday, the day before the game. Because I knew it was hard to fit even a brief interview into a coach's schedule the day before a game, I would write to the coach early in the week to tell him that I would call his office when we arrived on Friday, assuming that the game was on the road, or to tell him that I would be calling him at his team's hotel if the game was being played at our campus.

The UCLA coach in 1966 was Tommy Prothro whose father, incidentally, had been the manager of the Philadelphia Phillies in earlier years. When we arrived in Los Angeles, I called the football offices at UCLA, introduced myself to Coach Prothro's secretary, told her that I had written to the coach earlier in the week to tell him that I would be calling, and asked if she could arrange a five–minute period when I could meet with Coach Prothro at a time and place he would choose so I could interview him for our broadcast.

I immediately began to get a whole series of vague answers from the secretary. "No, Coach Prothro isn't here and I don't know when to expect him…. I'm not sure that the team will be practicing today and if they are, I don't know what time the practice will be held…. I'm not sure that I will be in touch with Coach Prothro any time today" and other such nonsense. I knew that there was no way that a football coach would not be in touch with his office the day before a big intersectional game.

I then called the UCLA athletic director and told him my problem. He asked me to call back and when I did, he told me that the UCLA team would be staying at the Ambassador Hotel in Los Angeles that night and that Coach Prothro had agreed that if I would call him from the lobby about mid–evening, he would come down to the lobby to be interviewed. I followed his instructions and called Prothro at about 8 p.m.

When Prothro came to the lobby, before I could thank him he said, "Let's get this over with." We then recorded probably the worst radio interview of all time. Every question I asked Coach Prothro was answered with just one word, either "yes" or "no." What a painful experience.

I don't know if he was angry that I had involved his boss to help me solve my problem and chose to be nasty just on this occasion. I had the feeling that he probably would have behaved the same regardless of what I did or didn't do. When we finished the "interview," I stuck out my hand to shake hands with him and thank him for taking the time. He ignored my hand and simply walked away.

After all this trouble tracking him down and going through the charade of a lousy interview, I eventually decided not to use the recording. I simply began the broadcast in the usual manner, introduced the interview with Joe Paterno, and then said, "I'm sorry that we will not be able to hear from Coach Prothro of UCLA. We were unable to reach him to record an interview."

We ended up losing a one–sided 49–11 game. If you have read Joe Paterno's book, *Football...My Way*, you know how that game ended. After my experience a day earlier, I was not surprised at Coach Prothro's decision during the final minutes of the game. That season, Joe had agreed that I could come down to the Penn State bench near the end of the game and as soon as the game was over, win or lose, he would allow me to do a five–minute interview that we would carry live over the Penn State Football Network.

When I reached the bench, the score was 42–11 in favor of UCLA. Almost at that moment, the Bruins scored and kicked the extra point to make the score 49–11. As you can imagine, the Penn State bench was not a happy place and I was not looking forward to interviewing Joe after that big loss. There were only a couple of minutes left in the game, and I expected UCLA to kick off and then go into a soft defense while Penn State tried to score a consolation touchdown.

Instead, despite a 38–point lead, UCLA went for an onside kick, recovered the ball, and threw a couple of passes in an effort to get another score. I have seen Joe Paterno angry on a couple of occasions during my years of association with him. But I have never, never seen him quite as angry as he was during those final minutes. To his credit, despite his anger, he stood on the Penn State bench with me and candidly and completely answered every question that I asked him. That could not have been easy for him. He never mentioned Coach Prothro, an early indication of Joe's professionalism.

I have since wondered many times why Coach Prothro acted as he did in regard to my interview request, and why he would even consider an onside kick with a lead of 38 points. It is only a guess on my part, but I believe it must have been a hangover from the game at Penn State one year earlier that UCLA won 24–22 and that was tainted by our "walkie–talkie" charge.

Anyone who watches football with any interest knows that one of the toughest decisions for a quarterback to make comes when he rolls out wide in a run or throw situation. The fans, of course, have the best seats in the house and can easily see if a quarterback should keep it and run or should throw downfield to an open receiver. How many times have you said or heard, "He could have made a first down if he had run for it" or "If he had thrown to number whatever downfield, he could have had a touchdown." It isn't that easy, of course, for the quarterback. He is being pursued from the rear and probably from the side, there is a hump on the field, and it isn't as easy as it looks to find a receiver downfield. Of course, he has to make a split–second decision.

Sometime during the second half of the 1965 game, one of the Penn State parking coordinators who supervised the traffic flow from the top of the press box and used a walkie–talkie to direct the parking staff, walked to the door of the broadcast booth and signaled me to come out into the hallway. He handed me his walkie–talkie and said, "Listen to this." When I put it up to my ear I heard, in addition to some static, a voice saying, "Go...go...go!" I wasn't sure what that meant and I kept the unit to my ear. A few plays later I heard the voice say, "Throw back...throw back...throw back!"

All of a sudden I realized what was going on. Someone in the press box was sending a message to the UCLA quarterback. On a roll–out, the press box voice was telling the quarterback to run for the sticks for a first down or more. Or, if there was someone open on the near sideline, and the quarterback had rolled out to the far sideline, the voice told him to turn around and throw back to the open receiver whom the quarterback probably never would have seen on his own. What an advantage for the quarterback.

With help like that from a press box spotter, even I could have played quarterback, at least until someone tackled me and two or three others landed on me. I had no idea who the "voice" was or where he was seated or standing, but I do know what he was doing. The traffic coordinator went to the Penn State bench and reported what he had heard to Penn State's coach, Rip Engle. I don't know if Rip did anything about it at that moment—we were still on the air wrapping up the broadcast during the post–game press conference—but I know that the matter did come up. Apparently the UCLA coach denied there was a receiver in the quarterback's helmet and that he was receiving instructions from the press box.

We'll never prove the truth and by now it really doesn't matter, I guess. Every time I think about that game and my reaction when the traffic control man put the walkie–talkie up to my ear, I have only one question I would like answered. If you were the UCLA coach and presumably knew what was happening between the press box and the quarterback, what would be your answer if the quarterback or some other player asked you, "Coach, why did we cheat and why didn't you let us try to win on our own?"

One More Time!

It seems that Penn State has always been a power in college football, although that isn't true. Nittany Lions fans disagree about when Penn State became firmly entrenched among the elite of college football. Some fans want to go back to the really old days of Bob Higgins, Charlie Way, and others who received personal accolades and awards. However, during the years I choose to think of as the "modern years" of Penn State football, the last 45 years or so, I think of Penn State achieving national attention and recognition beginning in the late 1950s. Although the Lions had a fine team in 1947 and tied Southern Methodist University in the Cotton Bowl, Penn State hadn't had a perfect season since 1912 and did not have another undefeated team until 1968. After then, the Lions would not have a losing season until 1988.

During the 1967 season, Joe Paterno made a call that took real guts, and it had much to do with the beginning of the great Penn State record. We had opened the season with an unexpected 23–

22 loss to Navy and had to go on the road to play Miami in the second game. It was unusually hot that fall, and the game was scheduled for the Orange Bowl on a Friday night. Joe was worried that his squad would have to spend a hot Thursday night and a hot Friday morning and afternoon in Miami if he followed the usual travel schedule and flew the Lions to Miami on Thursday. So after practice on campus on Thursday, the team took a bus to Pittsburgh and stayed in the air–conditioned hotel at the Pittsburgh airport. We boarded an air–conditioned plane Friday morning and flew to Miami. At Miami, Joe kept the team at the air–conditioned hotel at the airport Friday morning and afternoon. The team took an air–conditioned bus from the hotel and when they took the field for the game, it was the first time they knew how hot it was. Joe's explanation was that he didn't want his team wandering around Miami Friday thinking about how hot it was going to be for the game Friday night. Perhaps this has happened since, but I can't recall a team leaving on the day of the game, especially if they would have a four or five hour flight before they played the game.

The Lions defeated the Hurricanes 17–8 at the Orange Bowl. It was an important win for Joe Paterno's team because of the loss to Navy the previous weekend. Probably as important as the win was a gutsy move Joe made early in the game before either team had taken control. Anyone who follows Penn State football closely knows how Joe hates playing untested players in important games. He apparently had a lot of confidence in his sophomore class that year (freshmen were not eligible for varsity play then) because he sent in a whole group of them fairly early in the game. Joe obviously knew what he had in that class because it would serve as the nucleus, along with Mike Reid, of the great Penn State teams that, with the exception of the 17–17 tie with Florida State in the Gator Bowl that same year, went undefeated through 31 straight games. Who were some of these sophomores? Linebacker and later punt returner Dennis Onkotz, linebacker Jim Kates, defensive tackle Steve Smear, defensive end John Ebersole, defensive backfield stars Paul and Peter Johnson all were initiated in that game with Miami.

Probably the best–remembered game in that win streak was

the 15–14 win over Kansas in the Orange Bowl the night of January 1, 1970. That was the famous game when Penn State scored with only seconds left on the clock, making the score 14–13 with Kansas up! We passed unsuccessfully for a two–point conversion and then, because Kansas had had 12 men on the field during the extra point try, had another chance and Bobby Campbell ran it in on a misdirection play for a 15–14 lead with no time left on the clock.

I had an especially good seat for that game, which gave me an insider's look at what happened to give Penn State their second chance to win the game. There are always lots of social activities surrounding the major bowl games. At one of the luncheons, my wife, Betty, had a chance to renew her friendship with Jim Simpson, who would be the play–by–play announcer on the NBC telecast of the game. They had gone to a suburban high school in Washington, D.C., many years before, and they met again after all those years. I was one of the Penn State broadcasters that season and when Jim Simpson learned that, he asked if I would be willing to sit next to him during the telecast and feed him any information about the Penn State team that would help him to know the Lions better. I had never been in the middle of a network sports telecast and thought it would be an interesting experience. Simpson's partner for the telecast was Al Derogatis, former star center for the New York Giants, and I was assigned a seat between them.

I had a marvelous learning experience during the game, watching the broadcast team coordinate the instant replays, call for commercial breaks, decide to isolate the camera on a certain player before the play began, etc. The game appeared to be over as the clock wound down with Penn State seeming a long way from a chance to tie, much less win.

With Penn State near midfield, the players told us later, Bobby Campbell told quarterback Chuck Burkhart in the huddle to "throw the ball as far as you can to the left goalpost and I'll be there to get it." It sounded like the kind of play kids make up in street games and not a sophisticated play in a major collegiate bowl game. Burkhart went back, wound up and threw the ball as hard and far as he could. When it came down, Bobby Campbell had it! He actually would have scored if the throw had been a little shorter. Bobby dove as far as he could and it was right on his fingertips. A couple of inches longer and he never would have caught it. If it had been a foot shorter, Campbell wouldn't have had to leave his feet to catch it and could have run it in for the touchdown.

Campbell's magnificent stretching catch brought him down on about the three-yard line. The clock indicated that Penn State would have time for one—certainly no more than two—plays. Burkhart called for an off–tackle slant by Charlie Pittman, his best running back. They broke the huddle and, for some reason Burkhart later said he could never explain, he handed the ball to Pittman but never turned the ball loose. He pulled it back, put it on his hip, and ran a bootleg around his left end. Charlie Zapiec put a crunching block on Kansas' All–American end, John Zook, and Burkhart almost could have walked into the end zone.

This wasn't your usual run–of–the–mill bootleg. What made it different was the fact that Burkhart didn't call it in the huddle. He actually meant for Pittman to get the hand–off as he had called, but at the last second something told him to keep the ball. Since he hadn't told Pittman that he was simply to carry out the fake, Charlie reached for the ball that wasn't there and he was almost panic–stricken because he was sure that he had fumbled the ball.

Time had run out and there was only one more decision to make—kick the extra point and settle for a tie or go for two and win it or lose it right there. I'm sure that Joe Paterno never hesitated. This was a big bowl game and a chance to defeat a highly–ranked opponent and end the season with a big win. So he called for a pass in the corner of the end zone. You couldn't tell what play had been called or who the intended receiver was. We rolled right and flooded the end zone. Kansas also had everyone there and the play just seemed to go to pieces. The pass was right in front of the Kansas band and when it was incomplete, the band spilled out onto the field. Kansas fans all over the stadium began celebrating their 14–13 victory. But as we know, that was not the end of the story.

Up in the broadcast booth, Al Derogatis tapped me on the shoulder and passed me a note he indicated I was to pass on to Jim Simpson. I'll never forget what the note said: "This game is not over yet." Simpson looked over at Derogatis for an explanation and, without saying a word, Al pointed down to the goal line where a yellow flag lay on the field, and standing alongside was an official with his arms folded.

The official had a look that said, "There are many thousands of you here, but I am the only one who knows that this game isn't over." He had detected a violation, and it had to be against Kansas. After the officials huddled in the end zone, the signal came. Kansas had 12 men on the field during the extra point pass and the penalty was half the distance to the goal line. It meant that the ball was closer to the goal line because unquestionably Penn State would again go for a game-winning two points. Now, Penn State might call a running play.

So they lined up again. Burkhart gave the ball to Bobby Campbell on a counter play and he scored easily. So now it was time for heartbreak for the Kansas fans and near delirium for the Penn State fans. Change the scoreboard...leave the 14 points for Kansas, but let the Penn State score now read 15!

As you might guess, the post–game press conference was a noisy one with all kinds of questions fired by the very large press corps that had covered the game. Most of the questions were for the official who called the penalty. "When did you first notice that Kansas had 12 men on the field? Where was the 12th player lined up? Who was the extra man? What was his number?" The official played it very coolly. As a matter of fact, he seemed almost smug about his role. He told the press that there was no chance that either team could get by with an extra man on the field. He said something like, "That's a personal rule of mine. On every play I always count the number of players so if there ever is a 12th man, I won't miss him."

Most of the Penn State fans went back to the hotel with just one thing in mind. They were going to watch the replay of the game on a local Miami station to see if they could pick up the violation. Since the station didn't have time to edit the telecast, we had to watch the entire game to be sure we saw the last play. As I recall, the replay wasn't over until about 3:30 a.m. Sure enough, there were 12 Kansas players on the field for the first aborted extra point pass play.

But, as it turned out, the official who made the call should have played it modestly and simply said something like, "It's my job to count the players, and I was simply doing my job." The reason I say he should have played it modestly is that after Penn State took a complete look at the film and dissected it for coaching purposes, they discovered that the official who was so sure that he always counted the players must have been paying attention elsewhere. They found that Kansas had 12 players on the field for the three or four plays that preceded the extra point and we all wondered where was the official who said, "On every play, I always count the number of players." ■

5

In the Ring

■

with

■

Fred and Doc

■

It is hard to imagine these days, but there was a time when college boxing was a very popular intercollegiate sport. In the 1930s, boxing was probably the most popular indoor sport, and the boxing dual meets and intercollegiate tournaments packed Rec Hall. When I was on the campus in the 1940s, boxing still was a major sport, sharing the indoor spotlight with wrestling, which was a growing intercollegiate sport.

On many Saturday nights, Rec Hall held triple–headers—boxing, wrestling, and basketball. Boxing was so popular that freshmen in fraternity houses had the duty of getting to Rec Hall about 5:30 p.m. to hold seats for late–arriving upperclassmen.

In the early 1960s, university officials began to question the viability of boxing as an intercollegiate sport, and Penn State was one of the first schools to drop it. A few years after the Lions stopped competing in boxing, an NCAA champion who fought for Wisconsin died in the ring during a dual meet, and that was one of the final blows that removed boxing from the intercollegiate scene.

Two famous names from Penn State's boxing past are Steve Hamas, an outstanding heavyweight fighter, and Billy Soose, who turned professional after leaving Penn State and became middle-weight champion of the world by defeating Ken Overlin.

Among the most fondly remembered Penn State athletic figures is the man who was boxing coach from 1923 to 1949, Leo Houck. Leo is remembered for many funny things he said and did. But most of all, Penn Staters remember Leo because he called everyone "Fred."

Students, professors, his boxing team members, workmen who moved the ring onto the main floor, janitors, and university administrators…it made no difference to Leo; they were all Freds. I have never found anyone to whom Leo explained just why he called everyone by the same name. You could have been a friend of Leo's for a day or for every day that he was at Penn State; he called you Fred and you never knew why.

Leo was a well–known, successful middleweight fighter in the 1920s. Although he never was a champion, he fought many champions and defeated some in non–title bouts. The record shows that Leo never paid any attention to the size of the boxers he met in the ring. Although he was a middleweight, he fought light–heavyweights plenty of times. And, if my memory serves me right, when I looked up Leo's record in *Ring* magazine (the bible of boxing), he got into the ring with heavyweights more than once. He had the reputation of being one of the really tough guys to fight and beat, regardless of the weight.

Boxing in the 1920s was a really tough, unregulated sport. There was no television or television income, of course. There were few safety precautions. The fights were held in all sorts of arenas and halls. There weren't many technical knockouts (TKOs) in those days. If you were knocked down, the referee simply counted to 10 and, instead of a TKO, there was just a knockout, period.

When I first met Tommy Loughran, former world's light–heavyweight champion, at the Philadelphia Navy Yard when I was stationed there with the U.S. Marines, and told him that I was from Penn State, he asked if I knew Leo Houck. I said I had spent lots of time with Leo around Rec Hall and Tommy responded, "That Leo was one tough customer. He could box, he could punch, he could fight you any way he figured he could beat you, and he took a punch as well as anyone I ever saw in the ring."

There are literally dozens of Leo Houck stories I could tell here. My favorite story concerns the fact that for every single day of his life at Penn State, Leo ate his meals at the Corner Room. Leo was not a bachelor. He came from Lancaster and he and his wife had a number of children. When Leo was named Penn State boxing coach, the family moved to State College. Although I never found out the real reason why, Leo's wife never liked living in State College. Shortly after arriving, she took the children back to Lancaster, while Leo remained here. Any weekend that his team didn't have a match, Leo "hitched" a ride to Lancaster on Friday afternoon and back to State College on Sunday evening.

Now, he didn't "hitch" a ride the way a student might by standing out on Atherton Street with his thumb stuck in the air. Leo was such a well–known character that every salesman who made regular stops in State College knew about his "Lancaster on Friday and back to State College on Sunday" routine. So, beginning early on Friday afternoons, salesmen who were headed toward Lancaster stopped to find out if Leo had already gotten a ride. It's said that the same salesmen who were headed back in the direction of State College Sunday evening or early Monday morning would call Leo's home in Lancaster to see if he needed a ride. I don't know how many salesmen were in what I used to call "Leo's Transportation Company," but there were enough so that when I asked Leo if he ever got stuck in Lancaster or State College he said, "Not once. As a matter of fact, I usually had a choice of what kind of car I wanted to ride in!"

With that explanation of why and how often Leo had his meals in the Corner Room, I can finish my favorite story. Leo <u>always</u> ate in the very first booth in the Corner Room. I never knew how the booth could always be empty and available whenever Leo decided to eat. I asked him many times why he always found his booth empty. He gave me several answers ranging from, "I bought that booth a long time ago, and I only let certain people use it until I'm ready to eat," to "It's in my contract that I get to use the booth any time I want to, and if someone is already there, they have to move to another booth," to "You know how small Matty Mateer (one of the owners of the Corner Room) is. I told him that if I ever wanted to eat and the booth wasn't empty, I'd drop him with a left hook."

One day long after Leo had died, I found myself thinking about Leo and that front booth. After all those years, I think I figured it out. Leo used to spend much of his time across the street from the Corner Room in Graham's (I would demean the institution of Graham's by calling it just a newsstand). If the weather was nice, Leo sat on the bench out front; if the weather wasn't nice, Leo sat on a high stool inside the door. I finally figured out that at meal times, one of the waitresses would wave to Leo when the booth was empty and he walked across the street and occupied it as if he were royalty.

I was single in those days, and while I wasn't as loyal to the Corner Room as Leo was, I did eat many of my meals there and ate many, many dinners with Leo. Leo had a very unusual ritual. He was usually alone in his booth and no matter how well he knew you, he never invited you to sit down. If you did sit down and have dinner, he was always gracious and made you feel welcome. When dinner was over, he always made a point of thanking you for joining him. If, on the other hand, you came in and sat in the booth next to Leo's, he never said a word as you went by. It took me a while to figure out that Leo was really lonesome and that he enjoyed having someone eat with him. I also think he was bashful about inviting you, in case you would prefer not dining with him.

Dinner with Leo always ended with another ritual. He always ordered either a piece of cake or pie for dessert but, every night, after he had finished about seven–eighths of his dessert, he would call the waitress over. When she came to the booth he would say, "You know, this piece of cake (or pie) wasn't very good; it was much too dry. It must have been left over from yesterday." After she had assured him that the cakes and pies were made fresh daily right on the premises he would say, "Well, they must have put too much of something in it or left something out because it was very dry and I don't think I should have to pay for it. But I don't want you to get in trouble in the kitchen by making you take it back. So, if you can put a scoop or two of vanilla ice cream on what's left of it, I think that will moisten it up enough so that I won't mind eating it."

Every single night, the same scene was played out. The waitress would take what was left of Leo's cake or pie and bring it back with a fair–sized helping of ice cream on top. "Will this be all right, Leo?" Leo would take a spoonful of the ice cream and his reply was always the same, "Yes, that'll make it just about right." Of course, everyone knew the game Leo was playing, including management and ownership of the Corner Room. But it just didn't matter. Leo was a good guy and a scoop or two of ice cream just didn't seem to matter. The only person it mattered to was Leo, who really liked cake and pie, especially if it was topped with some ice cream…and the ice cream was on the house.

I think I could fill an entire book with Leo stories. But I only have room here for one or two more. Boxing practice always was held at 4:00 in the afternoon. The ring, which was on wheels, was placed in the middle of the Rec Hall playing floor for the intercollegiate matches. But because the floor also was used for other purposes—pick–up basketball games, badminton, intramural competitions, etc.—the boxing ring was wheeled under the balcony for practices. If you chose to, you could stand anywhere around the ring apron and watch the practice fights.

Leo always was the referee for the afternoon practice bouts. He said it was so he could get a close look at the fighters and see what mistakes they were making. But since he rarely said anything to the fighters in the course of a round, I always suspected that Leo wanted to be the third man in the ring so he could keep a close eye on the fighters to make sure that no one took an especially hard punch without him being able to immediately stop the bout.

I suspect this because of the instructions Leo always gave to the referee before any of our intercollegiate bouts began. For any Penn State bout, especially if the fighter wasn't very experienced or skillful, Leo would say, "Ref, I want you to watch me out of the corner of your eye. If my man takes an especially hard or damaging punch, or if he gets so tired that he looks like he can't defend himself, I'll stand up in the corner. The minute I stand up, you stop the fight and declare the other guy the winner." I can't tell you how many times that happened without the crowd knowing about it. What was obvious to the referee and Leo sometimes was not as obvious to the crowd. The result was that, over the years, dozens of referees took a terrific booing because the crowd thought that Penn State didn't get a square shake and the referee should not have stopped the fight.

The only shake that mattered was the shake of Leo's head when he stood up in the corner. I suspect that to this day, many Penn State boxing fans thought that a lot of the referees were "softies." If they had looked to the Penn State corner, they would have seen who the real softie was. After years of watching Penn State boxers in the ring, I can honestly tell you that I never saw a Penn State fighter take continued punishment. I've seen them cut, I've seen them knocked down, and I've seen them outclassed. But, I've never seen a Penn State fighter really hurt because the guy in their corner who was looking out for them was a rough, tough, ex–pro fighter who respected the difference between a guy fighting for business and a college boy trying to win a Penn State letter in boxing.

Leo's practices each week involved a series of elimination bouts in each weight class to determine who would be on the varsity team for the upcoming intercollegiate match. There were always plenty of fighters who wanted to eliminate for that weekend's bouts by challenging an incumbent who had fought the last time Penn State had a match against an intercollegiate opponent. Also, if you were good enough to be chosen for an elimination bout and you fought your fight, you qualified for the training table and that meant you didn't have to pay for dinner.

One particular elimination bout in the 135–pound weight class involved the defending Eastern Intercollegiate champion at that weight, meaning that if you wanted to fight an elimination bout you had to fight the champ, who was a murderous puncher. I remember the student who fought him this particular afternoon because of the way he was dressed. He wore a really old and tattered pair of shorts and had a decrepit pair of sneakers instead of boxing shoes. I remember thinking that he wanted to fight, even if he expected to take a licking, so he could have a training table dinner where you could usually eat as much as you wanted unless you were trying to make weight.

Right from the opening bell it was obvious that the challenger had fought some before. But it was equally obvious that he was no match for the champ. I remember thinking that when he realized that he had a relatively easy opponent, the champion would take it easy and carry the challenger for the entire three rounds. Some fighters might have, but remembering how young we all were, and realizing that the champ wanted to impress his coach, who was the referee, he began to hand out a pretty good licking to the challenger.

In the first round, the kid took a tough right hand and went down. Leo immediately kneeled beside him, talking to him to make sure that his head was clear. After taking a good look at his eyes, he let the bout go on. The challenger got in a couple of good licks the rest of the round, and into the second round he seemed to be almost holding his own until he ran into another right hand and went down again.

Standing next to me was an especially well–dressed student who yelled, "He's not going to get up, he's yellow." Leo said to the student manager who was timing the round, "Fred, ring the bell." Leo walked over to the ropes and called the well–dressed student over. "Fred," he asked, "did you ever wear one of these headgear? Did you ever put on the gloves? Have you ever been in the ring?" The student replied, "No, I never have." Leo then motioned to him to come around the corner of the ring and pointed to the three steps that were used to climb up into the ring. "Fred, I want to tell you something I hope you won't forget. Fighting's a tough business. Any guy who walks up those three steps, if he doesn't have to, he ain't yellow."

I never watch a live or televised bout without remembering that afternoon way back in the early 1940s. I wonder if the guy Leo told off also remembers.

One final story about Leo. I had mentioned earlier that Leo's family lived in Lancaster all those years while Leo lived in a rooming house that was next door to the rooming house where I lived. Where Leo lived always was a mystery to most people, but not to me. No one knew where Leo lived because he was always seen in only three places—sitting in Graham's eating pretzels or playing the pinball machine, at Rec Hall refereeing or coaching boxing matches, or eating his meals at the Corner Room. At other times he just seemed to vaporize and no one ever saw him.

I knew where Leo lived because at that time I was the wakeup announcer at WMAJ, which was half a block from my rooming house. We went on the air at 6:30 a.m., and I'd leave my room a little before that. Every morning as I came out of the rooming house, Leo came out of his house right next door. I was on my way to the radio station to begin the day with the "Star Spangled Banner"; Leo was on his way to Our Lady of Victory Church for the 7 a.m. mass.

Only once in my life did I spend an entire evening with Leo. I had a phone call one day from a radio station about 50 miles from State College. The town this station served was staging a big boxing show at the local high school and, because the gym was sold out, they asked if I would be willing to do blow–by–blow broadcasts of all the fights on the card. They offered me, as I recall, $50 for my efforts. That seems like a laughable sum of money, but since I was only making $80 a week then, it was a worthwhile use of my time. They also offered to pay 20 cents a mile for me to drive there. I can't remember the price of gasoline back in the '50s, but I'm sure I made a couple of extra dollars because gasoline was so cheap. They told me that they didn't have anyone in their town who was competent to judge the bouts and wondered if I knew Leo Houck well enough to bring him along to judge the fights. They said I could offer him $25 for his professional judging services. If you remember the lengths Leo would go to to get some free ice cream, you can imagine how he would jump at the chance to pick up an easy judging fee.

On the way to the fights, Leo let me in on something he thought I should know but had been hesitant to tell me for fear I would withdraw the offer of the judging fee. "Fred," he said, "I have lots of trouble staying awake in the evening, and after about 8 o'clock I'm always dropping off to take a couple of winks. I'll probably not have any trouble this evening because I'll be watching the boxers. But what am I going to do if I drop off during a round of two?" I said, "If that happens, Leo, I'll make sure that they sit you right across the ring from me next to the apron. If you drop off during a round or two, look over at me when the round is over and I'll signal you who I thought won the round." "How are you going to signal me?" "I'll pull my right ear if I think the guy in the right corner won the round, and my left ear if the guy in the left corner won." Leo asked, "What if the round is even?" I said, "If I think you ought to score the round a draw, I'll pull the end of my nose."

When we got to the high school gymnasium where the fights were being held, the place was jammed. And we were late getting started because there must have been a hundred people lined up to get Leo's autograph. Leo was a real celebrity in central Pennsylvania, and the audience considered it an honor to have him willing to come to their small town to judge their fights. What they didn't know, of course, was what Leo would do for $25.

After the introductions were made, the first fighters were introduced, the house lights were turned off, and the bell sounded for the first round of the first fight. I looked across the ring and there was the celebrity judge, my buddy Leo, fast asleep. His only saving grace was the fact that he was the kind of sleeper who didn't rest his chin on his chest when he was asleep. He belonged to the sleeping school that puts its elbow on the desk and rests the chin on the hand. Unless you were looking straight at him, you had no idea he was asleep. I've had lots of experience studying those kinds of sleepers in years of teaching at Penn State, and I could spot one in a minute.

The bell sounded to end the first round. Leo kind of nodded his head and opened his eyes. Giving absolutely no signal, he looked across the ring to me for my sign. I pulled my ear and saw Leo look down at the desk and mark his card. I'd like to tell you that Leo only fell asleep during a handful of rounds. Not so! He repeated the elbow on the desk and chin on the elbow routine through the entire 12 bouts. I don't recall if there was a knockout or two or if a fight or two was stopped, but if all the bouts went the distance, Leo slept through 36 rounds of boxing.

Either I was a terrific judge or the crowd had the utmost respect for Leo's expertise, because practically no decisions received a single boo when they announced the winner. I really felt sorry for the dozen or so boxers who had stayed in their robes to take a group picture with Leo. Practically every one of them asked him for any tips that he might offer to help their style. I never heard such generalities in my life—"You've got to keep your left up all the time" or "Keep your fists clenched tightly or you might break your thumb" or "Remember, fight the full three minutes of every round" or "Try and finish every round strong, especially the last one, to leave a good impression on the judge."

After Leo finished signing autographs, we got into my car and headed back to State College. I don't think I had driven two blocks until I looked over and there Leo was, fast asleep. This time he didn't go through the elbow on the desk and chin in his hand routine. He stretched out, loosened his tie, put his head back on the seat and snored through his open mouth.

When we stopped in front of his rooming house, I roused Leo, who said, "Thanks for the ride. Do you have my 25 bucks?" I was tempted to say, "What do you mean your 25 bucks? I broadcast all the bouts and I judged them, too. I think I ought to keep my $50 and the $25 judging fee, too." But I thought that since he was half-asleep, he might not know that I was kidding. I must have known Leo another 10 years or so after that night. He never said a word about our trip; nor did I. And I also never invited him to judge any more boxing matches.

Time Marches On—We Look Back and Ahead

The night of January 7, 1996, brought back a flood of memories for Penn State sports fans. That night the Nittany Lion basketball team played its last game in Rec Hall. Several nights later, Penn State and Minnesota played the first game to be played in the brand new Bryce Jordan Center, across the road from Beaver Stadium. It was appropriate for the Lions to close out their games at Rec Hall with a win over Wisconsin and to open the new arena with a win over Minnesota.

Thousands of Penn State alumni have their own recollections and memories of events that happened during their days as Penn State students, since Rec Hall was the site for boxing and wrestling as well as gymnastics and women's basketball, in addition to men's basketball. Since it sometimes seems that I have been involved with Penn State sports forever (I saw my first event in

Rec Hall in the fall of 1940), the athletic department asked me to write a "memory" article for the special program to be distributed at the final game.

I titled the article "Rec Hall Farewell Triggers Flood of Memories for Long–Time Lion Observer" and said, "For this retrospective I would like to borrow from the computer era and 'surf' through the computer of my mind to bring up from the past some of the most memorable events and performances from Rec Hall years."

I'm not sure why boxing was considered an appropriate college sport but it was, and it became arguably the most popular sport of the indoor season. There were many memorable fights in Rec Hall, including two that I want to tell you about here.

First, the late Chuck Drazenovich, outstanding blocking back on the 1948 Cotton Bowl football team, was talked into joining the boxing team by Leo Houck. Drazenovich was totally without ring experience, but you would never have thought that when you

Mickey Bergstein, who broadcast Penn State intercollegiate boxing matches, interviews Chuck Drazenovich following his national championship-winning bout in Rec Hall. Drazenovich also starred at blocking back on the 1948 Cotton Bowl football team.

saw him move around the ring throwing punches. I have always believed that Chuck could have made a strong run at the heavyweight championship of the world if he had chosen a boxing career instead of a professional football career with the Washington Redskins.

The defending NCAA heavyweight champion was Marty Crandall of Syracuse, who probably would not have argued about Chuck's ability after Chuck flattened him to win the intercollegiate heavyweight championship.

The second fight matched Penn State's 127–pounder, the late Glenn Hawthorne, with Dick Miyagawa of Wisconsin. The fight was during the 1947 season. Miyagawa had won the 1942 national championship while a student at San Jose State before serving in the military. He was a murderous puncher, while Hawthorne was quick with his feet and even quicker with his hands. It was a classic match, with Miyagawa stalking Hawthorne looking for one big punch to end it, and Hawthorne moving around the ring, in and out, with the Wisconsin champion's face right at the end of his wonderful left jab.

Glenn Hawthorne, the boxer, won over Dick Miyagawa, the puncher, and Penn State had another national champion.

Doc

There must have been a time when, in order to coach at Penn State, you had to promise to call everyone by the same nickname. Leo Houck kept from memorizing people's names by calling everyone "Fred." Another coach whose years on campus pretty much paralleled those of Leo was the popular wrestling coach Charlie Speidel. He and Leo had something in common in addition to their ears, which showed evidence of years in the ring and on the mat. Charlie called everyone "Doc." His rules evidently were the same as Leo's—if you were a wrestler, an administrator, a professor, a student, or just a friend to Charlie, you were "Doc."

At the time that Charlie was coaching the Lions (1927-1942 and 1947-1964), wrestling was an extremely popular sport that used to fill Rec Hall, especially for meets with traditional rivals like Lehigh, Pitt, Navy, and a couple of other teams. In more recent years, Penn State has enjoyed much success under Coach Rich Lorenzo, an Eastern Intercollegiate champion when he wrestled under Charlie Speidel, and another champion, John Fritz, Rich's successor. But despite the team's success during the dual meet season and at the national level, and despite Penn State's consistently high rankings, the wrestling team rarely draws the large crowds that Charlie's team drew.

There are probably lots of reasons for this because our gymnastics teams, which used to pack Rec Hall for Coach Gene Wettstone, also have not drawn sizeable crowds in recent years. And the basketball teams saw a drop in attendance, although the team started to fill Rec Hall under Coach Bruce Parkhill and now that we are in the Big Ten, interest in the basketball program has been revived with the appearance of teams like Indiana, Michigan, Michigan State, and Ohio State. With the new Bryce Jordan Center on campus and the success of Jerry Dunn, Parkhill's successor as coach of the Lions, basketball seems to be on the rise at Penn State.

A number of Penn State sports officials and participants gather in the equipment room at Rec Hall during the 1952 winter sports season. Shown from left to right are Mickey Bergstein, broadcaster; Ike Gilbert, graduate manager of athletics; Charlie Speidel, wrestling coach; Nick Thiel, lacrosse coach; Glenn Howthorne, NCAA boxing champion; and Skip Hosterman, All-American soccer player. Kneeling in front is Ridge Riley, Director of the Penn State Alumni Association.

In addition to football, basketball, and boxing, we used to broadcast the wrestling meets on the campus. I felt reasonably confident as a wrestling broadcaster. I knew the rules, understood the scoring, had a fair knowledge of the various holds, and studied the records of the opposing teams and individual wrestlers when they came to Rec Hall. I also knew Charlie Speidel because I often went to his afternoon practices to learn what I could about the sport.

One day he said to me, "You know, Doc, I've heard your broadcasts of high school matches and you do an okay job. You know what you see on the mat, but I think you ought to learn why wrestlers are doing what they are doing, why certain things work and why a wrestler can't get off the bottom or why he can't stay on top." I thanked him for his observations but, in my ignorance, didn't think I had to know all those things to be a broadcaster. Charlie persisted, however, and one day said to me, "Hey, Doc, why don't I get the manager to get you a uniform and you and I can roll around and I can show you a couple of things." That sounded like a good idea that could be fun so I went to the locker room to get my tights, shoes, and headgear.

When I looked at myself in the mirror in the locker room, I must admit I thought I looked like a pretty good lightweight wrestler. I would find out soon enough that there was more to wrestling than the uniform, and that it really didn't matter how good you looked to yourself.

Charlie cleared the mats and had his wrestlers surround the center mat where he was going to conduct his lesson. We walked out and Charlie announced, "I'm going to let you take me down." So, he sort of stuck his leg forward, and I took the bait. I got hold of his leg, lifted it into the air, reached back to trip his other leg out from under him, and we headed down to the mat. On the way down, something strange happened. I had one of his legs, the other leg was in the air, and both of my legs were on the mat. But somehow, when we landed on the mat, he was on top and I was underneath. My takedown had become his takedown and I still don't know what he did to me on the way down.

Then the "lesson" began. Charlie said, "Since I know so much more about wrestling than you do, it isn't fair for me to use my arms and my legs. You use your arms and legs and I will just use my legs and won't touch you with my hands or arms." I said, "You mean that you are going to stay on top and keep me on the bottom without using your arms?" "That's right," said Charlie.

So we went down on the mat with Charlie wrapping his legs around me and leaning back on his elbows, and I went to work. I tried to sit out, I tried to stand up, I tried to roll, I tried to pry his legs loose, I tried every bottom move I had ever seen a good wrestler make, and nothing came even close to working. I thought I could make it a couple of times, but just at the critical moment when I thought I was free, Charlie would adjust one of his legs and I was all wrapped up again. This went on for what seemed like a long time but was probably only four or five minutes. What happened was that I got so damned tired I eventually laid down and quit trying. If I had tried to wrestle 10 more seconds, I think I would have thrown up in front of the entire team.

If I had known the humiliation in store for me, I think I would have bolted for the locker room, gotten dressed, and never come back to wrestling practice. Actually it was a lot of fun and I really wasn't humiliated, just embarrassed. And I wouldn't have minded the embarrassment if I had learned anything about wrestling from the experience. But I only learned one thing: don't wrestle with Charlie Speidel. I hate to imagine what would have happened to me if Charlie had used both his arms and legs. I probably would still be trying to free myself!

I had known Charlie when I was an undergraduate and that friendship almost got me into trouble in my freshman year. As Penn Staters who were Liberal Arts students then might remember, there were several required courses for freshmen and sophomores, with two in particular that most students will remember— Physical Science 7, an introductory course in principles of physics, taught by Professor Henry Yeagley, who was a wonderful teacher, and Physical Science 8, an introductory course in chemistry taught by a jolly kind of guy, Professor Harry Van Velzer. You had to pass both of these courses before you could move into the Upper Division (junior and senior years).

At some point, Charlie Speidel decided that he should get his degree. I don't know what Charlie's earlier academic training had been, but I know that he did not have a college degree, and he decided that if he was going to remain coaching at the college level, he ought to have it. He enrolled in one course each semester and felt confident that in time he would earn his degree. In the particular semester when this story takes place, Charlie had enrolled in Physical Science 8. That course had many, many sections but, as luck would have it, Charlie ended up in the section I was in. Charlie immediately became friendly with Professor Van Velzer who, it turned out, was something of a college wrestling fan. Charlie, of course, called him Doc. I am certain that the professor took this as Charlie's shortening of his academic title of Doctor. I often wonder if Professor Van Velzer found Charlie's informal greeting disrespectful or merely friendly.

It was not easy to get a good grade in Physical Science 8. Many students had had no chemistry in high school or had had a very small smattering as part of a general science course. As a result, lots of students found themselves taking the course for a second time. That was not a desirable situation, so Dr. Van Velzer came up with a unique solution that the students liked and that, in the long run, helped them learn more chemistry. We had several exams during the semester. Every student had the same option. If you were not satisfied with your grade, you could come in on Saturday morning and take another exam that covered generally the same lectures or same chapters in the text. The rule was that you had to score 10 points higher when taking a re–exam. If you scored 10 points higher, you could take still another re–exam. But when you took a re–exam and didn't improve your score by 10 points, you settled for the highest score you had managed on any of the exams you had taken.

I don't remember what Charlie and I scored on the first exam, but I know we qualified to take a re–exam. I recall that I had a respectable score, probably somewhere around 70. Charlie's score was somewhere around 15 and he was panicked. He grabbed me in the hall and asked if I was going to take it again. When I told him I was, he told me that he could never get an additional 10 points. He said, "I hardly understood any of the chemistry terms and, even if I had taken chemistry in high school, it was so long ago that I would have forgotten everything. What am I going to do, Mick?"

I made this suggestion. "Charlie," I said, "Dr. Van Velzer seems to really like wrestling, and I think that he thinks you are a celebrity. Why don't you try and fast–talk him into the fact that you have been away from school for a long, long time, that you really want to take his important course and learn as much as you can, but that you don't seem to be able to get a decent score on the kind of exams we are going to have. Ask him what he would suggest."

As I remember it, Charlie never took an exam in the classroom. I seem to remember that the professor gave him an oral test in his office to see if Charlie could score a passing grade. In my view, although this smacked of favoritism, no one got hurt. Charlie went on to take a course here and there, but never earned his degree. If he had, and if he had had a hand along the way, my view would be "good for him."

Many years later, Charlie approached Eric Walker, the university president, about taking a sabbatical leave.

"Hey, Doc," he said, " I think I am going to apply for a sabbatical leave." "You can't, Charlie," Walker replied. "You don't qualify for a sabbatical leave."

"Why don't I qualify?" Charlie asked. "I've been here more than 25 years." Walker responded, "A faculty member doesn't qualify for a sabbatical leave if he is within one year of retirement." "Hey, Doc, I'm only 55 years old," Charlie said. "I'm not within one year of retirement."

"Charlie," Walker said, "every coach is always within one year of retirement!" ■

6

If This is State College,

Where's

University Park?

Isn't Penn State in State College, Pennsylvania? Well, sort of. Lots of folks think the name's been changed to University Park, Pennsylvania, and that's where Penn State is. Is that what happened? Is Penn State really located in University Park? Well, sort of.

How can a major university be located in two different towns? Well, that's not easy to manage…unless the president of the university just happens to have a brother who is the President of the United States. Is that what happened? Well, let me tell you the story of University Park, and you decide for yourself!

In 1953, Penn State was not yet a university. While it was a large and expanding educational institution, its official name was the Pennsylvania State College. The president was Dr. Milton S. Eisenhower, who previously had held several high–level positions in government and had been the president of Kansas State University in Manhattan, Kansas.

As Penn State neared its 100th birthday, it occurred to Dr. Eisenhower that the institution enjoyed the prestige, and was of appropriate size, to have earned designation as a university. He took the appropriate steps to achieve a university designation for Penn State.

As we moved toward the day when we would be recognized as a full–fledged university, Dr. Eisenhower was seriously troubled by the fact that, while we would be called a university, we would still have to show our location as State College. He feared it would be hard to get people to think of us as a university as long as the dateline on newspaper stories and the postmark on mail contained the word "college."

Those of us who had lived here for some time sort of enjoyed the confusion we caused when, for example, we made an out–of–town purchase and told the clerk that we worked at the Pennsylvania State College located in State College, Pennsylvania. Then began the real fun that went something like this: "Yes, I know that you are at the Pennsylvania State College, but what is the name of the town?" "State College, Pennsylvania, etc. etc. etc." So, most of us could sympathize with Dr. Eisenhower when he talked of the difficulty of trying to mix the words "university" and "college" while establishing what we were and where we were.

I received an invitation from Dr. Eisenhower's office to attend a meeting at which first steps would be taken to attempt to change the name of the community to eliminate the college–university confusion. It was a rather short meeting since not much discussion took place.

Dr. Eisenhower told the group that he was determined that the name of the borough be changed. He further told the committee that he had no personal preference for a new name as long as it did not contain the word "college." When someone suggested this would be a difficult change to bring about, Dr. Eisenhower said something like, "I'm sure that most of the residents of this community know how important Penn State is to the whole area. Since I've been here, I haven't asked the community for anything. I'm sure that if it is made clear to them that I <u>really</u> want them to change the name of the community, they won't deny my request." As far as he was concerned, the name change would soon be an accomplished fact.

As I recall, the committee he called together was called the "Committee of Forty." On the committee were those in the community whom the university deemed to be opinion leaders who would lend the weight of the positions they held, or their own personal reputations, to help win election for a new name. I was on the committee because someone believed that, as the general manager of the local radio station, I would be in a position to editorialize or lobby for the change. The other members of the committee were fairly evenly divided between those representing the community and those representing the university. No one asked any of us if we personally favored the change. It was assumed that since President Eisenhower favored it, we would automatically fall into line.

The first job we faced was picking a new community name to appear on the ballot. Under the law, voters could not be given several choices. The question on the ballot would read, "Do you favor changing the name of the Borough of State College to selected name?". We decided we should give everyone who would vote on the name change a chance to register his or her preference for a new name. We placed preference ballots all over town. I can't remember exactly how many preferences were registered, but a surprisingly large number of citizens voted, and the name getting the greatest number of votes was Mt. Nittany. So that was it. On Election Day you choose—State College or Mt. Nittany. Since State College is still State College, you know how the vote came out.

What you don't know is that State College won in something larger than a landslide. I had expected the result, but none of us thought the margin would be as large as it was. In the residential area north of the campus known as College Heights, the margin for the name State College was the largest in any precinct; in 1953, the vast majority of the residents of College Heights were Penn State employees or members of the faculty. The election proved that, given a chance to repudiate the boss once the curtain in the voting booth is drawn shut, large numbers of workers will take a shot at the boss.

During the campaign, it became clear to many of us that the name change was in trouble. Each member of the committee took informal polls to get some idea of how the tide was running. When we shared our poll results at committee meetings, we found similar responses to our question of whether someone would vote for the name change. Most of the answers went something like, "I may vote for the name change if the university will pay for all the stationary and invoices that I am going to have to throw away" or "I'll vote for the name change if the university will pay to have all my vehicles repainted with the new name" or "Who does the university president think he is? Just because his brother is President of the United States doesn't mean that he can come in and change the name of the town we've always lived in." My own findings were summed up by one of the borough's oldest residents who told me, "This town was named State College when President Eisenhower got here and it will still be named State College when he leaves."

So, it was obvious that there was work to do! Lou Bell was the Director of Public Information at the university and he chaired the committee. He went to Dr. Eisenhower with our guess that the campaign needed revitalization badly. He asked the university president to lend his personal prestige to the effort and suggested that he be allowed to schedule talks by Dr. Eisenhower to local service clubs, church groups, Chamber of Commerce, women's organizations, etc.

"It has to help if people in the community realize how much you want this change and how important you believe it is that we rid ourselves of the name State College," Lou told Dr. Eisenhower. However, when Lou reported back to the committee, he said Dr. Eisenhower responded, "I really don't feel that that's necessary. I have never asked this community for anything since I have been here and I am confident that, once they are told how important this is to me and how much I want it, they'll vote for the name change."

I remember thinking when I heard that, "The game's over. Now it's just a matter of running out the clock!" Confident that "the people will not deny me this simple request," Dr. Eisenhower asked Lou to schedule a "victory breakfast" at the Nittany Lion Inn for the morning after the election. The purpose of the breakfast, I assume, was to thank each other for our hard work and to congratulate each other on the big win. It was a quiet breakfast and, after the meal, there was a very, very short program. The only speaker was Dr. Eisenhower.

I cannot quote his exact remarks, but the gist of what he said was, "I guess the people of this town didn't understand how important it was to me and to the university to have a name which would make it easy for people to make the transition from a college to a university. I felt and continue to feel very strongly about this. So, I will tell you now that as soon as it can be arranged, there will never again be a news story sent off this campus bearing the dateline 'State College.' And as soon after that as possible, there will never be a single piece of mail leave this campus bearing the postmark 'State College.'" And with that he thanked us, and we exited the victory breakfast.

Was he true to his word? You bet he was! I don't remember how long it took, but it seemed like no time at all until the dateline on news releases read University Park, and we rather suddenly had our own post office in the Hetzel Union Building. When all letters and packages left the campus, they bore the postmark "University Park."

I really don't know and have no way of finding out if Penn State set a new record for the establishment of a post office in the shortest possible time. I also don't know how one goes about requesting a post office of your very own. Am I suggesting that someone called the President of the United States with a special request, or perhaps called the Postmaster General directly? Of course not! I haven't the faintest idea how "University Park" suddenly seemed to appear. I'll let each of you decide how you think it happened. But I feel certain that if our President Eisenhower didn't call the President of the United States, he certainly did call his brother!

Discount Stores Discover State College

As with so many other developments, State College was among the last communities to be "blessed" with the arrival of the discount store. Those of us whose jobs or personal travel took us to medium– and large–sized cities had known of this retailing phenomenon for some time, and the people of our community somehow felt cheated as stories of great bargains, name brand merchandise marked way below cost, and stocks of items never found in our town drifted back from the cities.

Finally, the news hit our daily newspaper—State College would have its very own discount store. A Pennsylvania–based discount chain operation had finally discovered the State College market, and there would soon be a Town and Country store in town. Let me tell you about my initial visit to our local discount store.

At that time, I was the general manager of the only radio station in town. In addition, I was on the air as the play–by–play announcer for local high school and Penn State football and basketball games. I also aired all of our local radio editorials and filled in on various news programs. I had one other important exposure: I was the announcer for the "Live and Twice a Day, Monday through Friday" origination of our very own "Jim and Jane and the Western Vagabonds" broadcasts. Remember, this was the 1950s, and State College was the smallest town in Pennsylvania with its own radio station. So real live musical groups were sort of local celebrities, and I was their announcer.

In addition, every Sunday night Jim and Jane and their group imported a country and western star from WWVA in Wheeling, West Virginia. This was a powerful clear–channel station with a country and western format and aired some of the biggest names in that part of the recording industry. These weekly Sunday evening live concerts were held at the Radio Corral, a big amphitheater with a hillside of long rows of logs on which sat three or four thousand fans. I was the stage announcer for those Sunday night get–togethers and became a near–famous personality because I was the guy who performed with Jim and Jane.

Gerry Abrams, one of the station's staff people who was a Penn State undergraduate at the time and went on to become a well–known producer of feature television films, came up with a promotional idea for the Christmas season that involved covering a tree with various denominations of folding money and asking listeners to guess the total value of the money tied all over the tree, which would be displayed inside the sponsoring retail store.

So Gerry and I went off to the local Town and Country because we had heard of the great bargains we were sure to find there. We did find the perfect–sized plastic tree that, as I recall, was priced around $9. After we dragged the tree to the checkout counter, I discovered that we didn't have a single dollar between us. The only thing I had in my wallet was a blank WMAJ check. I had just started to ask the middle–aged lady at the checkout counter if she would possibly take a $9 check from the radio station when she interrupted me with, "Say that again!" "Say what again," I asked. "Say what you just said." "Well, all I wanted to ask was whether…." That's as far as I got. She said, "I know you, you're Mickey Bergstein! I hear you on the radio all the time. I listen to you with Jim and Jane almost every day and I've seen you broadcast on WMAJ lots of Sunday nights at Radio Corral."

Then she asked me if I was in a big hurry, and when I said we weren't, she told me that she wanted me to meet her daughter, who was also a big fan of mine and who loved to listen to Jim and Jane and the Western Vagabonds. With that, she called over her daughter, who was running one of the other cash registers. The woman turned to me and said, "Say something for my daughter and see if she knows who you are."

I heard this semi–strangle behind me, and when I turned around, I realized that Gerry had half swallowed a handkerchief to keep from laughing at what was turning into a rather ridiculous shopping trip to buy a simple plastic Christmas tree.

I don't remember what I said, but before I was finished the cashier turned to her daughter and asked, "Who is he?" Her daughter almost shrieked, "That's Mickey Bergstein from Jim and Jane and the Western Vagabonds!" She launched into a long speech about how she really loved the show and me and never missed a daily or Sunday broadcast.

Finally, mother sent daughter back to her own cash register and, after telling me again how thrilled she was to meet me, she asked, "What can I do for you, Mickey?" I finally got to finish the sentence I had started about 20 minutes ago. "Well, we are really embarrassed because we have no cash to pay for the Christmas tree. All I have is a WMAJ check, and if you'll take my check, I'll pay for the tree and let you get back to work."

She said, "I'll cash the check if you can show me your driver's license," pointing to a big sign behind the cash register that said, among other things, "We will be glad to cash your check if shown your driver's license."

I heard a funny noise, turned around, and there went the other half of Gerry's handkerchief. How did this all end? I said, "I'm sorry, I don't have my driver's license." So she said, "I'm sorry Mickey, then I won't be able to cash your check."

Not Exactly the Crime Capital of the Country

Several periodicals and organizations regularly run lists of the most ideal places to live in America. State College is often included on the lists, with several studies placing us as high as Number One, and those of us who live here would agree.

For many years, our town was relatively crime–free and scientific crime fighting came late to State College. There were, of course, the usual crimes that required handling by our small police force—a stolen bicycle, fights when the combatants were emboldened by an excess of beer, the occasional theft of money from a dorm or fraternity house, some minor shoplifting, or occasional vandalism.

The police force did a reasonable job of enforcing the law for what was probably relatively low pay. Because I had worked as a newsman at the local radio station, I knew all of the police rather well. Occasionally, on a dull Saturday night, one of them would let me ride around the town and campus in a police car to help capture the flavor of crime fighting on a Saturday night in State College. One of the local officers was a particular favorite of mine because I enjoyed seeing him take what he perceived to be a highly professional approach to a relatively minor crime. Remembering the old Mayberry RFD television show, let me call him "Barney" and tell you about two particular "crimes" and his approach to solving them.

Our family's first residence was in a two–story garden apartment building that housed nine other families. When I want to tell my business classes about inflation and how it has crept up over the years, I tell them about the apartment that we rented for $48 a month. (When we moved to a similar apartment with an additional bedroom a couple of years later, our rent jumped all the way to $53 a month.)

I came home early one evening to find our neighbors agitated. One of the wives had told the other tenants that she had looked out the first floor window and was shocked to see a man exposing himself. When she screamed, the man ran down the alley and was gone. She immediately called the police, but they had not yet responded when I got home.

When "Barney" arrived, he immediately took control of the investigation. He walked up to the front door of the woman who had witnessed the exposure, rapped on the door with his flashlight and, when she came to the door, adopted his official crime fighting voice and asked, "Okay, where's he at?" I was tempted to interrupt and answer, "He's upstairs in the bedroom hiding under the bed," but was afraid he would have drawn his gun and gone bounding up the stairs.

After we told him that the criminal hadn't hung around, he informed us that he had been on the trail of this person and had almost apprehended him two nights ago. "This isn't the first time we've had a report on this fellow," he said. "We had a call four or five nights ago telling us that he had done the same thing right up the street. I really get mad when that sort of thing happens, so I decided that I was going to make this a personal thing and catch this guy in the act. So one night I parked my car under those trees up there. I slid down in the seat so he wouldn't see anybody in the car and planned to wait him out. Sure enough, in about half an hour, here he came. He was walking very slowly, sort of looking around, and I was sure that this was my man. I waited until he came even with the car window and, since I had been smart enough to wind down the car windows so he could hear me, I yelled, 'Hey, you! Stop right there!' That son–of–a–gun must have been pretty clever, because he outsmarted me. I had the car pointing one way and he ran the other way. So I had to start the car and try to make a U–turn, but the street was too narrow, and by the time I got the car turned in the right direction, the son–of–a–gun was gone. I drove around the block a couple of times; but there was no sign of him. Now I was really mad, and decided I was really going to catch that sucker. I skipped a night because I thought he would be too smart to come out two nights in a row. So I went out and parked under the trees the night after that.

"But this time I was one step ahead of him. I parked right by the entrance to that alley up there. I figured that whichever way he ran, I had him. If he ran the way he did the other night, I could just back into the alley and take off after him. If he went the other way, I was pointed that way and I'd run him down. Sure enough, I see a guy coming and even though it was dark, I was sure that it was him, there was something about the way he walked. So I slunk down in the seat and grabbed the knob on the spotlight. I figured that I wouldn't turn it on until he was right alongside of me, and when I turned it on, I'd get a real good look at him. As he walked towards the car, I kept the spotlight pointing right at him, but I hadn't turned it on, of course. He kept walking, and I kept moving the spotlight. Then he was right alongside my window. I'll bet he wasn't more than four or five feet away. I turned the light on, figuring I'd have it right on his face, and I yelled, 'Stop! I got you!' You know what some son–of–a–bitch had done? He had turned that spotlight around backwards and as soon as I turned it on, it hit me right in the eyes. All I could see were great big green balls, couldn't see a damned thing else. By the time the green balls went away, the SOB was gone again.

"But don't worry, I got him figured out now. I know how he operates and I'll be ready for him the next time." I said, "That's good figuring, Barney. Now that you've got his M.O. down pat (I figured he'd like that police talk), you'll get him next time for sure." I looked around and all the other guys seemed to have disappeared.

Actually, it turned out they were being kind to old Barney and were all hiding behind the trees with their handkerchiefs stuffed in their mouths so that Barney wouldn't hear them laughing. I wanted to say, "Barney, since you've almost caught him twice in this neighborhood, don't you think he might try another street on the other side of town where he figures you won't be able to nab him?" But I didn't say anything except, "Good work, Barney. Keep at it and be sure to tell us when you catch him one of these nights." Since I didn't read or hear anything about Barney apprehending his quarry, I assume the guy is still on the loose.

Barney and I crossed paths on another incident. It was in the late 1960s, during the time when there were serious protests everywhere. Many of our country's major cities were plagued with arson, looting, and confrontations with the police. Colleges and universities also were caught up in various protest movements. The campus unrest generally centered around protests against the war in Vietnam and included students electing to go to Canada to escape the draft, violence against draft boards, and general protests against authorities, including student strikes and students occupying campus buildings.

Some friends from Detroit, where such problems had been occurring, came for a weekend visit and, after dinner one evening, two of us drove downtown to buy an evening newspaper. We parked in front of a student apartment house that was just a few doors from the newsstand. As soon as we got out of the car, both of us were drenched with beer that had been thrown out of a third floor window. We looked up and saw two students who had put a quarter keg of beer on the windowsill and were spilling beer on anyone who walked by on the sidewalk below. They were more than inebriated; they were old–fashioned drunk!

I asked my friend to stay and watch the door to the apartment house while I went to the newsstand to call the police. I told the police switchboard what had happened and said, "It's bad enough they they're drenching people with beer, but I'm afraid that when the keg is empty they might throw the whole keg out the window and might kill someone."

They thanked me for calling and told me they would dispatch a police car immediately. Within a few minutes, a police car drove up with all three top lights flashing. The officer jumped out, didn't take time to close the door, and asked, "Okay, where are they?" It was Barney. I pointed out the window with the beer keg. Barney said to my friend, "Okay, you watch the side door and yell if they come out that way." Then I got my instructions. "You stay right here, Mick, and keep your eye on the front door. I'm going up to get them!" With that, Barney turned his flashlight on and headed up the steps.

Barney was gone a long time. We figured that he was inside the apartment taking names and reading the criminals their rights and filling out his report. After about half an hour, he came down the steps all by himself. He said to me, "Sorry, Mick, I can't do anything about those guys." "Why not?" I asked. "Because they've got the door locked!"

My friend from Detroit who lived within blocks of where there had been rioting recently almost choked to death laughing. "They've got the door locked? Do you know what the police would be doing in Detroit right about now? They would already have lobbed at least six tear gas canisters through the windows."

Penn State in the Troubled Sixties

Penn State is an idyllic setting in a beautiful section of central Pennsylvania. There are towering shade trees, acres of well–tended lawns, and flowers and bushes in bloom everywhere. There are wonderful facilities for learning and recreation and things move at an unhurried pace almost all of the time. It's the kind of campus most young people think of when they imagine going away to a college or university. I know it's the kind of place I visualized.

However, Penn State and other colleges and universities all over the country were not so peaceful and idyllic during a part of the 1960s and '70s. These were the days of the Vietnam War, and everywhere there were targets of anger and demonstrations and frustrations. Because young people seemed to have the strongest feelings about the war, much of the anti–war protest centered on remote campuses like Penn State's, as well as on the more activist urban campuses.

While the intensity and frequency of protests at Penn State did not match those at some other schools, it did create an atmosphere that had never before occurred on this remote and peaceful campus, and it often was scary.

Feelings were bitter and deep during those days and in retrospect, it was naïve to think that somehow our beautiful rural campus would be able to observe from the sidelines and not be touched by the protests. While there were various issues that drew student protests, there was one that seemed especially alien to our campus. While the confrontation lasted only 15 or 20 minutes, and involved just two people, it was dramatic enough for all who witnessed it to remember it for a long, long time.

As with many public buildings in the country, Old Main, Penn State's main administration building, has two very tall flagpoles on the lawn in front, one for the United States flag and one for the flag of the Commonwealth of Pennsylvania. During one of the student protests, someone decided it would be dramatic to deny the university the right to fly the U.S. flag over campus. So, sometime late at night, someone carried a rather heavy metal chain to the pole that flew the U.S. flag and intertwined it with the rope halyard used to raise and lower the flag. When the person in charge of raising the flag went out the next morning, he discovered that the locked chain made it impossible to use the rope halyard and reported this to the proper authorities.

The head of campus security at that time was Colonel William Pelton, retired from the U.S. Army. During his active duty career, Col. Pelton had been one of the original 250 U.S. Army advisers sent to Vietnam to provide training and advice to the South Vietnamese armed forces.

Col. Pelton was discharged after a long tour in Vietnam and was hired to head the campus patrol at Penn State. Late in the morning that the flag halyard was chained to the pole, Col. Pelton appeared alone on the steps of Old Main carrying a U.S. flag under his arm. The lawn in front of the building is rather large, and the colonel walked slowly across the grass to the base of the flagpole. The protestors who had gathered there saw that he had some sort of long metal tool in his hand.

As Pelton approached the base of the flagpole, one student detached himself from a small group of protestors who stood off to one side and away from the base of the pole. He asked Col. Pelton what he intended to do with the flag under his arm. Pelton replied, "I'm going to raise it to the top of the flagpole. We do that every day and we're going to do it today, even if you don't like it. It's a university rule that two flags, the United States flag and the flag of Pennsylvania, are raised every day. And that's what I'm going to do."

The student replied, "Like hell you are," and reached over and closed his hand around the chain, the halyard, and the lock that held everything together.

Pelton then raised his chain and bolt cutter, put the jaws around the chain, the lock, and the student's thumb, and said, "Look, son, I don't have any argument with you and you don't have one with me. I don't know what your protest is all about, but whatever it is, it's between you and the administration and has nothing to do with me. My job is to make sure that the flag flies every day. Now the flag is going up if you decide to keep your thumb or you decide to go through life without your thumb. Whatever you decide, the flag's going up. I'll give you a count of 10 to decide whether you want to keep your thumb or you want me to cut it off." He then began to count.

When he reached four or five, the student removed his hand saying, "You dirty son–of–a–bitch."

Pelton then calmly cut through the lock and chain, shook out the rope halyard, and slowly raised the United States flag. Most of the crowd that had gathered cheered. The protestors booed and yelled obscenities at the colonel. Pelton then wrapped the halyard around the pole, tied it carefully, and said to the student who had challenged him, "Son, I'm going to be here early tomorrow morning and just in case you decide to do something foolish, I'm going to bring along my chain and bolt cutter. I'm going to raise the flag again tomorrow morning and every morning for the rest of the week. You might want to think about it tonight and if you decide that you made a mistake and you really do want to go through the rest of your life without your thumb, you might be here tomorrow morning, and I'll see if I can't accommodate you."

The next morning, I was in the Corner Room restaurant drinking a cup of coffee, and I told the men with me about Pelton's confrontation with the protesting student. The question of whether Pelton really would have cut off the young man's thumb came up and nobody knew for sure what the colonel would have done.

That evening I called Pelton at home. I knew him well and I didn't feel uncomfortable talking with him about the confrontation. I asked, "Bill, if the young man hadn't taken his hand away from the chain, would you have gone ahead and cut off his thumb?" He answered with, "Mickey, I'll be very honest with you. When I walked out to the flagpole, I had no idea that it would come to a serious confrontation with anyone. So when he grabbed the chain, I didn't have time to think about it and I had no idea that his thumb would be involved. I don't know what I would have done if he hadn't removed his hand. But I do know one thing. If I had backed down and not raised the flag, I would have walked right into Old Main, gone to the president's office, and resigned my job. That story would have been all over the campus and I would have lost my authority, and credibility, and self–respect. Thank God he let me raise the flag." ■

7

JoePa, a Penn State Icon

One can hardly write stories about Penn State without includ-ing Joe Paterno. For those not familiar with the outlines of his career, he came to Penn State in 1950 when the Lions hired his college coach at Brown University, Rip Engle. Penn State had al-ways played single wing football and had no experience with the T–formation. Joe had been Rip's T–formation quarterback at Brown, and Rip asked Joe to come to Penn State with him and help install the T–formation with the Lions.

It had been Joe's intention to attend law school following his graduation from Brown but, to help his college coach, he agreed to come to our campus for a couple of years until the new forma-tion was established. There followed 16 years as Rip's assistant, primarily as quarterback coach and offense coach.

In 1966, following Rip's retirement, Joe was named head coach of the Lions. Decades later, he is arguably the most widely known college coach in America and a Penn State icon. Right from the start, Joe was a consistent disciplinarian and insisted on rules for his players and his program. With Joe, rules are rules, and the players know it. Here's one example of what Joe expected and still expects of his players and anyone else connected with the program.

Several years ago, Penn State began to feed the Joe Paterno pre–game radio show to several radio stations around the com-monwealth. Later, to reach a larger audience, the show moved to television and was aired statewide. As mentioned elsewhere in this book, our Quarterback Club luncheons are held Wednesdays at noon. Joe brings two of his players to the luncheon, and I interview the players in addition to Joe. The television producers decided that the players we interviewed at noon would be guests on Joe's show that evening. It was felt that the double experience would be good exposure for the players, and the lunch appearance would help them get ready for the television show.

This particular luncheon was held in the years when college students, along with many other men, began to wear their hair long. But there was one group of students that did not have long hair—members of Joe's football squad. I can't remember after all these years which player was our guest at the luncheon on this particular Wednesday. He came dressed in a neat shirt and tie

Penn State football coach Joe Paterno poses at a Fall press photo day with three quarterbacks (left to right)—Kerry Collins, Wally Richardson, and John Sacca.

and wearing a blazer. At one point during the luncheon, Joe simply said to the player, "You remember that you're going to be on our television show this evening." When the player assured Joe that he certainly did remember, Joe said to him, "You'll be a big hit because you're a nice looking guy. You'll make an even better impression with your hair shorter. I assume that you have time left on your schedule to get a haircut this afternoon so you'll look your best."

It was rather evident that the last thing on the player's mind was to get a haircut. He probably already thought that he looked his best. But he said to Joe, "I'll get it cut late this afternoon, Coach." I don't think that Joe really thought that the haircut was of major importance. I think he wanted everyone on the squad to notice how neatly trimmed their teammate was so they would know what was expected of them when it was their turn to be on television.

Another incident concerned Ray Shafer, a former governor of Pennsylvania. The governor was a very serious football fan who followed Penn State with a lot of interest. I'm not sure how many Nittany Lions games he saw, but it is my guess that while he was governor he missed few games. I remember one particular game at North Carolina State when the governor accompanied the team on its chartered plane. The usual seating pattern on our charter flights had the coaches seated up front, all of the players seated in the middle of the aircraft, and reporters, broadcasters, and other guests seated in the rear.

Shortly after takeoff, one of the flight attendants came back to ask the governor if she could get him something from the galley. The governor had just finished a busy day and seemed in a relaxed mood. He told the attendant that, if possible, he would really enjoy a martini. A short time later, the flight attendant came down the aisle toward the back of the plane carrying a martini on a tray. And right behind her came Joe Paterno.

As Joe passed each row of seats following the attendant down the aisle, the players in the rows stood and turned to look to the back of the plane. They knew a martini when they saw one and wanted to see who had had the courage to order one.

As the flight attendant was about to hand the governor his drink, Joe put his hand on her wrist and said to Gov. Shafer, "I'm sorry, Governor, this is an athletic team charter and the rules are set for the team and the rest of us follow the same rules. Since none of the players or coaches will have a drink, none of the guests on the plane will be allowed to have a drink. I certainly understand that you would like to enjoy this martini at the end of your busy day, but I'm going to have to ask you to pass on the drink. As I tell all of the guests who travel with us, if you would like to drink during the flight, I prefer that you take a commercial flight when that is possible."

The governor was gracious and, I suspect, a little embarrassed. He said to Joe, "I'm sorry, Coach. I should have known better. I just didn't stop to think. I was concentrating on how much I would enjoy this drink instead of remembering where I was and why my ordering a drink wasn't appropriate. I apologize for my poor judgment."

Joe thanked him for understanding and then Joe, the flight attendant, and the martini returned to the front of the plane. I respected Joe for insisting that everyone follow the rules. I respected Gov. Shafer for his immediate understanding and apology. However, I have a hunch that there are many, many coaches who would have looked the other way rather than confront the top official in the state.

While I certainly do not place myself on the same level as a governor, I, too, was on the receiving end of chastisement from Joe for breaking a team rule. When Penn State's football team travels, they all wear coats and ties. Those players who have earned team blazers in preceding years usually wear their Penn State blazers. The younger players wear sports jackets or suits.

I was on this particular trip as one of the game broadcasters, and I also was liaison with the phone companies involved in getting the proper broadcast lines installed in the press box and making sure that all of the member stations of the Penn State radio network were tied to the broadcast. I had finished my breakfast in the hotel dining room and was headed for the lobby. Immediately behind me came Joe Paterno. He said, "Mickey, I know that you know how to dress, and I certainly don't want to be critical of you, but if you are going to travel with us, I'm going to have to ask you to follow the team rules."

For the first time that morning, I realized that while I was wearing a sport jacket, I had a sweater under the jacket and a shirt, but no tie. I did as the governor had done and apologized to Joe, told him I was aware of his necktie rule, and that I knew I came under the rules, but hadn't paid attention to whether I was wearing a tie.

Joe notices everything and everybody. He told me many times that all of his rules were primarily for purposes of discipline, and that when players overlooked or got away with ignoring even small rules of discipline, it was a very short step to ignoring or overlooking something bigger and more important, so Joe and his staff always pay close attention to all the details. Anyone who has seen a Penn State football team play knows they always look disciplined and organized, win or lose. I remember a veteran sportscaster once said, "A Penn State football team never looks bad, even when they lose."

You can see lots of evidence of Joe's "we all follow the same rules" philosophy. Ever since Joe has been head coach, he has bucked the trend toward player individuality. Look at the Penn State helmets—no decals and no signs of individual recognition, just white helmets with one blue stripe and a number. Look at the Lions' jerseys—no stripes, no names on the back, no overabundance of numbers. And how about those black shoes? Penn State was one of the first schools to wear black shoes instead of white, red, or whatever color some schools choose to feature.

I'm sure that Joe's intention was to downplay individual recognition and accent the team concept. I find it very interesting to note how many other teams are now wearing black shoes and I notice, too, what seems to be a lessening in the decals, stars, numbers, etc. As a matter of fact, these last couple of years I have talked to players on the Penn State squad who indicated that the Penn State uniforms always appealed to them. One player told me, "I always wanted to be one of the players who wore those Penn State black shoes."

Although Rip Engle allowed it, I'm sure Joe didn't approve of Lenny Moore doing some very creative things with his shoes. Those days, players all wore high black shoes with longer cleats. Of course, all fields were grass; there was no Astroturf or other synthetic surface. Lenny Moore made his shoes very distinctive. He covered the upper part of his shoes with white tape, and he taped down to what today would be the top of the low–cut shoes. So from the stands, Lenny looked like he was wearing white spats.

I don't know if the coaches ever made a point of Lenny's shoes with him, but he continued to wear his taped shoes through his whole career. When I asked Lenny about the tape, he said, "Mickey, I just have to tape my shoes on. You've seen me run. I run real fast and when I get faking and jumping around, without the tape I'm afraid my shoes are going to fly off." My guess is that as long as Lenny continued to make the big plays he made throughout his career at Penn State, the coaches would have allowed him to use any color tape and as much tape as he wanted.

Paterno's Press

There's probably no sports figure in America who receives as consistently favorable press as Joe Paterno. In my work, I travel a lot and speak to a wide range of companies, trade associations, and industry groups. These groups range in size from perhaps 100 members of a corporate group to several hundred customers of a particular company, to perhaps 1,000 attendees at a national convention. I have been involved in this work for many years, and I must say that I have never spoken to a group of business people, regardless of the industry or the size of the group, where I have not been asked a question or two about Joe Paterno. Over and over again I am asked, "Is Joe as good as they say he is and the Penn State program as well–run and clean as everybody says that it is?"

I answer yes to both questions because through several de-cades of both official and unofficial connection with Penn State football and other sports, I have come to respect the program that Joe Paterno runs, and I know of no cheating in any of the sports at Penn State, including the football program. I do not say there has never been a single instance of rule–breaking or cheating in one form or another. I am simply saying that being reasonably close to the Penn State sports picture, I have never seen or heard of rule–breaking.

For many years, I was in a fairly good position to observe what was going on in the Penn State sports program. I personally was involved in broadcasting many of those sports. I also was a part–time teacher in various academic departments of the university and many, many Penn State athletes were in my classes. In addition, I traveled on the football team chartered planes and chartered buses. I numbered many of the coaches among my personal friends.

I tell you this because there probably was no individual who was in a more likely position to be asked for academic favors for an athlete in academic trouble. It would have been very easy for a coach to ask me to show special consideration for an athlete who was in one of my classes, or to ask me to speak to another professor friend of mine who could give a break to an athlete in his or her class. I must tell you that, in all my years associated with Penn State sports, I never was approached for a favor on behalf of an athlete by any university coach. I was never asked for a favor in person. I never received a note or a phone call asking for a grade consideration for a single athlete. I do not speak for the experiences of any other teacher or administrator at the university, I only speak for myself and my own personal experience.

In the mid–1980s, I received a call from a *Sports Illustrated* writer who was on the campus to write a story about Joe Paterno. He asked if I would be willing to meet with him to talk about Joe and tell him anything I knew about the coach and his football program. I told him I would be glad to meet with him, but also told him that I had no official connection with the Penn State football program and couldn't really speak for Joe or any element of his program. He told me he understood my position, but said that since I had spent several years as a football broadcaster and knew Joe, his coaches, and many of his players personally, he thought I could be a useful source of information. I agreed to meet with him the next morning. My office was on the seventh floor of our business building, and from my window you can see the Penn State football stadium, that at the time held about 83,000 people.

The reporter came to the office early the next morning, introduced himself and then immediately said, "Let me tell you why I am here. Joe Paterno has had nothing but favorable press for many years, and I don't believe that he can be that good or that his program can be that clean. I want to do a story to prove that Joe Paterno is the biggest fraud ever to hit major college sports."

I guess he assumed his opening line would have some shock value and that I would immediately begin sharing some "secrets" with him. I simply said, "You have a very tough assignment, if that's your goal, and I must tell you that anything I know about Joe or his program won't help because I can only say positive things on Joe's behalf."

The writer walked over to the window, pointed to the stadium and asked, "How does Joe keep enough dummies eligible to win so many games and keep that stadium filled?" I said, "I don't think you know Joe Paterno very well. Let me tell you a story about one of Joe's star players and how Joe handled a question about class attendance that involved that player. This particular player cut my class twice during the first two weeks, and when I met Joe at a Quarterback Club meeting, I mentioned to him that one of his players was cutting my class, and I thought he would like to know about it since I know he expects the very best academic effort from his players.

"Joe asked if I had spoken to the player about his absences. I told him that I had spoken to him twice, and that I wasn't going to speak to him again. Joe said I already had done more than I should be expected to do. He asked me not to tell him the player's name, but said that if he cut the class beyond what the rules allowed, he wanted me to flunk him. I asked Joe if he was sure that was what he wanted me to do. I said that the player might be his quarterback. He told me it wouldn't make any difference. He said that a player who cuts classes and suffers no penalty because of it would ruin his team. He went on to say that players tell other players and, first thing you know, everybody thinks you don't have to go to school if you play football for Penn State.

"'So,' he said, 'if any of my players cut your class, I would consider it a favor if you flunk them and send a strong message that I'm not kidding when I tell my players about their academic responsibilities.'" The writer asked me if Joe ever asked who the player was. I told him he hadn't. "Did you flunk him?" he asked. I said that I treated him just the way I treat everyone else. At the end of the semester I figured his grade, deducted points for his cuts (I believe he had seven or eight out of 45 classes) and he got a "D" in the class. Without his cuts he would have had a "B."

The writer stayed on campus for several more days and I ran into him one day outside of Rec Hall. "Did you tell Joe the kind of story you wanted to write?" I asked.

"I sure did."

"What did Joe say when you told him?"

"He said, 'Good! Promise me you'll do me a favor. After you finish talking to everyone you are going to talk to, if you find out any instances where we cheated or are cheating, promise that you'll tell me about it. I don't know of any place we aren't following the rules and if we aren't, I want to know about it because I want to get it stopped quickly.'"

About two weeks later, *Sports Illustrated* carried the story that the writer had come to campus to write. The story was unusually complimentary. It contained nothing negative and probably gave us another recruiting edge. The kind of publicity that the Penn State football program has earned has had a cumulative effect. I am not implying that Penn State coaches are able to recruit every player they go after. But I do believe that because of what people have heard and read about Joe and his program, we have been able to attract quality athletes who are willing to take on the responsibility of getting their degrees while participating in a high–level football program that takes a lot of time and requires constant attention to class attendance and assignments. The result is an impressive record of Penn State athletes who, in addition to the football honors they have earned, have earned the college degree that will allow them to hold their own in the field of work they choose beyond their football days.

While I have never specifically discussed with Joe his attitude toward reporters and the press, I am certain that he fully understands the value of healthy personal relations with members of the press, even when sometimes they are determined to write a negative story. I know that Paterno recognizes that if he cooperates with reporters and can make their job easier, it will pay long–term dividends for him and for his program. I know of two instances when Joe saw obstacles faced by the press and was willing to change his own schedule to accommodate their needs.

At the end of the 1967 season, Penn State was to meet Florida State in the Gator Bowl in Jacksonville, Florida. Joe took the team to Daytona Beach before the game to be able to practice in warmer weather. Jacksonville usually does not provide "southern" weather at that time of year, and Joe guessed that Daytona Beach would be a better practice site. Knowing Joe, I also suspect he felt that being away from the game site might give him and the team more privacy for their pre–game workouts.

Meanwhile, Penn State had scheduled a charter flight to Jacksonville for three or four days before the game for university officials, members of the press, families of the coaches, etc. On the plane along with other representatives of newspapers, radio, and television was Roy McHugh of the *Pittsburgh Press*. Roy had covered Penn State games for several years and was considered a regular member of the Penn State press corps. While talking with Roy on the plane, he told me that he couldn't very well cover the team from Jacksonville since they were in Daytona Beach, and so planned to rent a car and drive to Daytona Beach and stay there until the team moved to Jacksonville. He asked if I would like to go along. I could think of no good reason to stay in Jacksonville and so I joined Roy to drive to Daytona Beach.

We arrived at Daytona Beach at about 5 p.m. and checked into the team hotel. Roy phoned Joe's room and Joe invited us to stop by, agreeing to be interviewed for the next day's *Pittsburgh Press*. As soon as we arrived at Joe's room, he turned to Roy and said, "Roy, I have a real problem, and I hope you will understand my dilemma. I've closed our practice sessions to the press. I'm putting in some new offense and something different on defense, and I want to make sure that we have the advantage of some surprise when we get to game time. I don't know any of these southern writers, and I don't want to take the chance that one or more of them are especially close to the Florida State people and will talk to them about what we have been working on in practice. So I have closed practice to the press, and I hope that you understand that I can't close practice to the Florida press and allow the Pennsylvania press to watch us work out."

Roy began to protest. "Joe, I have to file a Penn State story every day and some days include sidebars with the main story. How am I going to cover Penn State without seeing the team practice?" Joe said, "Roy, I know this is going to be tough on you and I also know that you need to have enough copy to write your story. So if you are willing to understand my dilemma, I'll meet you here after practice every day, and I'll give you enough information that you can write your story. Fair enough? You have been a good friend of our program for a long time, and I certainly understand your problem. So I'll make sure that you have all you need to get your job done."

Roy was delighted and said the arrangement was more than fair and that he appreciated that Joe understood what it took for a newspaperman to meet his assignment. I'm not sure what arrangements Joe made to supply information to any other members of the regular press corps that followed Penn State all season long, but I'm sure he made similar arrangements to enable them to meet their deadlines. Do you think many other coaches worry about reporters' deadlines?

On another occasion, Joe did something for the press that I have never heard of being done before or since. On January 1, 1970, we were in Miami to meet Missouri in the Orange Bowl. The Orange Bowl is a particularly difficult bowl game for the press to cover, especially for reporters for morning papers. At that time, the Orange Bowl was the only game played New Year's night, and because of the length of the extravagant half–time show, the game didn't end until near midnight. This meant that a reporter for a morning paper had to do the story almost as the action occurred and could not spend his usual time winding up his story after the game.

Knowing the scheduling problems, Joe called together the reporters from northern papers who regularly covered Penn State and said he was aware of the problems created by a late game. He offered to meet with all of them in the afternoon of game day to share his game plan for that evening. He said that as the game progressed he might have to change plans to match the game situation, but he could share his plans as he had them before the game started. I couldn't imagine a coach taking that risk several hours before kickoff. If any of the reporters had chosen to violate Joe's confidence, or perhaps had a friend in the Missouri camp, it would have been a simple matter to reveal the Penn State game plan to the Missouri coaching staff. I am fairly certain that if that did happen, the Missouri staff would choose not to listen to any of this information as a matter of fairness and sportsmanship, but the possibility of leaks did exist.

I spoke to several veteran reporters who sat in on the game briefing by Joe. They were all surprised and greatly appreciative of Joe's consideration that allowed them to prepare some of their material ahead of time in the event that the game did run late. Is it any wonder that over the years Joe has received such favorable press coverage? Of course, his outstanding record as a winning coach also has much to do with his continuing accolades.

Many coaches I have known, or have had a chance to observe, seem to approach the press with the attitude that they are adversaries who will do you in if given a chance. Since he became a

Penn State University head football coach Joe Paterno makes a point at one of his regular news conferences. Throughout the years, Paterno has worked hard to develop a good relationship with the news media.

head coach, Joe seems to have taken just the opposite stance. Although I do not know this for certain, it seems to me that Joe realizes that the writers have a job to do, that they are entitled to respect as professionals, if they have earned that respect, that the publicity they provide for a school or team or coaching staff is important, and that a coach and his staff should do what can be done within reason to make the press' job easier, rather than harder, to do.

As an observer and as a Penn State fan, I read as much print coverage as is available when the subject is Penn State athletics. Although this is a statement that can't be proven—it is only an observation—I believe that no major football school or coach has received as much positive and favorable coverage as have Joe Paterno and his Penn State football teams. They have earned the exposure they receive, and I believe that they deserve all of it.

I'm Sure Joe Has Changed Over the Years, But It's Hard to See

I first met Joe Paterno when he came to Penn State as a brand new assistant football coach in the fall of 1950, and I've had the chance to get to know him better ever since. I'm sure that all of us have changed as we have matured and grown older, and I'm certain that Joe has, too. But I have found him to be the same basic person, despite his nationally recognized success.

One example of how Joe <u>has</u> changed is his diminished volatility during a game. I do not mean to imply that Joe is any less intense or doesn't have the same driving will to win as before. But if you had an opportunity to observe Joe during games, as I have, you would realize that his nature has become somewhat calmer as he has gained experience and maturity.

In the 1950s, Penn State's games were played at the old Beaver Stadium, before the current stadium was built and now crowds of more than 97,000 fans are typical for home games. During those years, the stadium press box had only two glass–enclosed broadcast booths. One was reserved for our local radio station that broadcast the games and also was the originating station for other stations on the Penn State Football Network. The other booth was reserved for use by the Penn State assistant coaches, who used this high location to send to the bench any observations about either team or about individual players. They had a phone in the booth connected to a phone behind the Penn State bench that was usually staffed by a coach on the field, the manager, or the reserve quarterback.

During the broadcasts, I was able to observe Joe in action through the sound–proof glass between the booths. When the game started, all was quiet in the coaches' box. As the game proceeded, and as the pace heated up, Joe's intensity also rose like a thermometer. By this time, he was standing and talking almost non–stop to the bench. If the game remained close, soon after the second half began, Joe had usually disappeared from the coaches' booth and, when I looked down to the Penn State bench, there he was, sharing ideas with Coach Engle and the other coaches. I have no way of knowing if Joe was expected to remain in the booth or if he was expected on the sidelines during the second half. All I know is that Joe usually spent the second half on the sidelines and didn't seem bashful about sharing his ideas.

Joe has changed, I think, as the years have gone by and, while you still see him being excited on the sidelines, he seems much calmer than he used to be, at least on the outside. But in a very close and important game, you can still see Joe fire himself up and take charge.

In other areas of their lives, you will find that Joe and his wife, Sue, have not changed much since he was a young assistant coach. The Paternos moved into their present home back in 1969 and raised their children there. I became aware of one physical change to the house in 1995 when I drove Sue Paterno home from a Special Olympics meeting on the campus. As we drove up, I noticed a large blue plastic sheet covering part of the roof. When I asked Sue about it, she said they were enlarging their kitchen and had to open up part of the ceiling to do it. She said she had told Joe something like, "If I am going to keep on making Italian food for the fall recruiting season, I really need more working space." I asked, "Do you really mean to tell me that you cook and prepare food for the families of all the recruits who visit during the fall season?" "I do," Sue replied. "I begin to prepare food and spaghetti sauce in early August and then freeze things so that we'll be ready when the season starts. When I asked Sue for the 1997 Homecoming how many people she and Joe would be entertaining after the game with Ohio State, she said their guests would number somewhere around 50 people. My point in mentioning this is that recruiting is a major component of running a Division I college football program. I'm sure that a single phone call from the Paternos to the university catering service would relieve Sue of all her cooking chores. I never asked her why she continues to cook, but I know them well enough that I'm sure she would say, "Joe and I want to do it that way."

One area in which Joe has <u>not</u> changed is the way he stokes his inner fires when a big and important game is upcoming. I suspect that this has to be an important ingredient in the makeup of every successful coach, but I cannot imagine any football coach in the country being more internally focused and intense than Joe Paterno.

Penn State football coach Rip Engle being interviewed by Mickey Bergstein at fall practice in 1954. Engle brought Joe Paterno to Penn State in 1950 as his quarterback coach. Paterno succeeded Engle as head coach in 1966.

At the end of the 1986 season, Penn State had been invited to the Fiesta Bowl in Tempe, Arizona, to play the University of Miami Hurricanes. It was almost a given that the winner would be the national champion. Many of us had watched several of Miami's games on television during the season, and beating them seemed to be a formidable task, to put it mildly.

A day or two before the Lions were to leave for the southwest to get ready for the game, I was walking on campus to the Penn State Creamery. I don't know why I would be making a run for ice cream on a cold and snowy night except that my love for Penn State ice cream overcame my good sense. Right outside the Creamery, I came across another Penn Stater who didn't seem to be minding the weather. It was Joe Paterno in his hooded blue coat that you often see him wear on the sidelines during games in cold

1973 Heisman Trophy winner John Cappelletti with his coach, Joe Paterno.

weather. I asked Joe how he felt about the upcoming game and he told me, of course, that Miami was an outstanding team.

While I can't remember what he said next, I had the distinct impression that Joe was cooking up some ideas and that he believed we actually could win the game. Perhaps Joe's game plan hadn't been finalized and, if it had, he wasn't likely to share the details with me. But as I walked away and wished him luck I said, "I don't know what you are going to do, but I feel much better about the game now that I have talked to you." He said, "I didn't tell you anything." "I know you didn't," I answered, "but you still made me feel better."

When I watched the game and saw the game plan that had us rushing only three men most of the time, putting everyone in the coverage and punishing the receiver if there was a completion, I wondered if Joe had that strategy already in mind when we met at the Creamery. Whenever the strategy was developed, Penn State won 14 to 10 and was named the national champion.

Game Day at Penn State

A home football game on the Penn State campus is a real happening. Beginning early Friday morning, maybe even Thursday night, motor homes and trailers, chartered buses, and cars begin to converge on the Beaver Stadium area. All four sides of the stadium are devoted to vehicle parking and by early Saturday the lots are full and tailgating is well under way. On top of everything else, there are helicopters overhead to make sure there is an efficient traffic flow. Going to a Penn State home game is a big, big event!

All of the roads heading toward the stadium are marked One Way, and if you aren't going to the game and just want to get to the supermarket, you'd better plan to use side streets. If you aren't careful, you could end up in a stadium parking lot even if you have no plans to go to the game. Believe it or not, many local people have found themselves at a tailgate even though they were only going downtown to pick up their dry cleaning.

One day in the 1997 season, my wife dropped me off close to the stadium and, since she wasn't going to the game, I mapped out a way for her to escape the traffic and get home quickly. I should have known better. She ended up in a wrong lane and kept being waved on in a direction she didn't want to go. She ended up making almost a complete circle before arriving back in our driveway.

Heading to a game a couple of years ago, we were in a slow-moving and very crowded long line of cars going toward a stadium parking lot. It was a three-lane road, and all the traffic was bumper–to–bumper.

Joe Paterno lives on the north side of State College, perhaps a mile or so from the stadium, and he is in the habit of walking to the dressing rooms before the game. As you are lined up in traffic, the last person you expect to see is the head football coach. I am sure that most fans would think he is in a staff meeting, making final changes to the game plan or something. But there he was, walking along the road.

Almost as if a magic signal was passed, car windows were rolled down, people began to greet Joe at the curb, and fans began to hand out pieces of paper or game programs, hoping to get Joe's autograph. He waved, smiled, and crossed the road, right in front of our car.

As soon as he recognized us and began to wave, I rolled down the window and asked, "Are you going to the game, Joe?" "What game?" Then the conversation took off something like this:

Me: "Penn State is playing Purdue today."

Joe: "Is it going to be a good game?"

Me: "It better be. If Penn State doesn't win today, they may fire their coach."

Joe: "I thought he had a good record."

Me: "He does, but Penn State fans are spoiled. They don't like to lose."

Joe: "What time does the game begin?"

Me: "1:30."

Joe: "I'll try and make it!"

By this time our line of traffic had been held up, and those in the cars around us heard an "inside" conversation. How many major college football coaches do you think walk to a big game? How many coaches would have taken time to have that conversation with us, especially in a line of traffic the day of an important game?

Major college football coaches are very busy with recruiting, coaching, staff meetings, public relations, lending their support to charities, and all of the other things that are part of running a large football program. Despite this, during the years that I was teaching, I could count on Joe taking time out to speak to my classes once a year.

A few years ago, I invited Joe to meet with my class in public relations. It was a large class with approximately 165 students; we filled all but 40 seats in the large lecture hall where we met. When I arrived at class that day, not only were all the seats filled, but there were a couple of dozen students sitting on the steps leading up to the back of the hall. Evidently the word had gotten out that Joe Paterno would be in my class and many, many students not taking that course had shown up.

In the very first row was a young boy whom I took to be 10 or 11 years old. I asked him his name, and that made him very nervous. I asked if he was registered for this class, and that made him even more nervous. "Well," I said, "I'll let you stay if you tell me why you are here." He said, "I understand that the Coach is going to be here." When I told him that he had heard right but that didn't give him an excuse to miss his own classes, he told me that he could always go to his own classes, but he'd never had a chance to hear the Coach. I let him stay, and I hope that he didn't get in trouble in school or at home.

On the first day of class in a recent semester, I noticed in the first row a heavyset young man who was one of the relatively few men not wearing a baseball cap. When I told the class that one of my rules was that "baseball season is over" and caps were not to be worn in class, he did not have to do anything to comply. At the end of the period, the young man came up and introduced himself. "Professor," he said, "my name is Scott Paterno. I think you know my parents." I told him that I had known them for many years. He began to talk about my rules for attending my classes, especially the "no caps indoor" rule. He said, "You know, Professor Bergstein, you sound just like my father." I said, "Scott, since I'm older than your father and have been here longer than he has, perhaps he sounds like me."

The Paternos and the Special Olympics

For the past several years, Penn State University has played host to the Pennsylvania State Special Olympics. For three days late in the month of June, the university facilities provide these handicapped athletes with a wonderful opportunity to compete against each other. They live in the university dorms and enjoy their meals in the dining rooms. As the teams enter the opening ceremonies with their various county delegations, members of the Penn State football team and other varsity athletes lead them.

Hosting the Special Olympics is a challenging logistics job requiring large numbers of buses and arrangements for every conceivable need of the athletes. Another consideration is transportation of athletes who require special help. Large numbers of volunteers from both the campus and the town are used each year.

Over the years, Joe and Sue Paterno and their children have been a key element in the success of the program. Sue is a very active member of the Special Olympics state board, and Joe is on hand each year to do whatever he can to make the handicapped athletes welcome in the community and on campus. The Paternos take part in the opening ceremonies for the games and are very visible in the closing ceremonies. Sue Paterno and many others who work so hard on the games seem to be everywhere during the competition. Unless you have taken an active role in the Special Olympics, you cannot visualize how much time and energy is involved in making the games run smoothly.

The closing ceremonies on the final evening are always a moving event. Eight hundred to 1,000 special athletes file into Penn State's Rec Hall along with their coaches, county volunteers, and families. They wear their county T–shirts and Special Olympics caps. The Paternos participate in the closing ceremonies each year, and don't think that these special athletes don't know it and don't look forward to seeing them.

It has always been fun for me, as master of ceremonies, to watch the men and women flock to Joe if they see him before the program begins. They come individually, or accompanied by a friend or family member if they need assistance. They bring their cameras for a coveted picture with the Paternos. They ask Joe to sign their caps, T–shirts, programs, and pictures. Several pull up their shirts and ask Joe to sign their bare backs. (I often wonder how long it takes to convince them to take a bath and give up Joe's autograph.)

When the officials finally clear everyone away from Joe, the program begins. After recognizing those who worked so hard on the games, I begin to introduce Joe to the large audience. I never come close to completing my planned introduction; usually I am only able to say, "And now we have a special friend who wants to say goodbye." That's when the chant begins— "Joe…Joe…Joe…Joe…" When Joe gets to the microphone with Sue, you never could hear a more appreciative welcome. Many of us used to wonder how many of these handicapped athletes, many of them quite young and many of them unable to read the sports pages even if they wanted to, would know Joe Paterno and want to see him. That question gets answered every year as his reception gets louder and longer and warmer with each succeeding Special Olympics.

In 1996, Joe was scheduled to be in Ohio for a fund-raising effort and so was not to be on the closing program. He decided at the last minute that he would try to make it and join Sue at the closing ceremonies. Joe indicated that he wouldn't speak, since the program was already set, but there was no way that the special athletes would see Joe and not set off their usual chant. So Joe relented, and what a reception he received. The moment the athletes spotted Joe standing behind the platform, you could have thrown the planned program into the wastebasket. They started chanting "Joe…Joe…Joe…Joe…" and didn't stop until he walked to the microphone to speak to them and say goodbye for another year.

I'm sure that the Paternos will be there next year and many more after that, even after Joe retires. They have become Penn State's special people for the Special Olympics.

The Soft Side of Joe Paterno

Many people view Joe Paterno as an "arms length" kind of guy. What they see when they see Joe is a man who is friendly, easy to talk to, interested in what they have to say, and always approachable. At the same time, Joe is not easy to get to know on a personal level and is, in many ways, a private person. It's not easy to remain private when you're as well–known a public figure as Joe is. Every once in a while, you get a glimpse of the soft side of Joe, and you somehow get the feeling that in public Joe seems determined not to reveal himself as a "softie."

When I was a Penn State undergraduate, one of my close friends was a student from New York who probably loved Penn State and Penn State sports as much, if not more, than any member of the alumni body that stretches all over the U.S. and into many foreign countries as well. His name was Art Gladstone, and he eventually was responsible for Joe Paterno revealing himself as an emotional and caring person.

For about 40 years, Art's dedication to the university amazed anyone who knew how much he lived and died with Lions athletic teams. Although he primarily loved the football program, he helped find athletes for basketball, wrestling, lacrosse, or any other Penn State team. Art spent most of his free time going to high school games to look for future prospects. He pored over the Long Island–area newspaper sports pages so he could compile information about dozens and dozens of high school athletes and what area sportswriters and coaches thought about their abilities. He became an information bank about Long Island high school athletes and was constantly sending this information to various Penn State coaches. You couldn't make a reasonable guess at how many hours Art devoted to learning about prospects for the Lions.

Art was not the kind of crazy fan you read about who seems to get his favorite team into trouble over a violation of NCAA rules. He was meticulous in knowing what an alumnus was or was not permitted to do, and never did anything that gave even the appearance of being out of bounds. He was simply a fan who wanted to make sure that Penn State coaches knew about as many outstanding high school athletes as possible.

One day, all of Art's friends on the campus received the devastating news that he had been diagnosed with a serious illness that would probably prove fatal. Art had friends everywhere and all, of course, were shocked at the news. When you saw Art, you couldn't believe that a man in such serious straits could continue to be so upbeat and so unchanged in his demeanor. It was as if there was nothing seriously wrong with him and he went on with all of his activities.

That fall, Art and his wife, Hermine, arranged to move to State College for the fall months. They never missed a home game, and I have a hunch that Art wasn't up to driving back and forth to New York between games. Now, fall football practices at Penn State are closed to the public and have been for many years. Stories are legendary about alumni boosters who come to campus and decide to "go up and watch the team practice." As they say on Broadway and at premiere athletic events, seeing practice is a "tough ticket."

But when Joe and his staff learned that Art had been stricken with his serious illness and had moved to State College for the fall season, Joe did something that we all found to be almost unbelievable. What Joe did for Art was the most important and caring thing anyone could have done for him. He allowed Art to sit in on all of his coaching staff meetings as they prepared for the upcoming two games. It had to be a wonderful dream come true for Art and when you saw him, he seemed unable to wipe a smile off his face.

If Art had survived, I'm sure that he never would have forgotten Joe's kindness. Those of us who were Art's friends can never look at Joe as we had before, especially in view of what he did when he learned that Art had passed away at his winter home in Florida. Joe, along with Tim Curley, the university athletic director, flew to Florida so Joe could speak at Art's funeral. Had he known what that would have meant to Art? Joe spoke movingly of Art's friendship and dedication and loyalty to Penn State and of his personal friendship for Joe and members of his staff and what they had meant to each other over the years.

I'm sure that football fans everywhere will continue to see Joe Paterno as they have always seen him—a coach who has continued to win without compromising himself, his staff, or his university. Art Gladstone's family and friends will also see him that way, but they will also know that there is an important additional dimension to Joe, because they saw it and felt it. ■

CHAPTER

8

Football Memories

Penn State has had many athletes who were outstanding in their sport while on the campus and then went on to excel in a professional sports career. For example, 10 of the players from the 1995 team were chosen in the first seven rounds of the NFL draft. Many others, over the years, have gone on in any number of fields—medicine, dentistry, law, business, education, and others. Among the Penn State graduates I have known, there is one who has had a uniquely broad career.

Most athletes are happy if they achieve star status in their sport; this man was a star in two sports. He was a star in the National Football League and, after his retirement from football, made his mark in many areas in his chosen field. I'm talking about Mike Reid, a true Renaissance man. If you want to see a young person who has had his eyes on a goal and used his educational years to prepare for that goal, I offer Mike Reid as an outstanding role model.

Many of us first became aware of Mike Reid and his star quality back in the mid–'60s when he was beginning to be recognized for his outstanding football talent as a member of the Altoona High School football team in Altoona, Pennsylvania. When you saw Mike on the football field, there was no question he would be a star. At Altoona, Mike played both linebacker and fullback.

As a linebacker, he dominated the field. He was big and strong and quick off the ball, and he could run. To use an old sports cliché, "He had a nose for the ball." After a play, when you found the ball carrier, you'd see Mike right in the middle of the pile. Watching him play, you knew he'd be a great linebacker in college ball…until you saw him play fullback. As I've said, he was big and he could run. Even when he was tackled, he "really moved the pile." Although he never played fullback in college or the pros, he probably would have been as outstanding at that position as he was at defensive tackle.

As happens too often, players who are slated to be stars are injured, and that happened to Mike. He injured his knee and was red–shirted to save a year of eligibility. When he returned ready to play, the coaching staff moved him to defensive tackle. Coaches often believe that a middle linebacker is too visible a target for certain kinds of blocks and certain types of players and is a high-risk position. Since a down lineman operates in a smaller space and most of the action seems to occur in front of him, he might have a better chance of avoiding the kinds of blocks that lead to leg injuries.

Mike became a dominating defensive tackle and, with Steve Smear at the other tackle position, the Lions had as effective a pair of defensive tackles as you would find on any team in any year. This pair has often been compared to a defensive twosome of later years—Matt Millen, who went on to win several Super Bowl rings with the Oakland Raiders, San Francisco 49ers, and the Washington Redskins, and Bruce Clark, who was the first junior to win the Vince Lombardi Award and later had a successful NFL career with New Orleans and Kansas City and then in the Canadian Football League.

Mike had two outstanding years after he returned from his knee injury, although there was one day when I was very afraid we had seen the last of Mike Reid in a Penn State football uniform. At practice one fall, the team was going through a "spot scrimmage" that includes hitting and tackling although the plays all start at the same spot. On this particular afternoon, Joe Paterno went at Mike Reid with some vigorous criticism of something Mike had done that was not up to Joe's standards. The only thing the sideline crowd could hear was Joe yelling something like, "Get out of here. If you don't want to play, get off the field." In effect, he appeared to have kicked Mike out of the practice. Mike took off his helmet and by the time he got to the sideline, he was steaming, almost in a rage.

Whatever had happened on the field and whatever Joe had said to him had him saying, almost to himself, "I'm going to give up this game" and "I've had enough" and "Nobody deserves to be screamed and yelled at this way." I was afraid that he might leave the field and head for the locker room, and after that who knows what might occur between Mike and his coach. Fortunately, Chuck Medlar, the head trainer, was right beside Mike. Mike was big and so was Chuck, who in earlier years had pitched baseball for Penn State and later for the Cincinnati Reds.

Chuck was a very calm man and seemed to have a settling effect on players when they needed to talk to someone other than their coaches or teammates. As big as Mike was, Chuck wrapped his arms around him over his shoulderpads and spoke to him in a calm, low voice. Nobody on the sidelines could hear what Chuck said to Mike, but he got Mike to agree to whatever he had said. At that point, Mike put his helmet back on and stood on the sidelines until Joe called him back onto the field and the incident was over. Happily for Mike, Joe, the staff, the team, and the fans, Mike stayed on to compile a phenomenal record for himself and help the team to two outstanding years:

- the Lions won 22 straight games in 1968 and 1969. Mike was one of the three team captains each year;
- The Lions won two Orange Bowl games, beating Kansas in '68 and Missouri in '69;
- Mike was named to every All–America team in '69, won the Outland Trophy as the nation's outstanding defensive lineman, won the Maxwell Award, and finished fifth in the Heisman balloting;
- he was first round draft choice of the Cincinnati Bengals in the NFL; and
- he was named All–Pro twice in his five–year career with the Bengals.

Football was not Mike's only sport. In 1967 he won the Eastern Intercollegiate heavyweight wrestling championship. Then, as a change of pace, he starred in a campus production of "Guys and Dolls," giving us an early look at his musical ability.

We have often wondered what it was that Joe told Mike that practice day and why he sent him from the field. A good guess might be that Joe was concerned with Mike's year off and the effects of the knee operation on his play. Is it possible that Joe wanted to get him mad enough so that he would come back into the scrimmage and show the coach how he could play, and at the same time show himself that he was over his operation and was tough enough to step back into the lineup? Just speculation.

After football, Mike went on to a successful career in music that continues to this day. While Mike was still in the NFL, he made some off-season appearances as a musician. On one occasion, he was piano soloist with one of the country's leading symphony orchestras. One of the television networks showed a clip of Mike's introduction to the audience. After being introduced as an All–Pro member of the Cincinnati Bengals, Mike came on stage in his formal white tie and tails. He walked to the piano, flipped out the tails of his jacket, and took his seat on the piano stool. Then, instead of moving the stool under the piano as usual, he reached out, grabbed the underside of the piano, and easily slid the piano toward him so he was properly positioned to begin his performance.

You might think that being an All–America college football star, a wrestling champion, an outstanding professional football player, and a soloist on the concert stage would be enough to earn a reputation as a Renaissance man. But Mike wasn't finished yet.

By pure coincidence, I was able to follow at least a small part of his new career as a performer at the piano. I was on my way to Owensboro, Kentucky, one day and after leaving the airport passed a Holiday Inn with a large sign that said, "Now appearing at the piano in our lounge room, former Cincinnati Bengal All–Star Mike Reid." Mike was beginning to pay his dues in another field of music. Not many months later, while I was at an IBM convention in Austin, Texas, one of the featured performers was country star Ronnie Milsap, who presented two songs by a rising composer named Mike Reid. If you follow country music, you know that Mike has had several songs at the top of the charts and won Grammy awards.

In 1995, Mike Reid and his musical group made an appearance at the Special Olympics at Rec Hall on the Penn State campus. Mike led the group, played keyboard, sang vocals, and had

written most of the numbers. What's Mike going to do next? A
story in a New York newspaper said that he was preparing to
premiere his first opera. What would you guess would be next
for him? Would you be very surprised if you were asked to vote
for Mike Reid some day for governor of Pennsylvania?

It's Much Easier to Quit

Over the years there have been many Penn State athletes, both
men and women, who suffered serious injuries and faced long
odds against them ever playing again. Many of them went to work
with doctors and trainers and, after months and months, returned
ready to compete. It is hard to realize the physical and mental
dedication that this kind of program must take and how much
pure work is involved.

I can cite the case of one of Penn State's great tailbacks, Blair
Thomas, who overcame what seemed to be impossible odds so
he could play football once again. Blair was injured during a simple
warm–up in the Lions' indoor practice facility. He suffered a very
serious knee injury that would require surgery and a long and
difficult rehabilitation program. Those who worked with Blair will
tell you that they cannot recall another athlete who worked any
longer or harder than he did. He had to sit out what would have
been his senior year and returned to the squad the following year
for an outstanding season, which earned him a Number One draft
selection by the New York Jets.

There have been other athletes who escaped serious injury
but, despite having great skill and ability, never had a real opportunity to become a front line player. This happens for a variety of
reasons, primarily being slotted behind a truly great player whose
abilities keep him or her in the number one position. I can only
imagine the mental dedication required to accept a back–up role
in the hope that "my chance will come and when it does, I have to
be ready."

Stephen Pitts was a highly skilled and widely recruited high
school player who came to Penn State in 1991. He joined what
was probably the most talented tailback group ever assembled at
one school at the same time. Along with Pitts, there was Ki–Jana

Carter from Ohio, who was later taken as the Number One selection in the 1995 NFL draft; Mike Archie, a record–brealking tailback in the tough western Pennsylvania WPIAL conference; and J.T. Morris from Virginia, who was switched to fullback and played almost immediately his freshman year. I'm sure that all of these outstanding players planned on being the team's star running back; obviously, that couldn't happen.

What did happen? Carter won the tailback spot and had an outstanding career with the Lions. Mike Archie, because of his skills as a runner, pass–catcher, and kick–returner, became a back–up and saw lots of playing time. J.T. Morris transferred out after one year. And Stephen Pitts saw only limited playing time.

After Carter graduated, Pitts and Archie went neck–and–neck for the starting tailback spot. Then Stephen broke a bone in his foot. By the time he returned, Archie had won the position. Did Stephen give up? You know that didn't happen. He played some at tailback and was a star on the "foreign team," the Penn State players who help get the team ready for their next opponent by playing the opponents' roles in practice. He was always ready to do whatever he could to help the team. Finally, others were injured and his chance came. Was he ready? Check the stats:

- 282 yards against Iowa, third highest in Penn State history
- 164 rushing yards against Michigan and 93 against Michigan State
- 77 total rushing yards in the games against Indiana and Northwestern
- 118 rushing yards in the Outback Bowl against Auburn.

Stephen helped the Lions with wins in five out of six games. If Stephen Pitts were less of a man, I'm not sure that he could have kept his high state of readiness, and his belief that he ultimately would have a chance to showcase his talents. In the games listed above, Stephen played like an All-American. He ran like a four–year starter. When you saw him on the field, you knew why he was widely recruited as a high school star. And you knew why he had earned the respect of everyone who followed Penn State football.

Penn State's annual football banquet honoring the senior members of the team is held following all the regular season games. That year's came between the win against Michigan State and the bowl victory over Auburn. At the banquet each year, one senior is chosen to speak for his teammates. That year it was Stephen Pitts. When he finished, he received as warm and sincere an ovation as I have ever heard at a Lions football banquet. By being there when he was needed and performing at such a high level, Stephen had become almost a folk hero.

The Great Upset of 1964

Penn State did not have a great football team in 1964; we lost six games and only won four. (Incidentally, that was the last losing season until 1988.) We took the 1964 team to Ohio State when the Buckeyes were ranked Number One in the nation and we had already lost four games. The press paid little attention to the contest in the week preceding the game. The feeling was that Ohio State was in contention for the national championship and Penn State with its 0-4 record certainly wouldn't test the Buckeyes.

As it turned out, not only did we beat Ohio State 27-0, but with one minute remaining in the third quarter, Ohio State not only had not scored but had not gotten even one first down. I don't know what the Penn State coaches had dreamed up to handle the Ohio State offense, but I do know that our quarterback, Gary Wydman, might have had the best ball–handling day of all time.

I was one of the Penn State broadcasters that day, and although we had the best seats in the house, even with our binoculars we almost never saw the ball. Wydman had the Buckeyes totally confused with his faking, and they didn't come close to being in the game. In those days, there was no more exciting place to watch a college football game. Michigan's field had more seats, but the 84,800 who packed the Ohio State stadium were a knowledgeable and unbelievably noisy crowd. But that afternoon in the fall of 1964, we might as well have been playing in a spring practice game as far as crowd noise was concerned. The home crowd was absolutely stunned, as was, I'm sure, the entire state of Ohio.

Members of the press and broadcasters usually traveled on

the same plane as the team. For some reason for that game, however, they were a few seats short and so we had chartered a four–passenger Cessna from Bunny Grazier of nearby Bedford, a well–known pilot, to handle the overflow.

There was Bunny; Ernie McCoy, Dean of the College of Physical Education; Jack Harper, a State College businessman who was a great fan of the Lions, and me. I tell you this because of an incident that occurred as we rolled down the runway in Columbus on our way back to State College. By the time we were leaving, the entire area not only knew about the monumental upset and the humiliating score, but they had gone into mourning and a pall had descended over the state.

As Bunny reached the end of the runway to take off, he called the tower to identify our plane and request permission to take off. Bunny said something like, "This is Penn State Flight 0023 en route to State College on Runway Four requesting permission to take off."

Through the receiver located over Bunny's head we heard the tower controller reply, "Penn State Flight 0023, you guys think you're pretty good, don't you?"

Bunny replied, "Yeah, we think we're pretty good, and you guys have a nice little team, too, because you did get a couple of first downs in the last quarter!"

From the tower: "Penn State Flight 0023, permission to take off with one proviso." As we headed down the runway and our wheels left the ground, we heard the final remark, "Penn State Flight 0023, don't ever come back!"

Earlier in that season, Coach Rip Engle had asked Ohio State Coach Woody Hayes if he would come to State College to be the speaker at the annual football banquet at the close of the season. Woody very graciously agreed. At the time, he probably thought that his speech to Penn State would be one of commiseration with lines like, "You guys gave us all we could handle that day" and "No team played us tougher than you guys did" and "I never saw a team four touchdowns behind play harder longer."

I'm sure he didn't expect that he would be speaking to a team that not only destroyed his club's national ranking but also actually shut them out. Woody had a reputation as a fierce competitor and a man who was very studious (he was known as an expert on the Civil War) and very gracious. He also was an amusing and engaging speaker.

That evening, Woody paid great compliments to our team. I'll never forget how he opened his speech. As soon as he came to the microphone he said, "You guys have a helluva team. You really kicked our butts." After paying gracious tribute to the team and several individual players, especially quarterback Gary Wydman, Woody went on to deliver an amusing speech. He told the team, for example, how important physical conditioning is to an athlete and that it was a year–round job, not just a matter of deciding to get into shape during the season.

To illustrate his point, he told us about one of his players who was an outstanding performer and a great professional prospect, but would never reach his potential if he didn't change his conditioning habits. It seems that this particular player had a great taste for beer and that kept him from his effective playing weight. Woody said that after practice one day, he asked the player to be in front of his dormitory at a certain time that night because Woody wanted to take him for a short ride to show him something important.

The young man was there on time, and Woody drove him to the outskirts of Columbus and stopped his car opposite the main gate of a well–known brewery. He said to the young man, "Do you see that? That's the XYZ brewery, and they brew lots and lots of beer. Do you notice how big that brewery is? Do you see how many tank cars there are over there to bring in the ingredients? Look at how many trucks are waiting there to take the kegs and bottles to hundreds of bars and saloons. I brought you out here so you can see how much beer they brew and to tell you that no matter how much beer you drink every day, you'll never be able to drink all the beer they brew!" The player turned to Woody and said, "Coach, I know I'll never be able to drink all the beer they make, but do you notice I've got them working three shifts a day to keep up?"

Woody, despite has bombastic reputation, knew how to lose a game graciously. He reminded us how noisy it was inside Ohio Stadium, regardless of the opponent and regardless of the score.

He told us that the crowd roared continuously whether the Buck-eyes were behind by a single point or ahead by six touchdowns. So Woody said he had developed a routine. When his team went on offense, he would call the quarterback over, grab the front of his jersey with both fists, and tell the quarterback the first three plays he wanted him to run in the series. Then, because he never wanted to give the quarterback an excuse in case he ran the wrong play or ran the plays out of sequence, he would say, "Now repeat after me." When he did this, he knew the quarterback could never say later that because of the noise he really couldn't hear what the coach had decided about which plays he would run and in which sequence.

Then he said to our team, "You guys were giving us a hell of a licking. You had our defense on the field practically the whole game. When you had the ball, we couldn't find it. When we had the ball, we were like the Rockettes at Radio City Music Hall—one…two…three…kick! So about halfway through the last quarter, we held you on downs for one of the few times that day and we were going on offense. So I followed my usual routine. I called over my quarterback, grabbed his jersey with both fists, and then said, 'Now repeat after me, Our Father, who art in heaven….'"

That was a gracious way to cap a speech by a losing coach. But for me, that wasn't the end of the story. Twenty–eight years later, I had occasion to tell that story. For many years, I have spent part of my time speaking to corporate groups, regional and national conventions, individual companies and their dealers and customers, etc. In 1992, I contracted to make a series of presentations to all of the Firestone and Dayton Tire dealers in the country. Firestone had recently been purchased by Bridgestone, and the new owners scheduled four meetings in various parts of the country to introduce themselves to their dealers and tell of their plans for growth and expansion. I was a speaker at each of those four meetings, which were scheduled approximately two weeks apart. Also on the program were four or five executives from Firestone, who were there to assure the dealers that there would be a smooth transition of ownership and to tell them plans for projected merchandising programs. Since we were together four different times, four lunches and four dinners and four social evenings, we got to know each other well and became friends.

One of the Firestone officials was an especially imposing man. He must have stood 6'4" and had an executive's bearing. At the last dinner, we were sitting around the table talking about sports. My tall friend told me that he had played for Woody Hayes at Ohio State, and I thought he should hear the Woody Hayes story about "Repeat after me, Our Father...." When I finished the story he said, "That's exactly the way it happened. I was the Ohio State quarterback that day."

The Prevent Defense

There is no football strategy that is the subject of more arguments and fan dissatisfaction than use of the prevent defense late in the game or during the final moments at the end of the first half. On one side of the argument are the fans who believe that the prevent defense has cost their team a victory. Lined up on the other side are coaches who are afraid that the opposing team will get a quick score on a long pass that will let them back into the game.

The prevent defense gave rise to the "two minute drill." Some quarterbacks have gained fame for their ability to direct that drill. Teams know that a team in the lead, trying to prevent a quick score, is going to drop men off the line of scrimmage, bring in an extra defensive back or two, and give up only short passes which, while complete, take time off the clock. These days, teams will go into a prevent defense at the end of the half or at the end of the game when they are ahead by only one touchdown or even by just a field goal.

Since passing games are so effective, they are afraid that if they play a normal defense, they might give up a quick touchdown and either tie or fall behind. Sometimes the prevent defense works; often it doesn't. There is nothing that enrages fans more than to watch their team dominate most of the game, controlling their opponent's passing game, only to allow the opponent to move down the field against a prevent defense and score a tying or winning touchdown or field goal.

At heart, all football fans are coaches. You know that's true when you sit in the stands or watch a game on TV with friends and hear all the second guessing. What's your vote on the prevent defense, at the end of the first half or at the end of the game? The Penn State–Georgia Sugar Bowl game at the end of the 1982 season that saw us win our first national championship is probably a good example. The Lions had dominated the first half and led 20–3, holding Heisman Trophy winner Herschel Walker pretty well in check. As time ran out in the half, Penn State played it "soft." Georgia went right down the field throwing the ball and scored right before the half ended.

The Bulldogs had appeared ready to lose the game when trailing by 17 points. Their late touchdown seemed to rebuild their confidence, and when they came out for the second half, they scored twice and took the lead. Penn State scored its last touchdown when Greg Garrity made a diving catch of a Todd Blackledge pass into the end zone, a picture that made the cover of *Sports Illustrated*. Although Penn State won the game, the Lions' soft defense at the end of the first half gave their fans nervous moments in the second half. The prevent defense is particularly anath-

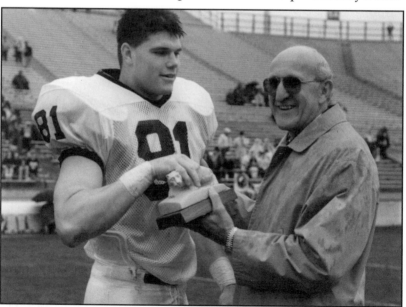

Steve Garban, right, recently-retired Penn State University Senior Vice President for Finance, presents Red Worrell Award to Kyle Brady at the 1993 Spring Blue-White Game. The award honors the most improved offensive player in spring practice.

ema to me since I saw Penn State lose a game probably as a result of the prevent defense.

The year was 1965, the opponent was the University of California, and the site was the California stadium at Berkley. Penn State had led most of the game and now was up 17–14. California had the ball at their own 48–yard line when they called a time out. The clock showed only two or three seconds left, time for just one play. Bob Prince and I were the broadcast team that day, working in a temporary booth that had been built in the top row of the stadium. The only things that protected us from a very long fall were two wooden railings that were the back of our flimsy booth.

I remember saying during the time out that I hoped Penn State would rush the quarterback to make him throw it on the field of play. My reasoning was that if the quarterback threw the pass on the field of play, the receiver would have to run a long way through lots of defenders to score. I didn't want to see a "Hail Mary" throw into the end zone that too often puts the result in the hands of Lady Luck.

I figured that the receivers would have to run 50 yards to get to the end zone and that tired players, in full uniform, probably would take seven or eight seconds to run that far. I thought that a normal rush could get to the quarterback before much time elapsed. Penn State fans who were listening to the radio that Saturday afternoon in 1965 probably still recall what happened.

Penn State went into a prevent defense and rushed only two or three linemen. The Cal quarterback stood in the pocket as all of the eligible receivers ran straight down the field and into the end zone. Penn State had dropped back a couple of linebackers, in addition to the defensive backs. I don't know how many players there were altogether in the end zone, but it sure looked like there wasn't very much room down there. The Cal quarterback threw a big rainbow 60 to 65 yards in the air. The ball came down almost dead center right in front of the goal posts. Penn State linebacker Ellery Seitz jumped up to swat the ball down. I don't know what happened, but when he hit it, it bounced up and sideways and a little Cal receiver named Jerry Bradley dove parallel to the ground and caught the ball for the winning touchdown.

What a disappointing way for Penn State to lose the game,

and what a long ride it was going to be back to State College. When Bradley caught the ball, Bob Prince jumped to his feet holding the microphone. As he did, his heavy metal folding chair fell over backwards and right through the wooden railings at the back of the booth. If the chair had fallen over the edge of the stadium, I am absolutely sure there would have been at least one fatality because it was a drop of several stories to the ground. Bob lunged for the chair, lost his balance, and almost went through the railing. I grabbed his sportcoat, he grabbed the chair, and order was restored.

Bob never stopped talking through all of the slipping and sliding that was going on. The score was now 20–17 in favor of California, and time had long ago expired. The Cal players were still on the field rolling around in a wild celebration. What a way to come from behind and win the game! Penn State, meanwhile, had left the field and gone to their locker room. The referee then did something that is probably in the rulebook, but I had never seen before. He sent one of the officials into our locker room and insisted that 11 Penn State players come out to line up for the meaningless extra point (meaningless unless someone had a three–point bet on the game, but that certainly wouldn't occur to a game official, would it?). Some of the Lions came out in their T–shirts, several had taken off their jerseys and came out in their shoulder pads and pants. One guy was wearing only one shoe. Cal kicked the point, and the game finally ended 21–17.

Ever since then, when the Lions go into a prevent defense, as we and practically every other team will do, I close my eyes and see 1965 all over again.

The President's Own Credit Card

Penn State had scheduled a new opponent for a two–game series for the 1959 and 1960 seasons. We would travel to Columbia, Missouri, for the first game, and Missouri would play at Beaver Stadium as our Homecoming opponent in the second. Until that time, Penn State usually traveled in a TWA chartered plane for road games that required air travel.

We always received the best of personal service from the airline, and they had a representative travel with us to make sure that all travel arrangements went smoothly. For some reason that was never announced but probably had to do with budget considerations, the Athletic Department was not able to sign a travel contract for the 1959 season without publicly bidding the charter business. No announcement was made that the football charter flights for the 1959 season would not be operated by TWA. The successful bidder's corporate name has long been forgotten, but their first charter flight for the Penn State team will be long remembered by those who were on that flight, including university president Eric Walker.

In those days, Mid–State Airport near State College was considered to be ill–equipped to handle any plane large enough to accommodate the team and traveling entourage. So, the team always traveled by bus to either Harrisburg or Pittsburgh, where the TWA charter could meet the group for the flight to the game site. We should have become suspicious when, instead of traveling to Pittsburgh or Harrisburg, we took buses to Mid–State Airport. As we arrived at the airport, there was a single plane of indeterminate color and dubious origin sitting on the runway.

The plane was sort of a faded blue/gray color, on the fuselage there was a painting of a dancer in a grass skirt, and under the painting was the name of the plane, Hawaiian Maiden. It obviously was a military aircraft left over from World War II and probably purchased at a surplus aircraft auction. When we arrived, the pilot and co–pilot were hosing down the aircraft to make it look presentable enough to carry the Penn State team.

Because of the configuration of the aircraft, a support to prop up its nose had been part of the original equipment but now was missing, and a prop had been jury–rigged to hold the plane in a more–or–less level position. Also, since the airport did not have a set of high moveable steps, which typically were rolled out to enable passengers to use a doorway high on the airplane, they had placed some sort of scaffolding next to the plane and we had to climb up the scaffolding to reach the aircraft door.

The inside of the plane did not have the usual lights set into the ceiling over each seat. Rather, there were square red flashlights wired to the overhead baggage racks. I should also tell you there was no internal public address system to allow the crew to talk to the passengers. Things like seat lighting and a sound system were of no value on a military aircraft that sometimes was used as a cargo plane by removing the seats. It was obvious that the charter company had tried its best to make the plane look like a regular passenger plane.

Head coach Rip Engle asked the stewardess which group the plane had carried on its last flight. "I wasn't assigned to the last flight," she said, "but I think they carried several racehorses." They apparently had removed the seats for the racehorse flight and, after a general clean–up, reinstalled them. I should say they reinstalled most of the seats because as I leaned over to speak to Dr. Walker, sitting across the aisle from me, my seat fell over on its side.

The final scary feature was the door. When the stewardess closed the door, it seemed to be securely sealed. I don't know if they had had trouble with the door coming open in flight, but I noticed that after the stewardess locked it shut, she further secured it by wiring the handle with something that looked like a coat hanger.

At about that time, the co–pilot called through his cupped hands to get our attention. He shouted the usual announcements about seat belts, flying time, etc. It was a pleasant surprise when the plane made a smooth taxi and takeoff, and we headed for Lambert Field in St. Louis, where we would board buses to go to Columbia, whose airport apparently did not have runways adequate for the Hawaiian Maiden.

Long before we landed in St. Louis, President Walker had made a decision. He called our business manager, Ed Czekaj, back to his seat and made it very clear that if we survived and landed safely in St. Louis, we absolutely were not going to tempt fate by trying a return flight on the Hawaiian Maiden. He told Ed to cancel the return trip with the charter company and contact TWA to see if they could have an aircraft at St. Louis to ferry us back to Penn State on Sunday morning, or even Saturday night, if necessary. Getting a large aircraft on such short notice apparently is not an easy job, and Ed had been given a tough assignment.

We landed in St. Louis and, as airline passengers usually do, we all started to move toward the exit door in the front of the plane as soon as the plane had rolled to a stop. Suddenly the aircraft began to tip forward and the stewardess started to shout, "Move back toward the tail. There is too much weight up front and we don't have a nose support for the plane. Stay at your seats and come forward two or three at a time so that the weight is evenly distributed and the plane does not nose down." If Dr. Walker had not already decided to cancel the return flight, this "don't stand the plane on its nose" incident certainly would have clinched his decision. We left the plane, said our individual prayers of thanksgiving, and then headed for the buses.

We won the game 19-8. During our broadcast, the telephone in the back of the broadcast booth was in constant use as Ed Czekaj contacted various airlines looking for a way to get us home Saturday night or Sunday morning. When the game was over and we had gone off the air, Ed triumphantly announced that he had been in touch with TWA and there would be a Constellation available to pick us up sometime late Sunday morning. So we took the buses back to Lambert Field, checked into the Holiday Inn at the airport, and spent the night. At dinner, we had plenty of laughs about the Hawaiian Maiden. It was easy to laugh now since we had safely made it on that old dinosaur.

(Incidentally, within a matter of months, we read in the newspaper that the charter company that had taken us to St. Louis had lost an airplane in the Florida Everglades, with many people killed. I never asked or even tried to find out if it was the Hawaiian Maiden. I'd like to think that it wasn't. The memory of our flight came back clearly again just a few years ago with the terrible plane crash in the Florida Everglades.)

Sunday morning, we assembled to be taken to the airport to board our TWA Constellation. But there was a delay in our departure because the TWA people had not received the paperwork authorizing them to carry us back to State College, and there would be no takeoff until the paperwork was in place. They told us they could not fly without some financial arrangement. They apologized, but said that company policy was "no money, no flight," and they had to follow company policy.

About this time, President Walker had had all he could stand.

He reached into his pocket, pulled out his American Express card and said, "Here, put the charges on this." To my surprise, they took the card and proceeded to load us aboard. I can't remember the exact amount, but I seem to remember Eric telling me the cost was around $10,000. I am absolutely certain that this was the only time that a TWA Constellation charter was paid for by a personal credit card. I assume that Eric had no trouble getting his money reimbursed from the university. I also noted that this was the last we saw of that particular charter company. I don't know how the contract for the rest of the season was resolved; I assume seats not bolted to the floor could have been adequate reason for cancellation.

How Much Do You Really Have to Run?

Matt Millen, a good television sportscaster, is one of the great athletes who played for Joe Paterno in the late 1970s. He was named to both the Walter Camp and United Press International All–America teams. In the National Football League, he earned three Super Bowl rings, with Oakland, Washington, and San Francisco.

When Matt played for the Lions, all the players who reported for pre–season practice in August were supposed to run a mile in a reasonable length of time. Sometime during the run, Matt simply stopped. He either couldn't or elected not to finish the run.

After being sure that Matt hadn't injured himself, Joe didn't take kindly to Matt's action, especially since he was the team captain and was expected to set an example for the rest of the squad. I don't know, of course, what Joe said to Matt, or what Matt said to Joe, but it ended with the coach deposing Matt as his captain.

After Matt's first year with Oakland, he was back on campus and visited the College of Business. I told him that I had never asked him what transpired between him and Joe because it was none of my business and since he was one of my students at the time, I didn't want him to believe he had to answer if he didn't choose to.

But that day in my office Matt told me what he had said to Coach Paterno: "I quit running because I never heard of a tackle having to run a mile in a game."

Sugar Bowl Revenge

The 1975 Penn State–Alabama game in the Sugar Bowl will never be forgotten by Penn State fans or, I suspect, by Alabama fans, either. That was the game when Alabama, leading 13-6, held Penn State to four downs on the one–yard line in as classic a goal line stand as I ever saw until the 1993 season when Michigan held Penn State at Beaver Stadium.

Penn State fans probably can recall each of the four plays that didn't gain an inch. Since then, I have heard football fans refer to that game from time to time, and almost every time the game is talked about, people seem to remember only that the game was lost right there on the goal line. What most fans seem to forget is that, except for an unforgivable mix-up, Penn State still would have had a great chance to win.

After the Alabama goal line stand, Penn State didn't fold. As a matter of fact, at that point the Lions came up with their own outstanding defensive effort. They held the Crimson Tide and forced them to kick. There still was time for Penn State to run at least several plays to try to win the game. Alabama kicked from its own end zone and Penn State had renewed hope for a win until someone on the Penn State bench made a monumental mistake.

I don't know if a coach made the mistake or if a player, in his excitement, was responsible for the error. But Penn State had 12 men on the field for the Alabama punt and, with the penalty, the Tide kept the ball and the game was soon over.

Penn State gained revenge, of a sort, during the 1982 season that saw the Lions capture their first NCAA national championship. The revenge didn't come against Alabama, which beat the Lions 42-21 during the regular season. Remember that 1982 Alabama game and one of the most bizarre plays ever seen? Fairly late in the game, Penn State lined up to punt. The videotape replay showed that the punter had dropped back the normal number of yards and one of his blockers, lined up to his left, had dropped back to block the outside rush by an Alabama player. But he moved too close to the punter and the result was that the Penn State punter kicked the ball right into the backside of his blocker. In effect, Penn State blocked its own punt!

After that, Penn State fell apart and gave up a couple of touchdowns to Alabama, which won the game by three TDs. If you were a betting man, what odds would you have given at that point in the season that Penn State would win the national championship despite the bizarre punt and the one–sided final score? But Penn State came back to win six consecutive games, outscoring Syracuse, West Virginia, Boston College, North Carolina State, Notre Dame, and Pittsburgh by a combined total of 201-48.

A triumphant Penn State community welcomed the team back after its dramatic last second win over Kansas in the 1969 Orange Bowl. Those on the platform for the rally included Coach Joe Paterno, Master of Ceremonies Mickey Bergstein, and PSU Athletic Director Ed Czekaj.

How did the football gods grant Penn State their revenge for 1975? Somehow, many, many teams managed to lose or tie a game before the end of the season and, despite the loss to Alabama 42-21, we were invited to meet Georgia in the Sugar Bowl and have a shot at the national title.

The Lions shut down the Georgia running game and its star, Herschel Walker, and Penn State was named the national champion after beating Georgia 27-23. Perhaps someone felt Penn State was owed a national championship after coming so close in 1968 and 1969 with two undefeated seasons and two Orange Bowl victories.

A Family Affair

Penn State has had several families that sent multiple family members to the Lions' athletic programs. Leading the list in sheer numbers was the Collins family from Cinnaminson, New Jersey. Five Collins brothers played important roles in Penn State's success over the years—Andre, 1986-89; Gerry, 1989-91; Philip, 1993-94; Aaron, 1994-97; and Jason, 1994-97. Andre played for the Washington Redskins for several years and now is with the Cincinnati Bengals. Aaron and Jason, members of the 1997 squad, are hoping for professional careers.

The Suhey family has sent four family members to the Lions football program. Father Steve was an All–American guard on Penn State's 1947 Cotton Bowl team. His son Larry played in '75 and '76, while Paul was with the Lions from '75 to '78, and Matt starred for Penn State from '76 to '79.

The Hostetler family also were key members of Penn State teams—Ron from '75 to '77, Doug in '76-'78, and Jeff in 1980. Jeff transferred to West Virginia University and has been a star in the National Football League with the New York Giants and Oakland Raiders and currently with the Washington Redskins.

A fourth family that made an important contribution to Penn State athletics is the Bahr Family, which gave Penn State father, Walter, who coached the Lions soccer team from 1974 to 1988, and sons Chris and Matt, who were outstanding place kickers for the Lions from 1973 to 1978.

Walter Bahr was a long–time soccer coach at Temple University, and his two sons were outstanding Philadelphia–area high school soccer players. They also were more than competent football place kickers, and Chris handled the punting duties for Penn State in addition to his kickoff and place–kicking responsibilities. Following his Penn State career, Chris kicked for the Cincinnati Bengals for 1976-79, for Oakland in 1980-88, and ended his career kicking for the San Diego Chargers in the 1989 season. He also took advantage of educational opportunities during his professional kicking years. By the time his athletic career had ended, he had earned a law degree, going to school during the off–season. He moved back to State College where he no longer practices law but is involved in business as a financial consultant and owner of a histology laboratory.

The university periodically brings to campus outstanding high school students who are contemplating enrollment at Penn State. On one occasion in recent years, Chris was asked to be one of the speakers at a banquet for these high school students and their parents. During the question–and–answer period following his talk, someone asked, "When you are going to try a long field goal, how do you decide just how hard you have to kick the ball to make the distance?"

Chris' answer was something I am sure is known to all kickers, and probably most coaches, but it came as a surprise to almost everyone in the audience. He said, "You never try to kick the ball harder, regardless of the distance. The object in place–kicking is to swing your leg exactly the same whether you are kicking an extra point or a 50–yard field goal. The next time you see a kicker kick an extra point, and he hits the ball solidly, see how far up in the stands the ball lands. He probably just kicked a 40–yard field goal.

"It's exactly the same as hitting a golf ball. You should swing the club exactly the same whether you have a short nine–iron shot or are trying to hit a long three–iron. Try for the same swing and let the loft of the club determine how far the ball flies. Next time you are on a golf course, or watching golf on television, see how smoothly the good golfers swing, regardless of the distance. If you watch a poor or mediocre golfer, watch and see how hard he tries to hit the ball when he is hitting a three or four iron. If he swings hard, he probably lunges, tops the ball, pulls it to the left, or makes some other terrible shot."

Matt Bahr followed his brother to Penn State and, while he was an equally fine kicker, he was a different personality who seemed to take a more light–hearted approach to the game. Matt went to the Pittsburgh Steelers in 1979 and kicked for them for two seasons. He spent the next 10 years as a productive kicker for the Cleveland Browns and then was with the San Francisco 49ers, New York Giants, Philadelphia Eagles, and New England Patriots. He remained a quality professional kicker through a long and productive career. Matt graduated from Penn State in electrical engineering and, in the off–season, has worked for Westinghouse and been involved in various business activities.

Both Bahr brothers came by their athletic ability naturally. Their father, Walter, played for the U.S. national soccer team in the World Cup in Brazil in 1950. That was the team that pulled off one of the most unexpected upsets not just in soccer but in all of team sports, defeating the English team in World Cup play. Soccer has never enjoyed the popularity in our country that it has in many other parts of the world. As a result, play in our country has never reached the level of expertise of other national teams, although there have been efforts lately to raise public awareness and thus the level of play has improved.

Both Bahr brothers were named to several All–America teams. In 1975, Chris was selected by *Time*, United Press International, the Walter Camp Foundation, and *Sporting News*. He led the Lions in scoring and hit four field goals from 50 yards out, including three from 55 yards. Matt broke his brother's percentage record, hitting 22 of 27. Matt also holds several NCAA kicking records—average field goals per game and most field goals per game. Those records were set in 1978.

Chris seemed to be the most reserved and unemotional during games. He always went about his job in a workmanlike way, and appeared quietly confident of his ability to make the kick when called upon. Matt, on the other hand, seemed more emotional and exuded an air of confidence when called upon.

At a Quarterback Club meeting, Joe Paterno talked about Matt and how he handles himself on the sidelines during a game. Joe has always said that he doesn't know very much about kicking or kickers and says, "I never bother the kickers or try to talk to them about their specialty. I leave that to the coach in charge of kickers, and I just hope that between them we get a successful kick when we need it."

Joe went on to say that he never seemed able to find most kickers when he was getting ready to call for a field goal. He said that each kicker has his own way of getting ready to go into the game. "One is tying his shoelaces for the third or fourth time. Another is getting himself ready with some sort of mental preparation and stands away from the rest of the team. Another is walking up and down behind the bench, giving himself a pep talk, and still another is kicking into the kicking net."

He said he never had trouble finding Matt Bahr. "As soon as we got near field goal range, Matt always seemed to be right beside me on the sidelines. Every time I turned around, I seemed to bump into him. He kept asking me over and over if I wanted him to go in and kick it. Matt always wanted to go in and win the game."

That attitude doesn't come as a surprise to me. One evening during Matt's freshman year, I went to Jeffrey Field, where Penn State plays home soccer games. I parked my car next to Matt's and we walked into the game together. As we walked in front of the stands at one end of the field, two attractive coeds asked him, "Aren't you Matt Bahr?"

Without even stopping, Matt turned his head, gave them a big smile, and said, "That's right, ladies. Number nine." As we walked away Matt said to me. "That's one of the reasons I decided to be a kicker."

Penn State and the Big Ten

For many years, Penn State was generally recognized as the sports leader as an independent school not affiliated with any conference. In football, Penn State and Miami were arguably the leaders as football independents in the entire country. In 1979 Penn State joined the Atlantic 10 in men's sports; it joined for women's sports in 1982. During their membership in that conference, the Lions captured more than 40 conference championships.

The Atlantic 10 was a limited conference for the Nittany Lions. Penn State fields teams in 15 men's sports and 14 women's sports. Because other conference members did not compete in as many sports as Penn State, and there was no conference in football, the Atlantic 10 did not appear to be the long–term answer for a major, nationally–recognized conference in which the Lions could compete. In addition, Penn State was having increasing problems trying to schedule an adequate number of teams that could compete at their level as more and more independents joined conferences and found it difficult to meet their conference obligations and still compete with the Lions.

Football coach Joe Paterno, who had built the Lions into a nationally recognized football powerhouse, had always wanted to bring to reality a strong all–sports eastern conference that would enable all of the stronger athletic schools to compete with each other and also receive national attention. He had proposed that Penn State join schools like Syracuse, Pitt, Boston College, West Virginia, and, perhaps, Army and Navy and other schools in the east with sizeable athletic programs in a new conference.

The effort failed when Syracuse, primarily, resisted giving up its membership in the popular Big East, a powerful and recognized basketball conference that provided much media exposure and income for its members. That conference included such basketball powerhouses as Georgetown, St. John's, Seton Hall, and Connecticut, in addition to Syracuse, Pitt, and Boston College.

Syracuse annually had led the nation in home basketball attendance. The Orange play their games in the Carrier Dome, and by using one of the two–deck football end zones and opposite side bleachers, are able to draw an average attendance of 30,000 per game. Syracuse would not give up their basketball income because they could schedule plenty of teams who would like to share in Carrier Dome dates.

According to media reports at the time, Penn State believed that the Orange wanted the best of both worlds—keep the Carrier Dome income and continue to share in the gate every other year when they played Penn State at Beaver Stadium where the crowds at that time numbered more than 85,000. At the same time, Penn State lost potential income when they played their every–other–year game at Syracuse before crowds of 50,000. Joe Paterno suggested to Syracuse officials that to level the income stream, when the agreement for the next six–game series was to be signed, four games be at Beaver Stadium and two at Syracuse. Syracuse objected because, according to a news report, it wouldn't be fair for Syracuse to "play two extra games at Penn State."

This seemed strange reasoning and unusual mathematics because the suggestion didn't mean two extra games. Usually the six games would be divided three and three. Paterno's suggestion meant only one extra game on the road for the Orange. But the issue never was resolved, and Penn State gave up its hopes for an eastern conference with their traditional rivals.

During the 1989 academic year, Penn State administrators and the Athletics Department reviewed the future of Penn State athletics in an effort to determine intelligent directions for the various teams. For many reasons, this review concluded that if the Big Ten conference was interested, it would be most useful for Penn State. That conference includes many land–grant institutions; its member universities have large enrollments; most have adequate facilities, especially in football and basketball; the conference enjoys a national reputation; and most members compete annually at a high level. In addition, both Penn State and the Big Ten value high academic standards. And so it was decided that Penn State would investigate whether the Big Ten had serious interest in adding the Lions to its membership. An approach was made to Stanley O. Ikenberry, Chancellor of the University of Illinois and, at the time, chairman of the Big Ten's Council of Presidents, with a request that he discuss the possibility of a Penn State membership with the other presidents.

The Big Ten is unique in that the presidents of the universities make major athletic decisions rather than the athletics directors and coaches. After quiet deliberation, the Big Ten presidents voted to extend an invitation to Penn State to join their conference. Penn State made its Big Ten debut in 18 sports during the 1991–92 academic year and was completely assimilated during the 1993–94 season. These discussions had been a well–kept secret and the announcement of Penn State's membership in the Big Ten not only came as a surprise but also triggered actions by athletics departments throughout the country. L. Budd Thalman, Associate Athletics Director at Penn State, described Penn State's decision and subsequent actions by other schools as "removing a small pebble which was holding up a major rock and, once the pebble was removed, it triggered a major rock slide."

Since 1993, the landscape of college athletics and the various conferences has undergone significant changes. The Atlantic Coast Conference and Southeast Conference both added new members. The Big East Conference, formerly only a major basketball conference, added football. The Southwest Conference began to come apart as its members sought new conference alignments. These realignments and the ensuing competition for conference affiliation by the various television networks changed not only the competition picture, but also the economic picture that found more and more schools and conferences aligning themselves with television to make sure they would earn their share of new TV dollars.

Whether this pattern will continue or expand is not yet clear but for the moment, more and more people are watching more and more teams and games than ever before. I think it is fair to say that Penn State's original move to leave the ranks of the independents to join the Big Ten was largely responsible for the new look of individual schools and the various athletic conferences.

How has Penn State fared in Big Ten competition? The 1993 season saw the Lions win six of eight Big Ten football games, losing only to Ohio State and Michigan; in 1994 the Lions won them all, going 12–0 and representing the conference in the Rose Bowl where a win over Oregon sealed a perfect season. In its first fully integrated season in the conference, the Nittany Lions and Lady Lions led all Big Ten teams in the inaugural Sears Directors' Cup Survey, an all–sports competition among Division I teams.

Penn State fans are now enjoying competition at a higher level in men's basketball at the new Bryce Jordan Center with its 15,000–seat capacity.

One of our traditional rivals, the University of Pittsburgh, is back on the football schedule. Penn State defeated Pitt in the 1997 season, and they will meet again in 1998, with future games depending on both schools' schedules. New schools undoubtedly will emerge to become traditional games for the Lions. Already, the Michigan and Ohio State games have taken on the air of traditional rivalries.

It's A Small World, And Getting Smaller

In 1986, I was invited to make a dinner talk to a large trade association meeting in Niagara Falls. After I had been speaking for 15 minutes, I noticed a man dressed in a jogging suit standing in the hall outside the dining room where we were meeting. I thought perhaps it was someone I knew, but it was a very large audience and the ballroom was long and narrow, so I couldn't get a good look at him. I spoke for about 60 minutes, and the jogger stood outside the open door for the entire talk.

As I was leaving the ballroom after my presentation, the man approached me and told me how much he had enjoyed listening to my talk. He said he hoped that his presence in the hall had not distracted me. I assured him he had not and said I had wondered if I should have recognized him, and whether he was someone I had met and should know.

It turned out that I never had met him, but he had heard me on an earlier occasion. He proceeded to tell me why he had stood in the hall and the circumstances under which he had heard me at an earlier time.

There was a fairly long period when I was associated with Penn State football and the Penn State football radio network. During several of those years, I was the color broadcaster for the games and, on a few occasions, had been the play–by–play announcer. The war in Vietnam was being waged then, and Armed Forces Radio provided many sports broadcasts to our troops in various parts of the world, especially Vietnam and other combat areas.

I remember that we were getting ready to broadcast the Penn State–Syracuse game when a man stuck his head into the broadcast booth and said, "Guys, I thought you ought to know that you are being heard on Armed Forces Radio today and maybe you can say a word or two to our troops out there." It really didn't matter that we hadn't been given more notice. We didn't do anything different during the broadcast, other than acknowledge that Armed Forces Radio was carrying the game and recognize the presence of military troops in the audience. We had been on the Armed Forces Radio network several times in the past, and it was fairly routine for them to carry our broadcast or the game broadcast from other schools.

The man in the jogging suit who had listened to my talk while standing in the hall wasn't really interested in my topic. It wasn't a matter of being unable to tear himself away from my stirring remarks. He said he was an FBI agent who was in the area for a convention and had gone jogging after dinner. As he was walking down the hotel corridor, he said, he heard a voice that apparently was being picked up by a speaker outside the ballroom. He said to himself that the voice sounded familiar, and he was sure that he had heard it before. The longer he stood there, the more positive he became that he was listening to a familiar voice. The more he thought about it, the more confused he became, although he was sure that he had heard my voice before. Right near the end of the speech it came to him.

Standing outside the ballroom, he asked if I had ever been in radio. When I told him I had, he asked if I had ever been a football broadcaster. When I owned up to that fact, he asked if I had broadcast the Penn State–Syracuse game in a particular season. After thinking back, I remembered that I had been the broadcaster for that game. He then told me that he had been sitting on the fantail of a ship off the coast of Vietnam, dialing his radio, and heard the beginning of the game. He listened to the entire game and, while many years had passed, recognized my voice as he walked down that hotel corridor.

So he listened to my business talk to the audience until it came to him—Penn State–Syracuse on a ship off the coast of Vietnam. I had two thoughts at that point. First, I couldn't imagine him being able to reach back and pull out my voice after all those years and all the voices he had heard in the meantime. My second thought was the recognition that in broadcasting, we too often get caught up in the action and fail to realize that you never know who is listening and where they are in the world.

Vietnam, as we know, was a lonely and dangerous place. We can't imagine how isolated the men who fought there must have felt. Can you imagine the emotions of a Navy man, thousands of miles from home, sitting on the deck of his ship and listening to a voice from home? I didn't ask him if he had been rooting for the Lions because it probably didn't matter at all. ■

CHAPTER

9

The Lady Lions

■

One of my favorite Peanuts cartoons quotes Charlie Brown as saying, "I never seem to know what's going on…right from the start my life has seemed strange." Then, after a moment's thought, he says, "I think I know what happened. I must have missed all the rehearsals."

That's the way I feel about the rapid growth of intercollegiate women's sports. Although I realize that women's sports have been growing over a number of years, if I don't stop and count back to when Title IX became a reality, it somehow seems that we didn't have an appreciable number of women's sports teams and then, all of a sudden, we did!

There always were a handful of "traditional" women's sports teams on campus, with the most recognized being field hockey. One thing that distinguishes field hockey from other sports is that only women play it. There have always been outstanding women athletes, of course, but comparatively few women's teams until Title IX.

Title IX is the federal law that said that any school that accepts federal funds has to be even–handed when distributing athletic scholarships; women are entitled to the same number and types of athletic scholarships as men. Further, women are expected to have the same size athletic budgets as men, same expenditures for uniforms, same travel budgets, etc. There was early skirmishing, of course, but there is little, if any, question that women's sports are an important fixture on the campus. Schools like Penn State have accepted the reality of women's sports teams and have expanded their athletic budgets to provide equal treatment for men's and women's sports.

The two Penn State women's sports that have had outstanding records in intercollegiate competition and, therefore, have drawn the most attention and largest crowds, are basketball and volleyball. They have had outstanding records under two excellent coaches—Rene Portland, coach of the Lady Lions basketball team, and Russ Rose, coach of the Lady Lions volleyball team.

Lady Lions Basketball

Let's talk basketball first. Many of you may not remember how they used to play women's basketball, but it was a very dull game. They used to play six players from each team on the court, three in the defensive half of the floor and three in the offensive half. A woman played either offense or defense and always stayed in that area of the court for her team. When a defensive player captured the ball after a missed shot, she could pass it or dribble upcourt. In either case, the ball was passed across mid–court for the offensive unit to take over.

Women's basketball today bears no resemblance to that old, boring game. The rules today are basically the same as men's rules. The women's teams run and shoot and defend and rebound; scores can exceed 100 points. The Penn State women have topped the 100–point total 22 times. Interest in their game is growing steadily. Since moving their home games from Rec Hall into the Bryce Jordan Center, the team has drawn more than 9,000 for a game three times and more than 12,000 twice.

Rene Portland came to Penn State from the University of Colorado, where her two–season record was 40-20. In 17 years on our campus, she had won 393 games through the 1996 season, giving her a winning percentage of 75.3 percent. Since the change from the Association for Intercollegiate Athletics for Women to the NCAA, the Lady Lions basketball team has been invited to 14 consecutive national tournaments. The Penn State program has produced two All–America players—Suzie McConnell, in 1988, who also was a member of the 1988 U.S. Olympic Gold Medal team, and Susan Robinson, in 1991, who also was the winner of the Wade Trophy, women's basketball's counterpart to football's Heisman Trophy.

I personally don't pay too much attention to national championships or any of the "All" teams. I question their validity because selection of teams and individuals is such an inexact science. When a team plays in a single–elimination tournament such as the NCAA basketball championships, too much is left to chance and too much depends on where and how a team is seeded. If a team is eliminated in one region, are we so sure they would not have reached the Final Four had they played in another region? Does a single loss to a team mean they would not have beaten that team in a round–robin tournament? I realize that a round–robin tournament is hardly practical or possible, but in my mind

Suzie McConnell, number 3, Penn State's All-American guard in 1988, drives against Louisiana State University's Teresa Witherspoon. Suzie was a member of the 1988 U.S. Olympics team that won a gold medal. She is the NCAA's all-time leader in season assists and career assists.

the team that emerges from today's tournament is not necessarily the best team in the country. In individual selection for "All" teams, far too many votes are placed because of regional pride, and I'm not sure that all the voters are competent to vote since they probably didn't see many of the players and teams they voted for play a single game, and their vote is cast because of what they read in the newspapers.

For the record, and to show the gain in skill and popularity of women's sports, we should note that since 1929, Penn State men's teams have won 22 national championships, while women's teams, since 1979, have won 13 national crowns and the gap will probably continue to narrow. In 1997, Penn State had 15 men's teams and 14 women's.

Alumni or friends of the university who periodically visit the campus will notice one change if they happen to walk into Rec Hall, which was the home of all indoor sports—men's and women's basketball, men's and women's volleyball, wrestling, men's and women's gymnastics, and boxing—and also home for a heavy schedule of intramural sports. Today, there is no longer a basketball court in the middle of the floor.

Volleyball Comes Center Court

After the Bryce Jordan Center was built, all home basketball games for both teams were moved there, and the floor at Rec Hall was painted and lined for volleyball. If volleyball continues to grow in popularity and fan support, one of these days that sport might also outgrow Rec Hall. As I write this chapter in the fall of 1997, the women's volleyball match against Michigan State drew more than 4,000 fans. As Coach Rose said, "It sure was nice to see the fan turnout for our undefeated team and to hear basketball tickets being promoted by the announcer at one of <u>our</u> games."

Russ Rose has had an outstanding record during his 18 years as head coach of the Nittany Lions. He has too many honors and awards to list here but, to give you some idea of the recognition he has received, his teams were never defeated when Penn State was in the Atlantic 10 Conference, a record of 49-0. His overall coaching record at the beginning of the 1997 season was 586-117,

Bonnie Bremmer, number 3, 1ˢᵗ Team All-American setter, sets up Penn State teammate Lauren Cacciamani, middle hitter on the NCAA All-American 2ⁿᵈ Team, in an intercollegiate volleyball game at Rec Hall.

a winning percentage of 83.4 percent, and he recently won his 600th game. He ranks second for wins on the all–time national coaching list. He has been named regional coach of the year and Big Ten coach of the year, and has been nominated nine times as national coach of the year.

His players also have won many honors and his teams have had at least one All–America player in 17 of his 18 coaching years at Penn State. During the 1996 season, Terri Zemaitis became Penn State's fifth first team All–American and two other players, Bonnie Bremmer and Angie Kammer, were named to the second team. Penn State has had, in addition, one three–time All America player, Lori Barberich, from 1982 to 1984. In 1986, she became Mrs. Russ Rose and is the mother of their four sons. Lori is undoubtedly Russ' greatest recruiting coup.

Liberating the Rec Hall Steam Room

When I think about the integration of women into so many activities on campus, I will always remember an integration effort that seemed very funny at the time, and still does. Many of you undoubtedly remember the early days of what has become known as the "women's movement." You would periodically read or hear about a woman or group of women who made an effort to integrate women into what previously has been a men–only activity or organization.

At that time, there was only one steam room in Rec Hall and only men used it. (Since that time, women have their own locker rooms, they are in joint physical education classes with men, and they share all facilities.) A small group of women decided that women, too, were entitled to use of a steam room and they made their feelings known to the physical education administration.

As I remember it, there were negotiations about the issue centering on whether to construct an additional steam room, establish specific hours of use, or other possible solutions. In the meantime, two women decided one afternoon that they wanted to use the steam room right then. So, with no prior notice, they wrapped themselves in towels and walked into the steam room that, at the time, was empty. I wasn't there, but an eyewitness reported it to me this way, "The word went through the locker room like wild-fire—there are two women in the steam room! Everyone was sort of paralyzed. Then, not knowing there were women in the steam room, a faculty member walked through the locker room wrapped in a towel and, as he often did following his workout, opened the door and disappeared inside the steam room. By this time, every man in the locker room was alerted to the fact that two women were still inside the steam room and that one of their colleagues had just gone in with the women. They expected that at any moment the door would fly open and their fellow professor would come roaring out. But nothing happened. Time passed and they all sat on their locker room stools wondering what would happen next."

After the usual length of time that a man would spend in a steam room, the professor casually walked out with his towel wrapped around his mid–section and headed for his locker as if nothing unusual had happened. When he was told that he had just spent considerable time in the steam room with two women he asked, "Were those women? I thought they were a couple of long–haired guys." One of the men in the locker room said, "Boy, you're really something. You're a Ph.D., and you don't know the difference between men and women."

Of course, the steam room issue was resolved. There was new construction and facilities became equal. Several months ago the saunas in Rec Hall were in the news. Apparently, some men had gotten in the habit of taking a newspaper into the sauna so they could read while enjoying the heat. But they also had gotten in the habit of leaving their newspapers in the sauna. The papers dried out and one day they caught fire. If some members of the women's basketball team hadn't seen the smoke coming out under the door and alerted the locker room personnel, there might have been a major fire. Both saunas were permanently closed and, as far as anyone can tell, there has not been any serious protest from anyone. So much for using steam rooms and saunas as a measure of gender equity! ■

10

You Meet A Lot of

Wonderful People

in 50 Years

As I look back on my past 50 years at Penn State, I am struck by how many opportunities I was given, how many people I have met, and how many directions my life has taken that were the result of opportunities and their timeliness. Perhaps things that have happened to you in your life also were matters of timing and opportunity.

During my days in the radio business, and the exposure I received because of a heavy schedule of sports broadcasting at the high school and college level, I received many invitations to speak or serve as toastmaster at area high school sports banquets.

One day, I received a telephone call from an athletics official at Clearfield High School, located about 45 miles from State College. The caller said they would like to invite me to be toastmaster at their annual football banquet. Because I had a busy broadcasting and speaking schedule that season, and was not eager to make a 90–mile round trip for what, as I recall, was very small compensation, I told the caller that I had a previous speaking engagement that evening and could not accept their invitation. The caller said, "That's too bad. It's going to be a very large affair, and we had wanted you to introduce our main speaker, Jesse Owens."

Jesse Owens had been one of my boyhood heroes. Perhaps you remember or have read about the 1936 Olympic Games that were held in Berlin, and the world attention that was focused on those games. This was during the rise of Adolph Hitler and his espousal of the belief that Germany was the master race whose genetic superiority would show them to be the greatest athletes in the world. He had lobbied for the 1936 games to be held in Berlin so he could put his theories on the world stage and receive all of the valuable propaganda he could milk from German success in the games.

The story of how a single black American athlete upset Adolph Hitler's plans has been told time and again. Jesse Owens won four gold medals in the 1936 Olympics. He won the 100– and 200–meter sprints and broad jump, and was a member of the winning relay team. Stories written at that time said that Hitler spent most of the Games in his ornately decorated private box and that he, personally, awarded medals to the winning athletes. The stories

Famed 1936 Olympian Jesse Owens was the featured speaker at a Clearfield High School football banquet at which Mickey Bergstein was the master of ceremonies. A high school official is at the right.

went on to say that Adolph Hitler, after all the talk of the master race, chose to avoid the picture of the Fuhrer awarding the gold medal four times to an American who was black; he left his box and delegated awarding the medals to one of the German sports officials.

As a young Jewish boy, I made Jesse Owens an instant hero, and now I had turned down a chance to sit with him and introduce him at a sports banquet, using a made–up excuse since I didn't want to drive 90 miles. I quickly told the caller that I believed I had made a mistake and had been looking at the wrong month's calendar. Now that I was looking at the proper page, I said, I could, indeed, be their toastmaster.

The banquet room was filled with sports fans who wanted to salute their high school players and, in addition, have an opportunity to hear a talk by a world–famous athlete. It may well be that there never had been an athlete of the stature of Jesse Owens visit Clearfield, and this was a rare opportunity for anyone interested in sports and sports celebrities.

Owens delivered a marvelous talk about how this country allowed him to fulfill his dream and how proud he had been to represent his country on the world playing field. He also detailed how his exposure, especially the snub by Adolph Hitler, led to worldwide publicity, and how all of that was translated into a successful business career and a lifelong connection with track and field.

One story he told was set after World War II, when the State Department adopted the practice of sending all–star athletic squads around the world to spread American goodwill through sports. Owens said he was a member of the first track team selected to take an extended trip under State Department auspices.

One of the countries his team visited was Persia, now Iran. He said that following the exhibition sports event, high government officials hosted a lavish banquet for the visiting Americans. He described in detail the golden plates and goblets and the ornate silverware and tablecloths that were used for the dinner. He also told the audience that they were served food that he had never seen before and said he tried never to put food into his mouth that he didn't recognize.

His hosts told the Americans that they were about to be accorded a high honor—they were served a very small uncooked bird that, in addition to being raw, was served with the head, bill, and feet still attached. This apparently was a symbolic gourmet delicacy that was served only to guests of the highest stature.

A young high school boy sitting in the second or third row interrupted to ask Owens, "Did you eat all of it?" Jesse said, "All of it? I didn't eat any of it! I don't know what anyone else did with his or her bird. All I know is that there was one guy who left the banquet with a robin in his pocket."

When Jesse had finished his talk and received a standing ovation, the principal of the high school rose and asked Jesse if, since he was staying overnight, he could be convinced to come to the high school the next morning so the entire student body and faculty could gather in the gymnasium and hear his inspiring talk. Jesse told the principal he would be glad to stay and address the entire school on one condition. He said, "I understand that you have two high schools in Clearfield, one public high school and one Catholic high school. Is that correct?" After the principal told him that he was right, Owens asked if the two schools ever had joint assemblies. When he was told that this had never been done, Jesse said, "I will stay over and I will speak to your students on one condition. My condition is that you have a joint assembly and invite the Catholic students to sit with your students and I will speak to all of them." The principal never hesitated. He said that right after the banquet was over he would call the priest who was in charge of the Catholic school and extend the invitation. He further indicated that he couldn't imagine the Father turning down the invitation, and he didn't.

When the banquet was over, Jesse asked if I would join him for a beer or two while he unwound after his speech. So the two of us ended up at the Clearfield Elks Lodge. By now, Jesse was an even bigger hero to me. His speech was so well delivered, he was so articulate, and he completely controlled the audience. Until this evening, he had been just a picture of a famous Olympian in the newspaper. Now he was a real person and there we were, exchanging stories at the Clearfield Elks on a snowy winter evening.

Jesse said to me, "You know, Mickey, life is a matter of timing and opportunity. Sometimes the timing of things in your life is all wrong. Things happen at the wrong time or you are the wrong age to take advantage of them. Or, many, many people of talent never are afforded an opportunity or when the opportunity comes, they aren't ready to perform at their highest level. Let me tell you about myself and the part that timing and opportunity played in my life.

"I was born in Alabama, and my daddy was a sharecropper. We had practically nothing. Sometimes you will hear people talking about their childhood say that they were poor but never knew it. Well, we were poor, and we damn well knew it. One day, my older sister left home to work as a domestic at someone's home in Cleveland. After a couple of years, she came home and said, 'Daddy, it's time to go!' So my daddy took a couple of tablecloths, laid out our clothes in them, and tied the four ends in a knot. He took some of the dishes and pots and pans, and we headed to Cleveland.

"I started this story by saying that life is a matter of timing and opportunity. Now I'll tell you how everything began to fall into place in my life. During recess one day, we were having races in the schoolyard. I was pretty fast and I don't think anyone beat me in any of the races. There was a man who looked like a teacher watching us run. After four or five races, he came over to me and asked, 'What's your name, son.' I said, 'My name is Jesse Owens, sir.' He told me that I looked like I could run pretty fast and then he asked me if I thought I could run faster than the bigger boys standing over there. When I said I didn't know if I could or not, he got four or five of the tallest boys to come over and he set it up for us to race up to the end of the swings.

"I guess it must have been 50 yards or so. I easily beat all of them. Then he brought over another group of taller guys and I beat them, too. Well, it turned out that the man was the track coach, and he got me a pair of track shoes and asked me to be on the track team. I didn't know a single damn thing about running, but he showed me how to dig a hole at the starting line, how to come up out of my crouch, and a couple of other things like that. The fifth race I ran I broke the city of Cleveland's 50-yard dash record.

The eighth race I ran I broke the city of Cleveland's 100–yard dash record. About the eleventh race, I broke the state of Ohio's 100–yard dash record.

"That's when everything began to fall in place and change the rest of my life. I was given a job and a scholarship to Ohio State. One afternoon in a dual meet with Michigan, I broke three national collegiate records and tied a fourth. In those days, they didn't hold tryouts for the Olympic team. The team was picked using the times and records of the best track men in the country. I was named to the team. I went to the Olympics, where I won four gold medals. This all happened on the world stage with all of Hitler's pre–Olympic boasting and all the other stuff that happened. When we got back to the United States, it seemed like every sportswriter in America was there to meet the boat. I must have been interviewed a hundred times, and everyone asked the same questions: 'Did Hitler really turn his back on you?' 'What did Hitler look like?' 'How did the Germans treat you?' 'Did the German press interview you and what did they say about you?'

"My interviews in the American papers appeared all over the country. We went on some all–star track tours. Some promoter even had me run against a racehorse. Every place I went, people seemed to know me. A couple of businessmen backed me in a public relations firm in Phoenix. I was offered dozens and dozens of paid speaking engagements. I prospered. My daughter was given an academic scholarship to Ohio State, where she became the May Queen.

"From the moment that track coach had me run against the bigger boys and I beat them, my life took off in a new direction. Timing and opportunity! I have often asked myself what would have happened if the track coach hadn't come out in the schoolyard and never had a chance to see me run. What if I had gotten a slow start in one of the schoolyard races and finished back in the pack? What if I had a serious injury in high school and didn't get a scholarship to college? But, none of those things happened. The timing was right! The opportunity was there! I was able to take advantage of the opportunity, and I was good enough to perform at a high level."

To illustrate the point he said, "I wasn't the only boy in our family. I had an older brother, Mercer, and he moved with us to Cleveland. My daddy was very law–abiding, and he immediately took me over to the school and had me enrolled because I was only 15 years old and had to go to school, though I'm not sure anyone would have paid any attention if I hadn't. My brother Mercer was 18 and didn't have to go to school. The family needed any money that Mercer could bring home. So I went to school, and Mercer found a very menial job.

"While I went to college and the Olympics and all the other wonderful things that happened to me, Mercer worked every day of his life as a menial until he passed away about six months ago. I'm not going to tell you anything more about Mercer, but I will tell you one thing—I never could beat him in a race!"

Early Vince Lombardi

Although his name will be forever linked to the Green Bay Packers and he always seemed to somehow epitomize the Packers and the way they played football, Vince Lombardi paid his dues as an assistant coach with the New York Giants, where he tutored an impressive list of all–time great NFL linemen. I was in his presence only once, but I will never forget the lesson he taught me and others who were hanging around him as he watched Penn State's football practice one fall day in 1954.

In those days, the practice field was alongside Beaver Stadium, which was still at its old location near the Nittany Lion Inn. There were no restrictions on fans standing along the sidelines during practice. (These days you can probably make it into where the gold is stored at Fort Knox more easily than you can get into a practice to watch the Lions prepare to play next week's opponent.) At any rate, on this particular afternoon, we all were gathered on the sidelines, along with Vince Lombardi, who was watching Penn State practice to scout players for the New York Giants.

Lombardi had a program from an earlier Penn State game, but while there were player numbers in the program, there were no numbers on the practice jerseys worn by the team. For those who are not familiar with college football practices, the first team wears one color jersey, the second team another color, and the third team still another. If a coach wants a player to practice with another unit, rather than take jerseys on and off over the shoulder pads, they have sleeveless jerseys that they slip on over their own jersey.

Without numbers on the regular and sleeveless jerseys, there is no way to pick out particular players if you don't know them pretty well. As it turned out, Lombardi was particularly interested in Roosevelt Grier, Penn State's outstanding tackle. Even in those days, Rosey was a very large 6'5", weighing around 240 pounds. There are many players today who are much bigger, but back then Rosey was considered more than adequately sized to be an NFL tackle.

Lombardi asked someone to point out Grier so he could focus on him during the scrimmage. The student to whom Lombardi had spoken said, "Coach, are you interested in Rosey Grier as a pro player?" Lombardi assured him that he was, indeed, interested in taking a good, long look at Grier. The student said, "You don't want Rosey on your team. He's too lazy. One play he'll look really good, and the next play you can't find him. He seems to go at top speed for a couple of plays and then loafs for several plays. He's lazy and couldn't play for my team."

Mickey Bergstein interviews Jesse Arnelle (left) and Roosevelt Grier at a 1953 practice.

Lombardi looked at the student and said, "That's a pretty tough thing you said about Grier, and I'm not sure you're right. Let me ask you something. Do you know how tall Grier is? Do you know what he weighs? Do you know how old he is? You'd better know all those things before you begin rating a player or saying that he is lazy or dogs it. Grier is a very large man. He stands close to 6'5", and I would guess that he's probably almost 250 pounds. Also, Grier is still 19 years old or may have just turned 20. You show me a player that young who is that tall and weighs that much and I'll show you a baby in football terms.

"A young guy that big isn't a loafer; he still doesn't have any stamina. That's why he seems to go at top speed for a while and then seems to drop out of action. He's getting his breath. Grier won't be a man with full strength and development until he's about 26 years old, and then you'll see a guy with the potential to be a great player."

Many fans probably don't remember, but Rosey was the first lineman taken by the Giants in 1954. He played in the National Football League for 11 seasons, the first eight with the Giants and the final three with the Los Angeles Rams. And, as Lombardi predicted, he seemed to get better every year. Does that student know that he owes Grier and Lombardi an apology?

People are always quick to express opinions about everyone and everything. This is especially true of sports fans, who have very strong, sometimes uninformed opinions about players and teams. Lombardi's evaluation of Rosey Grier should remind us to remember when we are quick with an opinion without facts or experience.

After football, Rosey Grier has gone on to a valued career. He first was prominent in television and then prepared for the ministry and has been recognized for his work with various charities and youth groups. You may also remember that it was Rosey who was with Robert Kennedy when he was assassinated in the kitchen of a Los Angeles hotel following a speaking appearance in the 1968 presidential campaign. Apparently, Rosey immediately used his body to shield Kennedy in the event there was more gunfire. I remember that one of the television networks tried to contact Rosey the next morning to get his eyewitness account, eventually going through the university to reach him. He gained the respect of many Americans when, instead of calling attention to himself, he simply expressed his personal grief and said he had nothing to add to the awful event he had witnessed.

Several years ago, Rosey returned to campus to be honored by the State College Quarterback Club. His wife and young son accompanied him. It was a family to be proud of, and Rosey delivered warmly–received and thought–provoking acceptance remarks. Roosevelt Grier was not only an outstanding collegiate and professional player; he is a warm and wonderful human being. Unlike many athletes who return to speak to teams on the campus, Rosey didn't dwell on the past. He tied the lessons he had learned on the campus and playing his sport to what he has learned from life as a social worker, youth leader, and ordained minister.

Coach Paterno originally had asked the Quarterback Club to invite back to our banquet players who had achieved meaningful success in whatever field they had chosen and who would serve as a role model for his players. Everyone in the hall that night saw and heard a player who met both of Joe's criteria.

More Than Haberdashers

The word "haberdasher" doesn't seem to be used anymore. As a matter of fact, I would guess that most college and university graduates haven't heard the word for the past 30 years or so. According to the dictionary, a haberdasher is "a dealer in men's furnishings." But now even the "men's furnishings" phrase seems out-of-date. Originally, a store designated as a haberdashery was a store that specialized in things other than clothing. It sold shirts, neckties, shoes, gloves, mufflers, etc. If a store sold men's suits, sport jackets, topcoats, etc., it was designated a "clothing store."

When I hear the term haberdasher, I only think of one person—Mr. Jack Harper. Jack and his Custom Shop for Men on West College Avenue is undoubtedly the most remembered retailer for Penn State men since the 1930s. Jack often showed me the list of Penn State men who, although they had graduated several decades ago, still wrote him to ask that he send them shirts, ties, trousers, jackets, and suits that "you know I would like and ought to have in my wardrobe." Jack kept their sizes on file, and when they lost or gained weight (mostly gained), they would send him their new dimensions.

I remember two special letters. One said, "Jack, my daughter is being married in three or four weeks. It will be a large and rather fancy wedding. Would you send me a suit that you think ought to be worn by the 'father of the bride'?" Another Penn State graduate wrote, "Jack, my wife and I are planning a rather elegant trip for our 35th wedding anniversary. We will be on a cruise and then will spend a couple of weeks at a fancy resort in the Bahamas. I have hardly any warm weather 'dress–up' clothes and accessories. Will you please send me everything I will need, and I will send along payment as soon as you let me know the amount?"

Is there any one man you would trust to pick out your clothing for important events? There would be one if you had ever seen or known Jack Harper. Jack was the most elegant man I had ever seen, and that's hard to carry off if you're as small as Jack was. I would guess he stood perhaps 5'4" or 5'5" and weighed maybe 120 pounds. He had a full head of white hair, always perfectly groomed, and I never saw him when he needed a haircut or trim. I often accused him of getting his hair cut every day or, more likely, in the middle of the night.

I'm not sure I ever saw him in shirtsleeves. I visited him in his office a couple of times a week for many years, and he was always seated at his desk with his jacket on. Most amazingly, he never had anything that remotely looked like a wrinkle in either his coat or his slacks. He wore the most beautiful suits and jackets and shirts and ties, and his shirt always looked like he had put it on less than 10 minutes ago. Did you ever know anybody whose belt and watchstrap were always a perfect match? And his shop always looked like he did, absolutely impeccable.

I first became a friend of Jack's when, early in my radio career, I called on him often to write his radio advertising copy. This was no easy task because he insisted that his copy be as impeccable as he was. Before I made a call on Jack, I carefully checked what I was wearing. I wiped my shoes clean, pulled up my socks, re–tied my tie and, if my sport jacket was a little rumpled, I didn't take off my outer coat.

As soon as I sat down in his office, I felt as though everything I was wearing was totally wrong and way out of style. I'm not even sure that Jack noticed, but I did. When I think of Jack, I always remember what a friend of mine, the late Jerry Weinstein, long–time editor of the *Centre Daily Times*, the local paper, once said about Jack and his outstanding store. Jerry said, "I would like to shop at Jack Harper's, but I don't own anything nice enough to wear into the store."

Jack passed away in 1984, and I miss my weekly visits with him. As Jack grew older, he began to drive less and less. He was a very devoted Penn State fan, and as a Penn State broadcaster I made a special arrangement with him. If an away game was within driving distance—Pittsburgh; Morgantown, West Virginia; Columbus, Ohio; Philadelphia; College Park, Maryland, etc.—I would drive Jack's car so that he could get to the game. It was on one of those drives that I gained an insight into Jack's personal philosophy of his business, and on another that I learned one of Jack's tricks to make sure that he looked perfectly dressed on all occasions.

We were playing Illinois at Cleveland Stadium in 1972, and I drove Jack, his son, and another friend to the game. When I picked them up, I was stunned to see Jack wearing a sweater. I had never

The late Jack Harper (right) a legendary State College haberdasher, joined Mickey Bergstein on the flight to the 1961 Gator Bowl in Jacksonville, Florida. Seated behind Mickey is Sunny Engle, wife of Penn State coach Rip Engle.

seen him in a sweater all the years I knew him. As you might guess, it was a beautiful pale yellow cashmere sweater. We drove west on the Ohio Turnpike and stopped at a restaurant for lunch. As we got out of the car, Jack slowly took off his sweater and carefully folded it. He then put on his sports jacket. One of the men in the car said, "Come on, Jack, we're not going to a dance." This was Jack's reply: "I have spent my entire adult life, with some success, trying to demonstrate to Penn State men how important it is to be appropriately dressed at all times, whether on the job, at a social occasion, interviewing for a job, or whatever. I don't know if there are any Penn Staters in the restaurant, but in case there are, I don't want them to see Jack Harper carelessly dressed and not at his best."

On another occasion, we went to a Penn State game with West Virginia in Morgantown. When Penn State was the opponent, the game was always a sell–out and the hotels and restaurants always were over–subscribed. Penn State had made arrangements for several of us to spend the night in a very unusual place. I still don't know where or what it was, but it certainly wasn't a standard hotel. We were housed in what apparently was an in–town men's club that had a few bedrooms for its members' guests.

There were so many in our group that the number of guest rooms was hardly adequate. So they had filled a large social room, that was complete with a bar and jukebox, with about a dozen folding beds that had been made up with fresh linens. It looked like a dormitory, and it turned out to be a different experience.

My bed was fairly close to Jack's, and I had a chance to watch him unpack. He had a suitcase that, when he unpacked it, reminded me of the circus when the clowns keep coming out of the small car until you wonder how everyone had managed to fit in the car. Jack kept taking clothes out of his suitcase, and I couldn't believe they had all been packed into that one bag.

In addition to the usual clothes and toilet articles, Jack unpacked **four raincoats**. Every time you saw Jack Harper, he was perfectly dressed for the occasion and for the weather. Now the secret was out! Jack had packed heavy and light dark–color raincoats and heavy and light light–color raincoats. So, regardless of what the weather might be—overcast or sunny, cool or colder—

when Jack walked down the steps at the stadium, he would be perfectly and immaculately dressed. And don't think that the Penn State fans at the game didn't notice.

When we got back to the "hotel," I asked Jack to show me how he packed and folded his clothes to keep them from being wrinkled. He showed me, and it looked fairly simple. When I packed for the dozens and dozens of trips I took in ensuing years (and I only packed one coat or jacket, not four), I never, never unpacked without my clothes looking wrinkled and rumpled. How did Jack do it? He simply wouldn't <u>allow</u> his clothes to wrinkle, and he must have willed them into obeying.

Over the years, Jack always had a student or two working in the store as apprentice salesmen. I knew several of them, and they all had one thing in common—they all had been meticulously trained by Jack Harper. The first thing they were taught was the proper way to clean and polish the front door latch to the store. This has been done since the day Jack opened the store, and it turns out there is a <u>proper</u> way to polish the latch and not everyone knows the secret. The second step in their training program was to learn the proper way to tie a necktie on a mannequin, either for display in the store window or on a mannequin in the store. This training took a long time and, when a trainee could pass the Jack Harper test, he then was allowed to trim the front window, under Jack's supervision, of course. I always look in the windows of men's clothing stores wherever I am, and I never, never have seen ties tied as meticulously as Jack Harper's boys tied them.

Because I enjoyed talking with Jack, and because Jack was one of my advertising customers, I usually spent a lot of time visiting his store. I especially enjoyed watching Jack measure a man for one of his tailor–made suits. He was a true professional and, if you were wearing a Jack Harper tailored suit, you probably were one of the best-dressed men in town. My wife spoiled me one year and bought me a suit tailored by Mr. Harper. I don't remember how many careful fittings I had, but there were many. And when I wore the finished suit, I felt like one of the richest men in town because Jack's tailoring made me look so elegant.

Another thing I enjoyed in visiting Jack's store was watching him fit one of the large football players who came in to buy a suit.

First, they would try on a ready–made suit, but that was an impossible task. Usually, the player couldn't fit the trousers over his large, well–muscled thighs. The next impossibility was to get a suit to fit him in the shoulders and chest and then, because it was probably a size 56 or 58, if it fit him in the chest, the jacket came down to his knees. So Jack went to work on a tailor–made suit as the only alternative. When the suit was finished and the player tried it on, he usually looked like a mannequin in the window of the country's most expensive store, assuming that he could tie a necktie the way Jack would teach him.

Even when Jack began to fail during his later years, he remained dedicated to immaculate dress. Clothing had been his life, and he viewed personal appearance as being at the top of the list for a man who wanted to be successful.

A legacy of his teaching was that all of the students who worked for Jack, and were taught by him, learned lessons they probably would never forget. The day after Jack's funeral, I went to the store to offer my condolences to his student employees. One young man who had learned to tie neckties the "Jack Harper way" said to me, "Mr. Bergstein, the person who tied Mr. Harper's tie could never have worked here. If he had a job here and tied ties that way, Mr. Harper would have fired him!"

Another well–remembered men's clothing store in State College was Kalin's, owned and operated by two brothers, Arnold and Bill. Kalin's featured a more informal atmosphere than you found at Jack Harper's. There was a shoe department that separated the men's furnishings section from the suit section and, especially over the noon hour, it was a gathering spot for men from town and the campus to discuss sports. It also was a place for discussion of the stock market and both national and world affairs.

Bill, the younger of the Kalin brothers, was a dear friend of mine and truly was one of the funniest men I have ever met. Bill didn't tell jokes; he just said funny things. For example, it was near Valentine's Day and a Penn State coed came into the store to shop for a gift for her boyfriend. Bill waited on her. The guy must have been a very special boyfriend because she looked at every possible gift item in the store, asking each time, "Do you think he will like this?" Bill was rather non–committal.

Finally, the young lady selected a pair of lilac–colored men's pajamas. After looking at the pajamas for a long time, she finally asked Bill if he would unpin them and hold the top up in front of him. Without a trace of a smile, Bill complied, looking rather mournful. The young lady asked, "If you were a man, would you like these?" Bill thought a moment and answered, "Just a minute, I'll ask my brother."

I spent a lot of time sitting around Kalin's when I should have been making sales calls for the radio station. I knew that if I stayed long enough and listened carefully, Bill would be sure to say something funny. I was there one day when the winter sale began. That's when Bill was at his best. A professor at the university, you could describe him as a frugal customer, was trying on a suit that was on sale. The suit was a Harris Tweed, a heavy, tightly woven fabric that was loomed in Scotland. I remember the price of the suit was $39, minus 25 percent for the sale. That price included a jacket, pair of pants, and a vest.

The professor was being waited on by a student who was working at the store while attending school. And the customer gave him a workout. First, the professor carefully checked the buttons. "Are these buttons sewed tight enough so they won't fall off? Did they use strong enough thread so the seams won't split?" The young salesman mumbled something like, "I'm pretty sure." Next, the professor asked if he could try on the coat and pants. He came out of the dressing room and, in the middle of the store, did several deep knee bends to see if the seams stayed intact when he stretched the pants over his ample behind. Next, he asked the salesman, "If I don't take the vest, may I take another pair of pants instead at the same price?"

The salesman was stumped. "Just a minute, sir, I'll go and ask Mr. Kalin." Now I knew this was going to get good. The salesman returned and told the professor, "Mr. Bill Kalin says that he would like to let you do that, but the store isn't getting many calls for single Harris Tweed vests this season."

Bear

There are relatively few people whose personality, and the aura that surrounds them, results in people recognizing them through a one–word nickname. One would be "Woody" Hayes of Ohio State. Another who quickly comes to mind is the long–time coach of the Alabama football team, "Bear" Bryant. Almost no one used his full name, and it's not often you see his full name in print. But when you mention Bear, even people who do not care for or know much about football often know who you mean.

Bear Bryant played an important role in Penn State football, even though the Nittany Lions played his teams only 13 times. In those 13 games, Alabama won eight and the Lions won five. The Penn State–Alabama games always seemed to have much riding on the outcome, and there are several that Penn State fans are particularly likely to remember.

The first time Penn State played the Crimson Tide was in the inaugural Liberty Bowl in 1959. That game was played in an un-likely city for a contest held at the end of December. It was played at Municipal Stadium in Philadelphia and really wasn't much of a game. Penn State called for a fake field goal on the last play of the first half. Second string quarterback Galen Hall, who was the holder on field goals, stood up and threw it in the flat to Roger Kochman, who ran it in. The final score was Penn State 7, Ala-bama 0.

What I remember most was not the game, but something I saw the day before the game at the team hotel in Philadelphia. When I left the elevator in mid–afternoon and turned down the corridor to go to my room, the entire corridor was full of men. The line ended at the door of the suite at the end of the hall. I originally thought there had been an accident of some kind, but there didn't seem to be any panic and it looked more like a receiv-ing line at a wedding or other social function. Actually, it <u>was</u> a receiving line—of former players who had played for Bear Bryant at Alabama.

The suite had been assigned to Bear, and these men had all come to the Liberty Bowl to see the game and renew their friend-ship with the coach. I don't know how many players had already come and gone, but clearly several dozen people had come to pay their respects to Bear. I didn't know very much about Bear Bryant or his coaching style, but the line outside his door told me one thing about him—obviously he had earned the respect of the men who played for him.

I remember Bear Bryant's last appearance at Beaver Stadium. Alabama came north very early for the 1989 game, arriving at the Holiday Inn at Burnham, about 25 miles from State College, the Wednesday before the game. In my experience, teams usually arrive at the game site on Friday or, perhaps, Thursday evening at the earliest. I don't know if Alabama arrived for every game on Wednesdays or if they viewed the Penn State game as particularly important, requiring extra time at the game site.

Sometime on Thursday, Bear Bryant called Jim Tarman, the Penn State Athletic Director at the time, and said he would like to bring his team to Beaver Stadium sometime on Friday for a pre-game practice session. He asked Jim what time on Friday would be convenient because he didn't want to interfere with Joe Paterno's Friday practice. Jim told him it wouldn't be possible to practice on the Beaver Stadium field since no team was allowed on the field prior to game time. Jim also told Bear that Joe's team didn't practice on the field prior to the game.

The 'Bama coach said this seemed fair and that he only wished to practice at the site where Joe's team would practice on Friday, and if it were to be on another field outside the stadium, that would be okay with him. He then asked Jim what time Joe would be practicing so he could ask for practice time either before or after the Penn State practice. Jim said he could bring his team over any time on Friday and not interfere with Joe's practice since Joe didn't practice on Friday. According to Jim, Bear responded, "Are you saying that Joe doesn't practice on a Friday before a game?" When Jim assured him that it was indeed Joe's decision not to practice on Fridays before home games Bear replied, "Joe must know something I don't know."

I'm sure that the decision to practice or not practice on Friday had nothing to do with it, but Alabama beat us the next afternoon. It was during that game that I saw a Bear Bryant gesture that I shall never forget and that, in my opinion, was the most memorable tribute a coach ever paid to his team. In almost a re-play of the 1975 Sugar Bowl game, described earlier, Penn State was on the Alabama one–yard line with a full set of four downs to score a crucial touchdown. I remember that this series of downs was even at the same end of the field as was the action in the Sugar Bowl.

Again Penn State tried it four times and, as before, Alabama held us right where the series had started four downs earlier. It was another really great Alabama goal line stand! I'm not sure how many of the 85,000+ fans in the stadium saw what happened next. I suspect that most Penn State fans were arguing against the last Penn State call, commiserating with their neighbors, holding their head in the hands, or looking at the Penn State bench to see Joe's reaction.

I happened to be watching Bear Bryant, and during the whole series of downs he registered almost no emotion. But when his defensive team came running off the field after their great stand, Bear walked out onto the field and met them about 15 yards in front of the Alabama bench. He didn't pat anybody on the back and he didn't single out any one of the players for his congratula-tions. As the players approached, he simply reached up and tipped his houndstooth-checked hat to his team in a wonderful silent gesture of respect. The entire incident probably didn't last 10 sec-onds, but to me it was a wonderful accolade from a coach to his team. I'll bet not one of those 11 defensive players will ever forget it.

John Thompson

The first night I met John Thompson was during one of his early years his first year as coach of the Georgetown basketball team. He brought his Hoyas to Rec Hall in 1973 to play the Nittany Lions. There really wasn't much at stake in the game. Both teams had respectable records, but neither was likely to go on to be-come a tournament champion.

For as long as I have been broadcasting basketball, I have been in the habit of watching the opposing coach to see how he handles himself. I am interested in how he seems to control himself and how he controls his bench and the players on the floor. Over the years, the rule makers have tried to pass all sorts of legislation to control basketball coaches. They have tried everything from rules to keep coaches in their seats to rules that stake out a fairly small coach's box, from which the coach is not supposed to stray. Nothing seems to work. Every time I look down, I see a coach edging up toward the scorer's table, out on the floor shouting instructions, walking along the sidelines working the referees and, in general, acting slightly or greatly out of control. Occasionally, a referee will call a technical foul, but they seem prepared to put up with a lot of abuse and harassment before they do. Occasionally, you will see a coach who seems in perfect control of himself and his players.

The first night I saw John Thompson, that was the thing that impressed me the most. In later years, as Georgetown has become a nationally–ranked team, Thompson seems to do somewhat more walking back and forth with his towel over his shoulder, but he still is far, far down the list of the "almost out-of-control" coaches. During the Penn State game, when John made a substitution, he made it quickly. The man substituted for came off the floor quickly and took his seat immediately. When a time–out was called, his players ran into the team huddle. They seemed completely disciplined, more disciplined than I have ever seen a college basketball team.

When you get into the final two minutes of a basketball game, the referees seem to take over. If you watch basketball, you know that happens very often. There always seem to be more whistles late in the game and, because time is running down, the whistles almost seem to dictate the outcome of the game. I suspect that because ball possession is so important, players play hard and take more chances late in the game. At the end of the Penn State–Georgetown game, with the clock winding down and the score tied, Georgetown was called for two infractions. Although I am emotionally a Penn State rooter (I've tried to hide that on the air, not always with much success, I suspect), it seemed to me that both calls against Georgetown were "homer" calls. In both cases, I thought the foul should have gone the other way. Penn State took advantage of their foul shots and won the game by a point or two.

After we did the final recap and game summary, we signed off the air, and I headed to the Georgetown locker room. Frankly, I didn't know what to expect. Would this 6'10" giant of a coach tear my head off? Would he be ranting about the two late calls that went against his team and probably cost him the game? Would he be berating his players for something they did or did not do late in the game? Would he even let me in the locker room?

As I approached the locker room door, there stood John Thompson like a giant doorman. I approached him with my tape recorder and microphone, introduced myself as the Penn State broadcaster, and asked if I could talk with him and some of his players. He was most gracious. He shook hands with me and asked which players I wanted to interview. After all these years, I remember that the player I asked for first was the team captain.

We walked into the locker room and Thompson called the captain's name. From the back of the room I heard, "Yes, sir" and he quickly came forward. Coach Thompson introduced me and said I would like to interview him. Incidentally, the locker room was quiet and orderly as the players put their uniforms into their traveling bags and put used tape into the wastebaskets, making you think they were a group of stockbrokers finishing a squash workout.

The other players I interviewed also were cooperative and polite. Then I asked Coach Thompson, "Did you think the two referee calls at the end of the game cost you the game, Coach? I thought they might well have gone the other way, especially the last call." Thompson proceeded to give some observations in a non–rancorous way. "They could have gone either way," he said, "(but) it doesn't really matter. I learned something in coaching a long time ago. If you are in a game, especially when you are playing a road game, you have to win the game yourself. You can't expect the officials to make a call that might cost the home team the game, especially if it is a large and active crowd. You will get a close call on the road occasionally, but you are a fool to count on it. My team had at least 20 places where they could have won the game and they didn't take advantage of their opportunities. When you can, you want to come into the final minutes with the lead you earned, and then you'll win most of those games. Don't ever count on the referees to win a game for you, especially on the road. Don't misunderstand me. I'm not just talking about Penn State. This holds true wherever you play and it holds true at Georgetown, too. We don't get the big break here, and you won't get the big break when you play at Georgetown. Referees are human, and that's the way it seems to work out."

I couldn't let the interview end there. I had to tell Coach Thompson what I thought about what I had observed that night. I said, "Coach, I want to tell you how impressed I was with your team, even though they lost. They are obviously well-drilled, they are disciplined, and they seem to know exactly what they want to do with the ball and where they want to be on the floor. And they played very hard. I also want to tell you how I admire their behavior in the locker room—no cursing, no throwing equipment around, no complaining, at least none that I could hear. Please thank your players for their courtesy. Finally, I must tell you how impressed I am with your whole organization. I know that you are brand new in this job, but I know that you are building a successful program and I wish you good luck with your team." He said, "Thank you very much for coming down to talk with us. Not many people want to talk with losers. Thanks for the interview."

Stan "The Man" Musial

Stan Musial was from Donora, Pennsylvania, and was an outstanding athlete at Donora High School, which was one of the chief sports rivals for Monessen High School, which I attended. He played football and was an outstanding baseball pitcher, but his best sport probably was basketball. Although he had at least one basketball scholarship offer, he chose baseball as his sport and began his career as a minor league pitcher.

I had an opportunity to talk with Musial about our high school experiences and his great baseball career several times in later years when he was one of the owners of a Florida hotel that hosted meetings for a company I was associated with and where the Penn State team stayed for an Orange Bowl game.

Many baseball fans will remember that Stan fell while shagging flies in the minor leagues, hurt his shoulder and, because of that injury, was moved to first base because he was also a good hitter. The rest, of course, is history. Stan's lifetime batting average with the St. Louis Cardinals was .331. He had more than 3,600 hits, well above the hitting level that baseball stars aspire to, and was named to the Baseball Hall of Fame. Stan spent his entire career with the Cardinals and you never heard a derogatory word about Stan Musial.

He and his wife raised a fine family and he was successful in business during the off–season and when his playing days were over. During his career, fans from Donora raised enough money to present Stan with a new Cadillac during one of the Cardinals' series at Forbes Field, the home of the Pittsburgh Pirates before Three Rivers Stadium was built.

I'm not sure how Stan felt about accepting such an expensive gift from his fans, probably none of whom could afford such a costly car. Perhaps he was embarrassed; perhaps not. I do know there was no gracious way he could have declined the gift without insulting his fans who were proud to honor their hero.

That's one example of ways in which fans almost deify their sports heroes. Many players are honored at the end of their careers. Not many are honored in mid–career, as was Musial. It is fairly obvious that the fans just wanted Stan to know how much they appreciated him as a man and as a player and how glad they were to have him on the Cardinals.

The Gunner

Anyone who has ever heard broadcasts of Pittsburgh Pirates or Steelers games or, for several years, Penn State football, will remember the name and voice of play–by–play announcer Bob Prince. If you don't remember the name Bob Prince, maybe you'll remember him by his nickname, "The Gunner." Along with many others, I was always curious how Bob had acquired this nickname, but every time I asked him, I got a different answer. I suspect that Bob felt he needed a nickname, for whatever reason, and that he liked the sound of "The Gunner" and adopted it.

I had the privilege of working with Prince on the Penn State football broadcasts. I also sat in the booth with him for several Pirates and Steelers games. My association with Bob began in the mid–1960s and lasted approximately 15 years, and 15 years with the Gunner is a couple of lifetimes with anyone else. More important than the chance to work with Bob was the fact that he became my friend. We shared hotel accommodations together, traveled over a large portion of the country wherever Penn State had a game, ate meals together in a variety of restaurants and diners, shared the dais at countless sports banquets and, finally, were together when Bob came as a guest lecturer in my classes many times.

One particular time, he was in town to serve as honorary chairman of the Second Mile golf tournament, and he came a day early to speak to my class. The class numbered some 250 students, and the larger the group, the better the show Bob put on. I had told the class at an earlier session that The Gunner was going to be with us on a certain date. You never had to use Bob's full name; he was "The Gunner," and everyone recognized that name. The class was absolutely full, with students even standing at the back of the large room and sitting on the steps. I introduced Bob and this is the way he began his talk:

"People often ask me how I got into the broadcasting business after they know that I was at Harvard Law School and fully intended to go into corporate law. I tell them how it happened, and I will share the story with you. First, I want you to know that some day I intend to write a book about my experiences in radio and television sports. I haven't begun to write it, but I have picked out the title. My book will be called 'I Never Should Have Danced With That Stripper!'

"When we were in law school in Boston, we used to take the afternoon off and go to burlesque shows at the Old Howard, a famous burlesque house. You are too young to remember, but at that time there was a national dance contest called the Harvest Moon Ball. The promoters of the contest held a series of sectional and regional dance competitions, with the winners advancing to the national finals. The finals were held at Madison Square Garden in New York City. This was before television and instant news coverage, so most people who saw the finals of the competition saw them as a feature of Fox Movietone News. This was a short feature on the news of the week that ran in conjunction with the feature film in movie theatres all over the country. That's how people 'saw the news.'

"The regional competition in the northeast was held at a famous nightclub on the outskirts of Boston. I had become friendly with Legs Lamont, one of the burlesque dancers at the Old Howard, and more or less as a lark she and I entered a sectional contest several weeks before the regional contest at the nightclub. I'm a pretty tall guy and a pretty good dancer. She was a sensational and very acrobatic dancer, and we did some pretty fancy dancing. I put her on my hip, then switched to the other hip, put her up over my head, etc. So we easily won the sectional. I didn't know it, but the regional competition was going to be filmed and shown on the Fox Movietone News. Fox showed the regional winners one week and then the national competition at the Garden in New York City the following week. Well, my partner and I won the Boston–area competition and qualified for the national finals in New York.

"At this time, my father was a general in the U.S. Army and was commanding a military base in the south. He and my mother went to the base movie theatre one night to see the feature. As it turned out, there was also a Fox Movietone News short being shown, and one of the stories was about the Harvest Moon Ball competition in which my partner and I were entered. My father had fallen asleep in the theatre when the dance competition flashed on the screen. My mother was stunned to see her son Robert doing wild jitterbug gyrations in the movies. She woke my father up and said, 'Look, there's Robert up there dancing with that girl.' By the time my father was fully awake, the news was over and he didn't see me in my dance routine.

"So the commanding general sent word to the projection booth that when the feature film was finished, he wanted them to show the Movietone News again. When they did, and the general saw me on the screen, my mother said that he almost went through the roof. 'What in the hell is that damn fool doing down in New York dancing in that contest? He's supposed to be in law school and he ought to be in Cambridge studying. This is the end of his fooling around in school.'

"Let me tell you guys that this was not the first time I had been in trouble with the general. He had put me on probation any number of times for any number of what, in his mind, were ridiculous actions. And when I went to Harvard, he told me it was my last chance. The next day, I had a call from the general. He told me that I had run out the string, and he wanted me to withdraw from law school and go get a job somewhere. Further, he told me that I had drawn my last penny from him or my mother, and that I was now on my own personally and financially.

"I had an aunt in a small town outside of Pittsburgh, and she had always helped me out in the past. So I hitchhiked from Boston to Pittsburgh and went to my aunt's house. After she greeted me and gave me a welcoming kiss she said, 'Robert, the general called. He told me to give you one night's lodging, to feed you at breakfast time, and then to send you on your way. If I wanted to give you any money, he absolutely told me that the limit was one dollar.' So I hit the road again.

"I had another aunt in Washington, Pennsylvania, about 25 miles south of Pittsburgh so I hitchhiked to see my second aunt. The general must have been very busy on the phone. When I got there, it was the same story. 'Robert, the general called. He told me that you were to have one night's lodging, breakfast, one dollar, and to be on your way.' So she kicked me out. I had run out of money, and I had run out of aunts.

"Without boring you with the details of my job search, I will tell you that I got a job at a local radio station where I was lucky enough to find an opening. I told them that I had some broadcast experience when I was a student at the University of Oklahoma (one of his earlier academic stops) and, since I have a pretty big voice, I was able to fake a newscaster's style and got the job. After a couple of months, Jack Craddock, the number two broadcaster with Rosey Rosewell on the Pittsburgh Pirates network became ill, and they held auditions for his spot. By this time, I had a pretty good radio voice and always was a baseball fan so I asked for an audition and got the job. After a couple of years, Rosey retired and then passed away and I inherited the top job."

My favorite Bob Prince story happened in Fort Worth, Texas, where Penn State had gone to play Texas Christian University.

The TCU athletic staff hosted a press party the night before the game, and one of the Fort Worth reporters there was wearing a pair of purple and white cowboy boots with a horned frog stitched into them. Prince fell in love with those boots and tried to buy them from the owner. When he found out that the guy wouldn't sell, and that the boots weren't nearly big enough to fit him anyway, Bob decided that he just had to have a pair of those boots. It turned out that the man who hand–made the boots lived in a small town outside of Fort Worth. Bob got the man's name and contacted him to arrange to have a pair specially made for him.

Our broadcast team followed the same routine for every game. After breakfast, I would arrange for a cab to be at the hotel at 10:30, and we would head for the stadium. We got there early so I could check with the phone man assigned to the broadcast, check through to the 40 or so stations on the network, talk to the engineer who would handle the broadcast, organize time cues, and that sort of detail. Meanwhile, Prince would visit both locker rooms to check on any lineup changes, to see if there were any players' numbers that were changed, and to talk with both coaches about the game. At least that's what Bob was supposed to do. Most of the time, he would disappear before the game and I, or someone else, would check with the locker rooms.

Bob had supreme confidence in his broadcast ability and he never worried about the correct player numbers and other details he considered too minor to be concerned with. He felt that he could pick everything up as the game unfolded, and usually he was right. Instead of being in the locker room, we might find Bob socializing in the press room with the writers or even find him in the other team's VIP box, getting to know the athletic director or university president.

After breakfast on this particular day, Bob was nowhere to be found. Bob would never deign to sleep in a simple room and always insisted on occupying a suite. He was not in his bedroom at the suite that morning and was not in the dining room having breakfast. After asking around, I couldn't find anyone who had seen Prince. Ten–thirty came and went, as did eleven o'clock, and still no Bob Prince.

As we approached 11:30, we wondered if we should call the

police and report Prince missing. Instead, we got a cab and headed to Amon Carter Stadium. Game time was 1:30, and we were to go on the air at 1:10 with the lineups and pre-game color. As 12:30 passed with no Prince anywhere, I began to think that I would have to do the entire game. Normally, I was the color announcer and handled the pre–game show, time–outs, half–time interviews, etc. Bob was the play–by–play man.

I quickly began to make up a spotting board that would list the players by position. Normally, that is the responsibility of the play–by–play announcer, and I had seen Bob's spotting board the night before, but wherever he was now the board was with him. As we approached 1 p.m., I was convinced that something had happened to Bob and I would have to do the entire game. I had done several high school games by myself, and I knew that I could handle it, but we were worried about Bob. I was sure that he wouldn't miss the beginning of a broadcast unless something beyond his control had happened.

It was now 1:10 and we went on the air with no Prince anywhere in sight. I ran through the pre–game information, gave the starting lineups, but didn't say anything about Prince not being there for the play–by–play. The referee called the captains to the center of the field, tossed the coin, and the captains made their choices and ran back to the huddles. The teams took the field, the kicker teed up the ball, the referee raised his hand and at that very moment, the door to the broadcast booth opened and in walked Bob Prince with his spotting board under his arm. He wasn't even in a hurry. He leaned over my shoulder, put his hand over my microphone, and asked two questions, "Who won the toss?" and "Who's wearing white?" And that was the extent of his pre–game preparations.

He casually took his seat and proceeded to do a highly professional broadcast. I guarantee you that no listener had any inkling that Bob wasn't totally prepared and had all of the information that he needed at his elbow or on the tip of his tongue. They also had no inkling that I had completely soaked my shirt with nervous perspiration, and that during the first time–out I would probably try to strangle Bob.

When we broke away for individual station commercial announcements, I asked him where in the hell he had been all morning. He said, "Did you see those great purple and white cowboy boots that writer was wearing last night? I called the shoemaker and arranged to have a cab drive me out to his place (about a 50–mile round trip) so that I could be fitted for a pair just like them." And that was that!

I found Bob to be a real enigma. Although many who knew him would probably disagree with me, I found him to be a complex guy. The reason they would disagree is that he almost always had his "public face" on when they saw him. Bob was always "on" when he was with others. That was as true if he was in a room with four or five people as when he was toastmaster at a banquet for a thousand people. Bob appeared to be the ultimate extrovert. I say "appeared" because unless you caught him in an unguarded moment, you would only see him as the same storytelling, laugh–getting guy you saw the last time you were with him. Although I would never claim I actually got to know him as we traveled together, I did have a chance to see the emotional and caring guy that he could be and, I suspect, often was, although mostly in private.

Mickey Bergstein (right) and Bob "The Gunner" Prince (center) worked together for 15 years. This picture was taken in the press box during a 1951 football game at Beaver Field. The man on the left is Ernie Berkaw, who handled statistics and game highlights for Prince as a hobby.

Bob was widely in demand as a luncheon and dinner speaker. He was an outstanding toastmaster, and when an organization in Pittsburgh began planning an event, the first potential toastmaster who always came to mind was The Gunner. He had the ability to bring something extra to an event. His whole style lifted the affair and the other speakers to a higher level and he almost personally could assure the success of a speaking program.

While so many people in the Pittsburgh area knew him for his various public roles, for a long, long time, very few knew of his private role. Outside of Pittsburgh, there is a large and impressive school dedicated to improving the lives of the handicapped and the mentally retarded. The name of the facility is the Allegheny Valley School for Exceptional Children. Many people, of course, knew of its existence; few knew that one of the major benefactors for the school was Bob Prince.

For many years, apparently, Bob contributed to the school the fees he earned in his "outside" work—speeches, banquets, and other paid appearances. He apparently never spoke of his private charity, and few knew of his generosity to the school. If you drive onto the grounds of the school close to the Greater Pittsburgh Airport, you will see an impressive group of red brick buildings that house and serve the school's residents. There is one building that is sure to capture your eye and attention. It is a rather large gymnasium named the Robert Prince Gymnasium, and it owes its construction and existence to the generosity of Bob Prince. Because he never spoke of his interest in the school, I never learned how and why he had become so involved in the welfare of the handicapped and retarded.

Someone in Pittsburgh learned of Bob's interest in the school, and they planned a large banquet to recognize and pay tribute to his generosity. I was told that Bob agreed to a banquet in his honor only if all the funds that were raised were given to the school. It was a large, well–attended banquet in the main ballroom of the Pittsburgh Hilton. The affair attracted many celebrities, including F. Lee Bailey, Hugh O'Brien, and many easily–recognized people from sports and the broadcast and print media.

I attended the banquet because I wanted to help honor Bob and it was my full intention that I would sit well back in the hall and not interject my presence into the celebrities who joined Bob at the speaker's table. I thought I would write him after the event to tell him that I had been there and to offer my personal congratulations. I also wanted him to know how important I felt it is for recognized people to affiliate themselves with the handicapped and retarded populations.

Somehow Bob, in looking out over the hall before the banquet began, saw me standing in the back and signaled me to come up to the speaker's table. He introduced me to all of his celebrity friends and was very kind in his remarks about my broadcasting abilities and how he felt about our work together. He then asked the group to excuse us, and we walked to a private area behind the speaker's table.

At this point, I must give you some background regarding what Bob said to me in our short meeting there. Some years before, my wife and I had given birth to a daughter who, unfortunately and unhappily, had suffered a brain injury before or during the birth process and, at a later date had undergone very serious brain surgery. Because Bob was no longer connected with Penn State sports and I seldom saw him, I really didn't know if he knew of our daughter's medical problems. I knew that I had not mentioned it to him or had ever had an opportunity to discuss it with him.

Bob told me that he had heard of our daughter's birth and subsequent medical problems, and he wanted to offer his help. He reached into his wallet and took out a card on which he had written two telephone numbers. He gave me the card and said, "This first number is my unlisted home phone number. The second is the unlisted home phone of a very skilled pediatric neurosurgeon on the staff of Children's Hospital here in Pittsburgh. I have told him about your daughter, and what I have been able to learn from a couple of your friends.

"If you ever have any serious difficulty and need help, please call me at this unlisted home phone number. If you cannot reach me, call the second number. The doctor knows all about you and will not be surprised by your call. Between us, you can be sure that your daughter will receive the very best treatment that the doctor and hospital can provide. I hope that you won't ever have to use these numbers, but if you do, you'll have the help you need. I also want you to know that any medical help you receive won't cost you anything. The financial end is all taken care of."

With that, he said something funny, we shook hands, he cut me off when I tried to thank him, and he was gone. I knew that if Bob ever cried, he made sure he did it in private; that wouldn't have suited his public image.

If you are not familiar with Pittsburgh sports, it's difficult for me to explain what an icon Bob Prince had become. Whatever his broadcasting or public service assignment, he always performed at the top of his game. In addition, he understood Pittsburgh and the particular ethnic mixture of the city and the steel towns that surrounded it. He had probably, at one time or another, stood at the bar of every ethnic club in every little town in the river valleys that surround Pittsburgh. He remembered everyone's name and made reference to people and organizations in the area during his broadcasts. He started all kinds of promotions and made them work.

During the 1960 baseball pennant drive that culminated with Bill Mazeroski's home run against the Yankees that nailed down the World Championship for the Bucs, Bob started a really outrageous promotion called the Green Weenie. He arranged for someone to manufacture thousands of green rubber hot dogs that they sold to fans all over the Pittsburgh area. When there was a key point in the game, for instance, if the Pirates had a one run lead and the other team had the bases loaded with no outs, Bob would have everyone at the park take out their green weenie and wave it at the batter. And he'd tell all the fans at home to point their green weenies at the radio.

It certainly didn't work every time, but it worked often enough that to this day some fans credit Bob Prince and the green weenie for the Pirates winning the National League pennant and the World Series.

He had babushka games, when all the ladies were asked to wear babushkas (a head scarf worn primarily by eastern European women). They would wave the scarves at critical points in the game to scare up evil spirits or whatever Bob wanted to use them for.

Because of all his community involvement and widely accepted promotions, Bob Prince really was Mr. Pittsburgh and he deserved the title. After years of service with the Pirates, Bob apparently had several run–ins with his sponsors and the originating station on the Pirates Network and was fired. Unbelievable! Bob Prince fired? You've got to be kidding. Who would be dumb enough to fire The Gunner?

Within a day or two, the city had organized a Noon protest parade in downtown Pittsburgh. Large crowds of people lined the streets and cheered wildly as Bob rode by atop a fire truck. There was a tremendous outpouring of protests with letters to the editor and calls to radio stations. But the decision stood and The Gunner was gone.

A few years later, when Bob was stricken with a malignancy, he was hired back to do the Pirates games. I'm sure that it was intended as a gesture of kindness, but it really was too late. Bob obviously had slipped physically. The great Voice of the Pirates wasn't what it had been, and while he tried for his old style and enthusiasm, it wasn't there any more. Bob missed more and more home games and road trips and finally succumbed to his illness in 1985.

I don't care what the medical certificate says; I'll always believe that Bob Prince died of a broken heart.

The Only General I Know

As you know, Penn State is a very large university that performs many functions and provides much information and many services to a wide range of individuals, corporations, industries, and technologies. Most Penn Staters aren't aware of the many activities and programs offered by the university. The great majority of our students are here for only four years, and when they return, it's for alumni activities or for sports, usually Nittany Lion football.

One of the areas in which Penn State has a national and even international reputation is executive management programs that are provided to domestic and foreign companies. For several years, I spent most of the month of June as a faculty member for one of the four–week management programs.

For one of the programs, I taught industry executives, rank-ing government officials and officers of several branches of the military. The presence of an Air Force colonel in that class gave me an opportunity to develop a friendship with him and to show the Penn State colors on many future occasions.

The colonel's name was Eugene J. Habiger and, at the time, he was commanding officer at Barksdale Air Force Base in Shreve-port, La. Habiger is an outstanding Air Force officer, as seen in his rapid rise through the top officer ranks. Since being at Penn State in the late '80s, he has received steady promotions. Recently, my wife and I received an invitation to ceremonies at which he be-came a four–star general.

One of my duties as faculty director was to present an evening program to the class and then engage them in a discussion on the material presented. Several months after that executive manage-ment class had been graduated and had gone back to their indi-vidual jobs, Col. Habiger called and asked if I would consider coming to Barksdale AFB to speak to his Strategic Air Command officers at an Officer's Muster. I was happy to accept his invita-tion, especially since he promised to give me a close look at the operation of the Strategic Air Command and the pilots who flew the B–52s that were the backbone of the defense effort.

I must tell you how impressed I was with the caliber and qual-ity of the SAC pilots and their crews. I could not imagine a more fit and obviously prepared group of men anywhere, and I came back from my visit totally confident in our country's ability to carry out its assignments and mission.

The morning after my talk, I had one of the most interesting experiences of my life. I joined the crew of a tanker plane and participated in a refueling mission over the Gulf of Mexico. I sat in the pod underneath the tanker next to an Air Force sergeant, while another plane came up through the mist and, after being hooked up to the tanker plane through a hose that is only 38 feet long, proceeded to be refueled in mid–air. The planes were so close to each other that I could see the sunglasses of the pilot of the plane being fueled. After filling the lower plane with fuel, we separated, our plane went below the other plane, and the fuel was returned to the tanker. What an exciting experience it was for me to see true professionals at work and to feel that I was not only a spectator, but also part of it.

When we came on board the plane before we took off, I was introduced to the pilot, the co–pilot, and the sergeant who would handle the actual hook–up between the two planes. When he was briefing me as to what we would be doing, I somewhat naively asked for my parachute. The pilot told me, "Sir, you won't be wearing a parachute. In flight, there is no way you will be able to exit the aircraft." I really hadn't thought I would be wearing a parachute, but thought I might as well ask.

When we landed following the exercise, I went to the front of the plane to thank the pilot and co–pilot for their briefings on our mission and for their hospitality in making me feel a part of the crew. When I prepared to leave, I said to the pilot, "Major, you are obviously a first-class pilot. If you weren't, you wouldn't be in charge of this multi–million dollar aircraft." Then, I thought I could have some fun with him. I told him, "You are a pilot and I am a college teacher, and one of the things I teach is public relations. When we got on the airplane and I asked about a parachute, you told me there was no way I could exit the aircraft. If you don't mind, I'd like to suggest that there is a better way to say that, especially to a coward like me. Instead of saying that there is no way to exit the aircraft, a pilot good at public relations might say something like, 'Sir, after careful thought and research, the United States Air Force has decided that in the event of some trouble, the very best and safest thing you can do is to stay with the aircraft.' I think that might make non–fliers feel much better about their chances."

I was only kidding at the time, and I'm sure that he was correct in telling me that there was no way to exit a giant tanker. But after thinking about it, there probably is a more diplomatic way to convey the information to passengers. Or, if the pilot wanted to go to the other extreme, he could put a big sign right inside the entry door. The sign could say: "TO OUR PASSENGERS. PLEASE DO NOT ASK ABOUT PARACHUTES. YOU WON'T LIKE THE ANSWER."

Punchy Rogel

One of the toughest football players ever to play at Penn State, or for any other team, was Francis Rogel. No one would recognize him as Francis. Few would recognize him as Fran. To everyone who knew him, he was simply Punchy Rogel, and he was a helluva football player. He was the fullback on the Lions' 1947 Cotton Bowl team, and there never was a player he couldn't block, or an extra yard he wouldn't somehow make. He was as intense a competitor as Penn State ever saw in any sport or on any team. After being graduated from Penn State, he joined the Pittsburgh Steelers and had many productive years as their starting fullback.

One night, Rogel and his girlfriend went dancing at Ollie Kohlbecker's Limedust Inn in Coleville. I will not try to describe the Limedust Inn; the name speaks for itself. As Punchy and his girlfriend circled the floor, three graduate students began to make remarks that he found offensive and insulting. After several times around the floor, and continued remarks from the three students, Punchy told them that if they weren't going to stop the annoyances and insults, perhaps they should go outside and settle it physically. They agreed.

As he crossed the road into the field, Rogel decided he shouldn't try to face all three at once. So, he said, "I reached over, tore one guy's shirt off his back, punched the second guy, and the third guy may still be running."

Sometime later the man he punched brought assault charges against Rogel, and someone arranged for Rogel to see Paul Campbell, a local attorney who later became a judge in Centre County. (Incidentally, Paul Campbell filled in as State's wrestling coach when Charlie Speidel went into the Navy during World War II.) Paul Campbell passed on the rest of the story to me.

He went to the plaintiff's attorney and between them, since no real damage had been done and the question of instigation wasn't clear, they got the plaintiff to agree to drop the charges if Rogel would apologize. Rogel originally refused on the grounds that he didn't start it, his girlfriend had been insulted, etc.

Paul convinced him that there was no point in continuing the case, that he should apologize and let the matter be dropped. Rogel finally agreed, and a meeting was arranged in Paul's office with Paul, the plaintiff's attorney, the plaintiff, and Rogel in attendance. Paul reviewed what had happened to this point, turned to Punchy and said, "If you will apologize to this man, he will drop the charges and the matter is closed."

Paul told me that Rogel gave the other man a hard–eyed stare and then said, "Okay, I'll apologize. If you see me on the campus or around town and want to say hello to me, I'll say hello to you. If you see me and don't want to say hello, you can go screw your-self."

Frank Patrick and His Yellow Convertible

Every time I read about a school athletic department or team coach or some zealous alumnus being involved in procurement of a car for use by a star athlete, I am reminded of a story that was told to me by the late Frank Patrick, for many years the defensive backfield coach and kicking coach for Penn State's football team. Frank was an outstanding backfield star with the University of Pittsburgh Panthers in the late 1930s and was a teammate of the fabled Marshall Goldberg, who gained National Collegiate Hall of Fame honors for the Panthers. Frank did all of the kicking and was the starting fullback on those outstanding Pittsburgh teams. He later played fullback and was the kicker for the Chicago Cardinals of the National Football League.

The University of Pittsburgh team was coached by Dr. Jock Sutherland, who was one of the most famous and successful coaches of that time. Sutherland was a licensed dentist, although I'm not sure he ever practiced. He was very tall and dignified, and his almost austere presence commanded respect. He rarely, if ever, spoke directly to his players, preferring to communicate instructions to the squad through his assistant coaches. The story Frank Patrick told me concerned one of the very few times that Coach Sutherland spoke directly to him, and it concerned what the coach considered a violation of his own and one of the athletic department's rules.

If you are familiar with the Pitt campus and athletic facilities, you know that Pitt Stadium is most of the way up a long, steep hill, and that the practice fields are even further up the hill. That meant quite a hike before a tough practice session. Frank told me that on one particular Saturday, he had had an especially good game. Exiting the locker room, Frank was approached by a Pitt fan who congratulated him on his game and said he would like to do Frank a favor. He handed Frank the keys to a yellow convertible and told him it was his to use until the end of the season. He said he wanted Frank not to have to walk up the big hill so he would have fresh legs for the remaining games. Frank was delighted! There were very few cars around in those late Depression years; few students had a car, and no one had a yellow convertible.

The next day, Frank proudly drove his new possession up the hill to football practice. When practice was over, the backfield coach approached Frank and told him that Dr. Sutherland would like to see him. Dr. Sutherland, incidentally, was a bachelor and had an apartment at the Pittsburgh Athletic Club, located right off the Pitt campus. The coach told Frank that Dr. Sutherland would expect him at his apartment at about 7:30 that evening. Frank got all dressed up and drove his convertible to the Oakland section of Pittsburgh where the Pitt Athletic Club was located. He rang the bell for Dr. Sutherland's apartment and was told to come in.

Dr. Sutherland, as I said, was a very grim looking person, not noted for his levity or his smile. He was sitting behind his desk and motioned for Frank to come over and stand in front of the desk. As Frank told the story, the coach went on writing for several minutes and then, as if noticing Frank for the first time, looked up and said, "Frank Patrick, it seems that you don't care to walk around the campus like all of the other students and all of the other players. It seems that you think that it's a good idea for you to ride around campus and up to football practice in a fancy car that someone either gave you or loaned to you. Frank, I think it is a bad idea. I think that you should walk to practice like all the other players. I would suggest that tonight you find the person who provided the car you are driving, and I would strongly suggest that you thank him and return the keys to him and that you never again take back the keys to that or any other car. If you do that, Frank, I will see you at practice tomorrow. If you do not return the keys tonight, I will send you back to East Gary, Indiana, where I found you! That's all, Mr. Patrick."

When he finished the story, I asked Frank what he did. "What do you think I did? I drove all over town until I found the owner of the car, thanked him, and then gave him back the keys and took a street car home. Playing for Jock Sutherland was tough, but it wasn't as tough as going home to East Gary to work in a steel mill!"

I only met Dr. Sutherland once, and since he had been such a major sports figure when I was a boy, I must admit that I was in awe of him. I cannot remember just why he was in State College, but I received a phone call from someone in the Penn State athletics department asking if I would like to have Jock Sutherland as an interview guest on my nightly sports program. I jumped at the chance to meet this famous coach, and I certainly did want him to be on my radio show that evening. When I met him at the studio, he was even more impressive than the pictures I had seen of him. He was very tall, well–dressed, and struck me as a very formal person.

The interview went very well, although I can remember only one of the things I asked him about. There were very few bowl games in those days and, of course, the Rose Bowl was the premier game, the goal of every team in America. Coach Sutherland had taken his team to the Rose Bowl, and I asked about his preparations for such a major game.

In those days, teams usually played only eight or nine games during the regular season, which ended by Thanksgiving. That meant about a six-week break between the final season game and the bowl game. I asked Dr. Sutherland how he could keep a team ready and eager to play since they had such a long period of inactivity. I can still remember his answer. He told me there was no way any coach could keep a team sharp and ready to play after such a long layoff, if the players didn't want to play in the game.

He pointed out that for many of the players, including the team's stars, their college football careers were really over. Unless they wanted to use this game to impress the few professional teams, most players had already put their college careers behind them and, if so, this became just another game. He said there was no way a coach could make players feel that winning the game was important if they didn't already believe it. He then told me what he told his team when they accepted a post–season game.

"I told them," he said, "only one thing will win the game for you and that is your own personal pride." He told them that he would do everything he could to get them ready as far as offensive and defensive game plans and strategy were concerned, but that their personal physical condition and their mental approach to wanting to play and win the game was strictly up to them. He then told me that he had learned this lesson through experience and that getting ready to play a bowl game was totally different than a regular season game. He ended by saying that if there was no personal pride involved, you could forget about winning the game.

The last time Coach Sutherland had taken his team to the Rose Bowl, Pitt won. I'm sure he was more than happy to share the credit with his team.

I asked Frank Patrick about this "it's up to you" philosophy of Coach Sutherland in regard to getting ready to play a bowl game. Frank said, "That's what the coach told us, but we all knew one thing—you had better accept his challenge and get ready to play, both physically and mentally, especially if you were an undergraduate and expected to play next year."

Ben Schwartzwalder, The Orange, and Things That Are No More

I don't know how many sports fans share my disappointment that we don't play some of our long–time traditional opponents any more. I understand why schedule changes are made, and I understand that the economics of collegiate athletics has led to new conference sizes, new bowl game alliances, and lucrative television scheduling. While I understand these changes at an intellectual level, I have a hard time accepting them at an emotional level.

I have been emotionally involved with Penn State winning and losing since I first arrived on the campus in 1940. In addition, because of my radio sports connections for many years, I came to know other teams and their coaches and athletic administrations. I have been in all of their stadiums and gymnasiums, and I have been at ringside and matside for boxing and wrestling. I somehow thought that I would always be able to watch Penn State play Syracuse and Pitt, and while I never was especially fond of either school and hated to see us lose to either of them, I did look forward to our annual grudge games and must admit that I miss them.

I understand that things seldom remain the same and that change is inevitable, but that doesn't make me enjoy watching us play football against Iowa and Indiana as much as I used to enjoy our games with Pitt and Syracuse. I certainly wouldn't second–guess our decision to join the Big 10. I am sure there are advantages in this affiliation. I am sure, for example, that over time our basketball program will benefit in recruiting and competition, and we probably will enjoy greater national exposure in playing teams like Indiana, Michigan, and Ohio State, along with the others. And in all likelihood, our new scheduling will benefit us financially.

Having said all that, I remain nostalgic about our old schedules with teams like Syracuse. We played 68 football games with Syracuse beginning in 1922, and won almost twice as many as we lost. Regardless of the record, I can tell you that it never was easy to beat Syracuse, especially after Ben Schwartzwalder became their head coach. I am sure that anyone who ever suited up for a Penn State–Syrause game will tell you about those tough contests.

Coach Schwartzwalder played a very simple offense, and he knew exactly what kind of players, especially offensive linemen, he wanted to recruit to make his system work. When you played Syracuse, you knew what to expect. The Orange played an unbalanced line. That means, of course, there are four linemen on one side of the center and two on the other. On the strong side, Syracuse always, and I mean <u>always</u>, had two broad–beamed and beefy tackles, and the point of the Syracuse attack was usually right over those big linemen. Syracuse always, and again I mean <u>always</u>, had a big and powerful fullback to run behind their big unbalanced line. The most famous of those Syracuse fullbacks was probably Larry Csonka, who went on to an outstanding career in the National Football League.

It was critical that you get an early lead against the Orange. Because of their offensive plan, if you got behind, you almost didn't have time to catch up. Syracuse invariably used up all but one or two seconds of the time they were allotted between plays. They never fired in and out of the huddle. They used as much time as possible to get a play under way without drawing a penalty for delay of the game. The quarterback went into a long count and they snapped the ball at the last second. Their big linemen fired out, the big fullback bulldozed right in behind them, and it was tough not to give up yards. Meanwhile, the clock ticked on.

Syracuse rarely got a first down on first or second down in a series. If they were in your territory and probably wouldn't have to punt the ball on fourth down, they rarely made the sticks on first, second, or even third down. Too many times to suit me, they made the first down on fourth down. Meanwhile, again, the clock ticked on.

Of course, Syracuse had more than their share of outstanding tailbacks. When you mention the late Ernie Davis, you are talking about a Heisman Trophy winner. And Floyd Little was a genuine All–American tailback and punt returner whom I was very, very glad to see graduate. But in the main, Syracuse controlled the clock and beat you with their time–consuming and powerful attack.

We did many, many broadcasts from old Archbold Stadium on the Syracuse campus. It was a cold concrete stadium where the fans sat right on the concrete steps that comprised the seats. The press box was an archaic relic. In our broadcast booth, for example, a telephone pole went straight up through the booth and the announcers communicated with each other by leaning back and talking around the pole.

One of the highlights of a trip to Syracuse was the chance to spend some time with Bob Drum who, at one time, delivered golf tips of questionable value on the CBS national golf telecasts. If you watched those telecasts, you probably remember the big, round guy they called "The Drummer." Bob had been a sports writer with the *Pittsburgh Press* and covered many Nittany Lions games. He also told me that he was the ghostwriter on at least some of Arnold Palmer's golf books and had written Bobby Layne's football book. Layne, of course, was the Pittsburgh Steeler quarterback.

For one game Bob, who was employed as a public relations host for one of the electronic companies in the upstate New York area, came to the game to help us out by spotting players for one of the teams and feeding us background information on the Syracuse team. Bob really knew the game of football and was delightful to be around, if you could keep from laughing during the broadcasts when you read some of the candid notes he passed to the announcers. Bob also was in the habit of betting on almost anything.

For example, when Syracuse came out for the second half of this particular Penn State game, they were to receive the kickoff. The ball went into the end zone and the Orange put the ball in play on the 20–yard line. During a hold–up on the field to check difficulty with the clock, Bob turned and offered to bet that Syracuse would begin a drive, use up more than 10 minutes on the clock, wouldn't get a first down in fewer than three downs more than once, wouldn't throw the ball more than twice, and if they scored, there wouldn't be more than four minutes remaining in the third quarter.

Who do you think won the bet? He did! Syracuse used up all of the time possible between plays, they ran their fullback practically every play, they never took a timeout, every first down took them three or four plays, they threw the ball only twice for a completion, and when they scored, they had used up slightly more than 11 minutes in the drive. If you knew Bob, you can imagine him laughing so loudly that they could probably hear him back in Pittsburgh. Can you imagine the frustration for a team that is losing to try to stop a touchdown drive that lasts 11 minutes?

Through the years of the Penn State–Syracuse rivalry, there were many controversial incidents. One that I remember involved some calls in a game that Penn State lost and, as it later developed, the official who was involved in several of the calls was a Syracuse graduate. No one made any charges, but that was the kind of heated controversy that seemed to follow so many of our games with the Orange.

I remember another game at Archbold Stadium that was typical of the Penn State–Syracuse antagonism. The teams lined up for the opening kickoff when suddenly there were lots of arms waving and attempts to get the attention of the referee. Finally, Penn State coach Rip Engle had the referee on the sidelines and kept pointing to a player on the field. He was indicating that Fred Mautino, Syracuse's outstanding defensive end, had what looked like a cast on one of his hands. The rule states that certain kinds of injury coverings are permitted, but that hard casts are not allowed.

While the crowd in the stadium waited, and while we tried to tell the radio audience what was going on (although we didn't have the faintest idea), the officials were unwinding a long, white Ace bandage from Mautino's hand and wrist. We assumed that they were trying to discover if there was a hard cast underneath and if it was properly wrapped to protect the other players. They finally got it straightened out, re–wrapped the hand and wrist, and the game began about 10 minutes late. Just another example of the suspicious nature both teams had when it came to their game. I must tell you that this running feud did have a happy ending.

Many years later, Ben Schwartzwalder had retired from his coaching position at Syracuse and his Penn State "enemy," Rip Engle, had also been retired for several years. The State College Quarterback Club decided that, as a salute to the long rivalry between the two teams, it would invite Ben to attend our annual football banquet as a special guest and at the same time would pay tribute to Rip.

To see these two old football warriors together at the head table was both heartwarming and amusing. You would have thought they were the greatest buddies who ever lived. They told stories about each other, and when they were called to the microphone they embraced each other. All of the acrimony and all of the accusations, real and imagined, seemed to have flown away. As Rip put it when he was at the microphone, "Ben and I never really had any trouble with each other." Those of us who had been through all the battles knew better, of course. But, what the hell! We had seen some great games. The arguments gave us lots to talk about, and all that was left were two old football coaches reminiscing at the microphone. Wasn't that a great way to end it? And does anyone remember the scores of any of those games?

There is one Penn State–Syracuse game, won by the Lions 21-20, which many older fans should remember. It is not remembered because it was a recent game; it was played in 1955. It is not remembered because it involved one of Penn State's outstanding teams; our record that year was 5–4. It is remembered because of the outstanding performances of two football greats who were matched against each other and are now enshrined in the NFL Hall of Fame—Syracuse's Jimmy Brown and Penn State's Lenny Moore.

In that game in old Beaver Stadium, both Brown and Moore rang up outstanding offensive statistics. But you must remember that at the time, teams played single platoon football. Both men played tailback on offense and safety on defense. In retrospect, it seemed that when Jimmy Brown was off on a long run, Lenny Moore made the tackle that kept it from being a touchdown. Likewise, when it looked like Moore was going to break loose for a long touchdown run and only one man could keep him from scoring, it was Jimmy Brown.

Lenny gained 152 yards that day and Jimmy 159. Although they did not keep track of tackles, it seemed as though both were making tackles all afternoon. Brown had unbelievable statistics in addition to his rushing total. As Ridge Riley, long–time Penn State alumni director, wrote in his weekly football letter sent to alumni all over the world, "Brown seemed unstoppable, running both inside and outside. He averaged eight yards per carry. We never stopped him for no gain. He caught two of the passes tried by Syracuse, one for a touchdown. He scored three touchdowns and kicked two extra points. He intercepted a pass and returned three kickoffs for 95 yards."

You often see great performances by one player, but you rarely see two players having great performances on the same field in the same game. This was one of them!

One final note about how football has changed over the years. If you don't have a really fine quarterback who can throw the ball effectively, you probably don't win a great number of games. In this Penn State–Syracuse game, Penn State threw eight times and completed four, for a total of 54 yards. Syracuse passed five times and completed two, for 21 yards. The total passing yardage in a close one–point game—75 yards!

My most enduring memory of the Penn State–Syracuse football rivalry was the 1959 game at Beaver Stadium that won the national championship for Syracuse. It was a game to make both teams proud of the way they played. Although it was not the last game on the Syracuse schedule, it was generally agreed that if they could beat Penn State, they would probably wrap up the national title.

Both squads had outstanding stars. Syracuse had Ernie Davis at tailback, who won the Heisman Trophy that year. He was drafted by the Cleveland Browns but, before he could play his first professional game, was stricken with leukemia and passed away. Penn State had All–America quarterback Richie Lucas, who was drafted by Buffalo of the NFL and Washington of the AFL. He went on to a professional career with the Buffalo Bills. Penn State had a fine sophomore tailback, Roger Kochman, who also was drafted by the Buffalo Bills and later suffered a leg injury in a game with Houston that ended his professional career. He went on to an executive position with Bell Telephone. Andy Stynchula was one of the Penn State tackles. Andy played for many years with the Washington Redskins and later perished in a highway accident.

Penn State scored first but missed their first extra point of the season, leading 6-0. That would be the last time the Lions had the lead. Syracuse came back to score three straight times and go up 20-6. Then, all of a sudden, Penn State was back in the game. Roger Kochman took a Syracuse kickoff and ran it back for a 100–yard touchdown. Trailing 20-12, Penn State went for the two extra points and missed.

Penn State kicked off to the Orange and knew that they had to get the ball back with enough time to score twice. The Lions smothered the Orange offense and forced them to punt. Elsewhere in this book, I quoted the man who said, "If you say you can, or you say you can't, in either case you're probably right." Well, Andy Stynchula must have decided that "I can," because he came up with a sensational block of the Syracuse punt.

I know how sensational it was because a picture of it hangs in my home along with other Penn State sports pictures. On most blocked punts, someone on the kicking team makes a mistake. Someone will miss an assignment and leave a player unblocked. Someone will miss the outside man who comes in on an angle and gets to the ball. Usually there is someone who falls asleep and blocks the wrong man. None of these things happened this time. The picture clearly shows that the three Syracuse blockers were lined up, shoulder to shoulder, in front of the kicker. Stynchula didn't try to go around the blockers and didn't try to split them and go through to get to the kicker. He got his 240 pounds off the ground and went over the blockers. The picture clearly shows Andy's hand blocking the ball with his body horizontal to the ground. The blocked kick went out of bounds on the one-yard line.

One play later, Penn State had its third score, missed a two point try, and now was down 20-18. There still was plenty of time on the clock, and the Beaver Stadium crowd was betting that if Penn State could get the ball one more time, there was no way Syracuse could keep the Lions out of the end zone.

Penn State wrestling coach Charlie Speidel once said, "If you want to win a national wrestling championship, sooner or later, in one match or another, there comes a time when you head into the last period ahead by just one point, and you have to hold the other guy on the mat for the full three minutes. I don't care what he does—rolls, somersaults, stands up, or whatever—to become a champ, you have to hold him until the bell rings." There is another version of what it takes to become a national champion, this time in football. There probably will come a time when you're ahead by only one or two points, you have to go on a drive, late in the game, probably into the wind, make no mistakes, draw no penalties, move the sticks and keep the ball until the clock runs out. Or, if you are behind and need a score, you have to go on that same drive, with the same precision, and score the winning touchdown. That is exactly what Syracuse faced that day in 1959 with the national championship probably on the line.

Penn State kicked off to the right sideline, right to the player that Syracuse hoped would get the ball, Ernie Davis. The ball came down tight to the sideline. Davis wasn't sure that it would go out of bounds and didn't want to take a chance that it didn't. He fielded it on about the six–yard line, lost his balance, and fell out of bounds. Now the crowd sensed that the Lions would hold them and get one more chance to win the game.

The Orange never lost their poise. They drove down the field, took lots of time in the huddle, didn't draw a penalty, didn't fumble, didn't throw the ball away, and made four first downs on the way to running out the clock. Penn State never got the ball back. A heartbreak for the Lions, who had fought so hard to come back. A national championship for Syracuse, who did just what a champion has to do! ■

11

Penn State Potpourri

■

Most Penn Staters probably know of Eric Walker's modest beginnings. He rose from a financially–deprived family to become Penn State president. He earned the Horatio Alger Award, which pays tribute to those achievers who have a record of great accomplishments after overcoming very modest beginnings. There are at least two other Horatio Alger Award winners with Penn State connections—Dr. Milton Eisenhower, who preceded Dr. Walker as Penn State president, and Robert Schwartz, an accounting graduate who rose through the ranks of the Metropolitan Insurance Company to become president and then chairman.

Eric Walker came to the United States from Canada and worked his way through Harvard University. He told me a story of those days that is worth repeating. There was a diner in Cambridge where Eric found the best food bargains. He told me he often fleshed out the modest meal he could afford by asking the waiter or waitress for a cup of boiling water. He then poured ketchup from the bottle on the counter into the water to make a cup of warming tomato soup.

When you look around the Penn State campus you see one result of Eric Walker's presidency in the physical facilities he helped bring. You might also note some of the university's outstanding faculty who were recruited during his administration. I was especially pleased when the Board of Trustees voted to name one of our newer buildings the Eric A. Walker Building because that decision was an exception to a university policy against naming buildings after living persons. The university has since named several buildings and even entire colleges after living alumni, faculty, and administrators.

The Hershey Medical Center

Probably the most impressive accomplishment of Eric Walker's presidency is the Milton S. Hershey Medical Center. The center houses the Penn State College of Medicine and the University Hospital in Hershey, Pennsylvania. This is how it came into existence.

Milton Hershey established the Hershey School for orphaned boys many years ago. The physical facilities of the school, incidentally, rival those in the finest preparatory schools in the country. Founders Hall, for example, is like no other building I have ever seen at any school or university.

As the years went by, apparently there were fewer and fewer orphan boys who were candidates for admission. The entrance requirements were changed to allow for the admission of orphan girls, but in time the number of orphan girls also dropped. The admission rules then allowed for admission of boys and girls from broken or troubled homes who might benefit from the education there. Apparently, the money in the endowment for the school continued to grow until significant funds were being accumulated beyond the needs of the school. An approach was initiated with trustees of the school and those responsible for the handling and growth of the Hershey Trust that had established the school.

It is my understanding that the basis of Penn State's approach was that it was evident from all the projects he had funded, and through the trusts he had established, that Milton Hershey had dedicated his life to individuals and families who could benefit from the assistance he could provide. Further, the argument was made that if Mr. Hershey were still alive, he would prefer that the monies be used for the benefit of humanity, rather than simply accumulating. On that basis, plans were made to approach the court with a request that Mr. Hershey's will be altered, and that monies in the trust be diverted from the original intent, which had been satisfied long ago, to establishment of a medical school and teaching hospital to be staffed and operated by Penn State University.

The appropriate legal steps were taken and the result was a ruling by the court that agreed that Mr. Hershey's trust would allow for establishment of a Penn State College of Medicine and accompanying hospital. Further, the court ruled that the school and hospital should be located in Hershey and that the school should specialize in the education of family doctors, rather than specialists, with the feeling that Mr. Hershey's dedication to the family would best be realized by the education of doctors who would agree to serve the family and its primary medical needs. I still remember the day that the medical school's establishment became a reality.

Eric Walker was a very active man who participated in many sports. He was a dedicated golfer, tennis player, and hunter who enjoyed the outdoors. He also was an ardent squash player. As a matter of fact, we never had squash courts until he became president. When a wing was added to Rec Hall during his tenure, a number of squash courts were included in the plans. Eric played at the end of his busy day and had a number of friends he played with, usually Ralph Rackley, Dean of the School of Education, and Larry Perez of the engineering faculty.

Every once in a while, his regular partners were not available and his secretary would call to ask if I would be available to play squash with Dr. Walker. Of course, I always made myself available the way one does when the boss calls. On one particular day, I received a call from Eric's secretary, who told me that he had been in Hershey and had had an especially long day and would be very happy if he could unwind with a couple of games of squash. I told her that I would, of course, like to play and would meet him at the courts.

Eric walked onto the squash court and almost immediately said, "You are in the radio business, and I am going to give you a scoop, but you can't use it. If you leak this information, it will be very bad for me and I, in turn, will make it very bad for you. Will you promise to keep it a secret so that the news can be released in Hershey and through the courts in Harrisburg?" I promised, of course. He said, "Well, today I got $50 million for the university to build a medical school in Hershey, and we are going to build one of the finest schools and hospitals in the country."

As the story of the hospital and medical school unfolded, it turned out that the Hershey trustees had provided $50 million to construct and equip the hospital and medical school, but nothing to maintain and operate them. Since the medical school and hospital have grown impressively, I would guess that the university administrations and state legislatures have been able to provide adequate funds to give our state a wonderful medical facility.

A Faculty Club for Penn State

For several summers, Eric hosted a golf tournament with the proceeds placed in a fund to be used to build a tennis court and golf clubhouse on the newly–expanded university golf course. At the conclusion of play in his tournament, Eric hosted a dinner at the Nittany Lion Inn where he awarded prizes and made appropriate remarks.

At the end of one of those dinners, Eric told a story that probably none of those present had ever heard before and all found most unusual and interesting. It concerned an early attempt to build a faculty club on the campus, pre–dating, of course, the faculty club that eventually was built and, for various reasons, failed. That club was built during the administration of Dr. John Oswald, and the building has since been converted into an executive education classroom.

Eric told the group that he had wanted a faculty club for many years and believed that the Penn State faculty deserved such a facility. Many universities, of course, have had faculty clubs for many years. Eric said he never had been sure how the money could be raised since he didn't think it would be appropriate or wise to ask for funds from the legislature in Harrisburg. He then talked about industrialists from Pittsburgh who have second homes in the Ligonier area of western Pennsylvania. Among others, members of the Mellon family have been residents and landowners in the Ligonier area for many years. That area also houses the Rolling Rock Country Club and, more recently, the Laurel Valley Country Club, which has as members many of the important corporate people from Pittsburgh.

Eric told us that after many of these people had acquired their farm property in Ligonier, it developed that the soil was sub–standard and not very satisfactory for any crops they wanted to raise. They contacted Eric and asked if our School of Agriculture could be of any help to them. Some of the experts from the Ag School went to work on the project and, within a few years, apparently were able to greatly improve the soil so the land could be productive.

At about that time, the landowners and gentleman farmers decided they would like to raise some prize cattle and again called on the Penn State experts, this time in animal husbandry, to advise them on how they might build up the kind of herd they wanted to have. This advice apparently paid off, as had the soil advice, and they proceeded with their plans for raising cattle.

Eric told us that one of the men involved in both projects was a member of the Mellon family of Pittsburgh. He called Eric and told him that they were all in Penn State's debt for the outstanding land and livestock advice and would like to pay the university back by giving something of value. Eric said he had been tempted to ask for a faculty club, but thought it would be too expensive and ambitious a request. He tried to think of another university need. Mr. Mellon must have had some contacts on campus because he said to Eric, "I understand that you have been wanting a faculty club, and I think that we might be able to arrange for you to have one."

Eric told us he was stunned. Mr. Mellon suggested that he send an architect to the campus to scout for an appropriate site and to begin to draw plans for the club. Sometime later, the famous architect I. M. Pei called to arrange to visit the campus. After looking over the campus, Mr. Pei said that the large, sweeping lawn in front of the Hetzel Union Building would be the ideal spot for a faculty club. Without actually having a decision on the site, Pei proceeded to draw the plans for the club.

Sometime later, Eric recalled, Mr. Mellon called and said that he and Mr. Pei would like to come to the campus to show Eric the preliminary plans for the club. When they arrived and rolled out the plans, which neither Mr. Mellon nor Eric had seen previously, Mr. Mellon immediately said that the facility wasn't large enough. He said the club should include squash courts and a swimming pool and should have a few rooms where distinguished visitors to the campus could be housed.

Eric was pleased and very surprised. But he said he then saw there could be an internal problem he would have to address. He had not consulted with any of the Penn State faculty and was sure there would be objections raised if a faculty club was to be built without any faculty input, regardless of how nice the club might be. Eric thought he should begin thinking about appointing a faculty committee to review the plans and offer their input and ideas. He said he called Mr. Mellon, explained the sensitive internal situation he faced, and asked Mr. Mellon to put the project on hold until Eric could take the proper steps to secure faculty input and approval. Mr. Mellon apparently understood Eric's problem, and they left it that Eric would contact Mr. Mellon and Mr. Pei after some time had passed and he had had time to further involve the faculty.

At this point, Eric stopped in his narrative, took a long pause, and concluded by saying, "You all realize, of course, that the club never got built. The reason it didn't get built was that Mr. Mellon died."

Bill Schreyer and Spider Remembered

In the early 1980s, I was teaching in the university Marketing Department and also held the title of Director of External Relations, a fancy name for corporate and alumni fund-raising. In that capacity, I was involved in a fund-raising program called Corporate Associates, which identified a number of corporations that would financially support our College of Business and would send several executives to campus twice yearly to participate in an information exchange program with other executives from companies also involved in the program. One of the earliest companies to join the program was Merrill Lynch, whose president at the time was William Schreyer, who later became the corporation's chairman and who, until 1997, was president of the university's board. Both he and his company have been extremely generous financial supporters of Penn State.

Schreyer, along with his eventual successor at Merrill Lynch, Dan Tully, attended one of our earliest Corporate Associates seminars. The subject was "The Changing Marketplace," and I was one of the speakers. At a later date, Schreyer asked Dan Tully to find out if I would be willing to come to New York to present my topic to a group of Merrill Lynch marketing executives. I was flattered by the invitation and agreed to participate.

At that time, Merrill Lynch was headquartered at One Liberty Plaza, an impressive new office building in which the company occupied a number of floors. I arrived early for my talk, and a secretary escorted me to the boardroom, where the meeting would take place. The centerpiece of the room was an enormous table surrounded by burnt orange leather chairs. The back of each chair had a brass plate engraved with the name of the director who sat there. High in the office building, the boardroom had a view of the Statue of Liberty, Ellis Island, and the Atlantic Ocean.

At exactly 9 a.m., the massive doors opened and approximately 35 marketing managers came into the room and took places around the table. Before he introduced me, Dan Tully told me that Bill Schreyer would be unable to attend the session as an important matter had suddenly arisen. He then asked if I would have time, following my talk, to stop in Bill's office for a visit. Could I find time to visit with the president of Merrill Lynch? Are you kidding?

I should point out that although we were not close personal friends while students at Penn State, Bill and I had known each other and occasionally visited each other's fraternity house. His Sigma Phi Epsilon house was just down the street from my Phi Sigma Delta house. When I got to his office, he greeted me very warmly. There were two other Merrill Lynch executives in the office. I can't remember their names, but do recall how much deference they showed their boss.

Bill and I did some reminiscing about Penn State, talked about prospects for the next football season, and inquired about mutual friends at the university. He apologized for not being able to stay for lunch because of an important meeting, but invited me to be the lunch guest of the other two men in the room. He said, "Our executive dining room is right through that door. Can you stay for lunch?"

I said, "I don't know. Is the food any good?"

At that point, the two executives looked at me in a new light, wondering who this is who talks so irreverently to their boss.

Schreyer's quick answer was, "The food here is a helluva lot better than the hamburgers Spider used to serve us at the Raths- keller."

Now I really had the attention of the two men who were to host me for lunch. I apparently was an old friend of their boss and that called for the red–carpet treatment. (A note for non–Penn Staters: The Rathskeller was the beer and hamburger place in town and the man behind the grill, who specialized in rather greasy but delicious hamburgers, was known only as "Spider." I am ashamed to admit that his last name was not known to me, and perhaps to none of us. "Spider" was "Spider" and, as far as I knew, he had been at the Rathskeller forever.)

About two years after my visit to New York, Schreyer was asked to return to the campus as an Alumni Fellow. This is to honor the accomplishments of a man or woman who graduated from Penn State and went on to achieve important recognition in their field. It is a lifetime designation. The recipient is presented a large medal that was created exclusively for Alumni Fellows and spends days on the campus sharing career experiences with un- dergraduate and graduate students as well as the faculty.

One of the classes that Schreyer visited was my large class in public relations, which met in a classroom that many Liberal Arts students will recall, the large lecture hall in 121 Sparks Building. I introduced Schreyer to the class by saying something like, "There are several ways to rise from the bottom to the top of a corporation. You can take the zigzag route in which you move from one com- pany to another, always upward, and then you may be brought back to your original company as the man on the top of the pyra- mid. Or, you can do it the harder way. You can start at the bottom and go straight up through the pyramid, passing many people along the way up, until you arrive at the top as president or chairman. Our speaker today, Mr. William Schreyer, followed the harder route. He went to work as a broker in his hometown of Williamsport, Pennsylvania, and rose steadily through the ranks until today he is Chairman of the Board of his important company, Merrill Lynch."

Schreyer's first remark was, "Professor Bergstein, there is a third way to get to the top; to marry the boss' daughter. Since I didn't do that, I had to work my way up through the ranks."

He then delivered a most interesting, informative, and entertaining speech. When he had finished, he asked the class for questions. A handsome student sitting in the back of the class raised his hand and asked, "Mr. Schreyer, do you have any daughters?"

After the class was dismissed, I got an insight into how deeply Schreyer felt about Penn State, demonstrated many times since by his service and financial generosity. He said to me, "See that chair over there?" With that he walked over to a chair in the third or fourth row on the right side of the lecture hall and sat. "This is the seat I sat in the last time I was in this room many years ago, and I can't even remember the name of the professor. Is there a photographer around? I'd like to have my picture taken with me sitting in this seat so I can send it to my family."

Fortunately, Penn State had a photographer following him around so we could prepare an album to present to him as a memento of his visit. Bill Schreyer is a famous and important man in the world of finance. He probably has had his picture taken thousands of times. But I would be willing to bet that none of them are as prized as a photo of him, Chairman of Merrill Lynch, sitting in the classroom where he sat as a teenage student, wondering what the future held for him.

Jesse Arnelle: Up the Ladder

On a Saturday night in 1996, 1,500 people attended a gala dinner to help dedicate the new Bryce Jordan Center across the street from Beaver Stadium on the Penn State campus. This magnificent building gives Penn State a facility that has been sorely needed as the university has continued to grow to its present size, now numbering more than 36,000 undergraduates on campus in University Park alone. This new building gives men's and women's athletic teams a large and attractive facility for their home games. It is large enough to allow centralized graduation ceremonies instead of having individual college graduation ceremonies held in different buildings all over campus. The Jordan Center also can seat more than 15,000 for concerts and other entertainment events.

On stage for the dedication were the university president, Dr. Graham Spanier; Dr. Bryce Jordan, former Penn State president for whom the building is named; and Dr. Joab Thomas, Dr. Spanier's predecessor as president. Also on stage were representatives from state government, which had provided much of the funding for the building's construction, and university trustee Jesse Arnelle, four–time Penn State football and basketball letterman from 1951 to 1954, who still holds many of the school's basketball scoring records. Arnelle was one of the first "big men" to play basketball at Penn State. Jesse was an extremely graceful 6'5" who was almost unstoppable playing inside in the Lions' offense. His height is not impressive these days, with basketball's big men standing from 6'7" to 7'+, but in the early '50s, it was a lot of height.

During the speaking program, I took special notice of Jesse. Because of his size and erect posture, he towered over everyone else on the platform. Jesse was always well–dressed, so when you see him, you see a tall, lean, well–dressed man who, in addition, has a deep, attention–getting voice. He is an imposing figure, and always has been. As Bill Campbell, long–time editor of *Intercom*, the in–house campus newspaper, said, "I was in the same freshman, class as Jesse and even when he was a 17–year–old kid, you had to notice him because he was so imposing."

As I sat there, my mind recalled all the associations I have had with Jesse since he first walked onto the Penn State campus in 1951. Because I was our basketball broadcaster in those days, and the squads only numbered 10 or 12 people, it was relatively easy to get to know the players on a personal level. This is not possible, of course, in football, even if you spend a lot of time in the locker room and traveling with the team on the road. The sheer numbers limit your personal associations to just a handful of players.

Right from the time he stepped on the floor at Rec Hall for practice as a freshman, you knew that here was a player with star quality. Before he was finished, he had scored 2,138 points and, 42 years later as this is being written, he still is the all–time scor-

Jesse Arnelle, all-time Penn State leading scorer, rebounds against Georgetown in a 1953 game. He later became president of the university's board of trustees.

ing leader for Penn State basketball. In Jesse's four years at Penn State, the Lions went to three NCAA national tournaments, including making it to the Final Four in 1954. He became an outstanding student leader and was named All–University student body president in his senior year, the first and only black student to hold that position.

As I thought back, I could recall a number of times when Jesse and I had an opportunity to discuss serious matters. One occasion followed the basketball team's participation in a tournament in Oklahoma City. The tourney was scheduled over the Christmas school break, and the team had returned to State College while the rest of the students were still away on holiday recess. I was walking down College Avenue when I ran into Jesse outside the New College Diner (now, as you might suspect Ye Olde College Diner), and he asked if I had a minute or two to talk about something that had happened on the trip to Oklahoma City.

We took a booth inside the diner and had a cup of coffee. Jesse was obviously upset and told me that while they were in Oklahoma City, four of the players had shared a cab. Before they pulled away from the curb, the driver turned around and said, "You guys will have to get out of the cab because I won't drive him," pointing at Jesse. After exchanging some hot words with the cab driver, the group got out of the cab. Since I didn't know Jesse very well at this point, I had no idea if this sort of insult had happened to him before. I can only guess that in New Rochelle, New York, where Jesse had been an outstanding football and basketball player and where his family was well respected, this probably had never happened. He probably had had to put up with insults here and there, but not in his hometown.

Remember, too, that Jesse was only an 18–year–old sophomore with limited exposure to people like that cab driver. I can't remember exactly what I said after Jesse had unloaded his feelings. I'm confident I didn't just mouth platitudes and cliches because we went on to become friends for more than 45 years.

The State College Quarterback Club has a tradition of inviting a former player who has distinguished himself in his chosen field to come back and address the members of the football team. Returnees have included doctors, lawyers, successful businessmen, educators, and others from a wide variety of fields. One year during the 1960s, we invited Jesse Arnelle to come back to the campus and tell the players and guests of the club "What Penn State Means to Me." It turned out to be a night long remembered by those in the audience.

Jesse delivered what, to me, was a timely and important speech. After telling the audience how much he had enjoyed his university undergraduate years, he then told of the disappointments and discouragements he had experienced in his return to the campus. I cannot quote exactly what he said, but it essentially was that he felt the university did not appear to be a leading force in the recruitment of black administrators, faculty, and students. He expressed the thought that if we were willing and able to recruit black athletes, why couldn't we do a reasonably effective job of recruiting in the other areas. He then asked that the Nittany Lion statuette that we had given him as a gift for the occasion be retained by the Quarterback Club and said he hoped that he could return and accept it when there had been more racial progress on campus.

As you can well imagine, not everyone had the same positive reaction that I did. I liked it because it was timely, it was an extremely thoughtful speech, it dealt with an issue that was beginning to be a major concern of some of the leading universities, and it was a subject that was being discussed in the political arenas. To make it a remembered speech, Jesse delivered it in a very thoughtful and masterful way.

Others felt that it was delivered at the wrong time and in the wrong place. That's too easy a criticism to make, and you hear it too often. When some of the audience told Jesse at a reception following the banquet that they thought his timing was wrong, he said that this was the only occasion to which he had been invited, and there were many university leaders in the audience whose position allowed them to begin to think about solutions for the concerns he had raised. Although it was a jolting speech then, within a fairly short time it became a subject that was being discussed at universities and colleges and companies throughout the country. If you read that speech today, it would be very mild.

Since that night when he suggested that the university should take a more active role in providing educational opportunities for minorities, Jesse went on to a successful career in the law. He is a senior partner in the San Francisco law firm of Arnelle, Hastie, McGee, Willis, and Greene. In addition, he serves on a number of corporate boards in a wide range of businesses.

Has the university moved forward in the area of minority recruitment of students, faculty, and staff since Jesse made his speech? It has worked very hard in this area. Former president Bryce Jordan, for example, started going along with a university admissions officer to Sunday worship services in the Philadelphia area to tell minority congregation members of Penn State's commitment to increasing educational opportunities for minority students and offering to enroll students on the spot if they could qualify academically. I know that the university has a wide range of loan programs to help financially disadvantaged students attend Penn State, and there are other programs as well. From 1987 to 1997, minority student enrollment increased from 6.5 percent to 10.2 percent, and minority staff employment increased from 3.2 percent to 7.4 percent. I am confident that Penn State will continue to extend educational enrollment and employment opportunities to minority populations.

At the beginning of this section, I listed the speakers who were on the platform for the dedication of the Jordan Center and identified one of them as university trustee Jesse Arnelle. The "rest of the story" is that Jesse Arnelle, who made his mark at the university in basketball and football, and who was the alumnus who had shocked many in the university community with his Quarterback Club speech, was introduced that evening as "President of the Board of Trustees of our university, Mr. Jesse Arnelle."

Have We Made Real Progress?

I recently heard a discussion on one of our major television networks that was concerned with the question of whether real progress has been made in improving the lot of America's black population since *Brown v. Board of Education* was handed down in 1954. That important Supreme Court decision declared that schools could no longer be segregated, and that it was impossible for schools to be separate and still be considered equal.

Unquestionably, increased educational opportunities for the minority population have dramatically improved the lot of middle and upper income persons who were able to participate more fully in the educational process. As a result, there are more blacks who are college and university graduates, more doctors and lawyers, more people who have risen to upper and middle management positions in business and industry, more people with graduate degrees, etc. At the same time, however, there are many inner city areas in which, because of the makeup of the population, there is still much *de facto* segregation, with the result that, as there are increasing numbers of middle class black Americans with better educations, there also are dramatically more poor inner–city people who have been almost untouched by school integration and, as a result, remain in poverty.

The one part of life in which the rules of education and accomplishment seem to be different is sports. While it is true that most of our highly paid professional athletes originally called attention to their talents while competing at the high school and collegiate levels, they are almost immediately lifted to high levels of income, not because of what they have learned in the lower school grades, but because of their superb athletic ability. While one might argue that the school system starts these athletes on their way, I maintain that exposure through the media and the dollar value of both collegiate and professional sports is primarily responsible for the high income levels that are enjoyed by both black and white.

I originally became involved with the media and collegiate sports in the late 1940s, when I had my first opportunity to broadcast sports at Penn State. I began my career as a broadcaster of college football, basketball, boxing, and other assorted sports. I have tried to remember the role of the black athlete then, and whether important changes have occurred that have increased their level of acceptance and comfort as they have competed at the collegiate level.

I have always been proud, as a Penn Stater, of some of the pioneering steps taken by our university in the treatment of black athletes. The November 6, 1946, *New York Times* carried the headline on the sports page "Penn State Game with Miami is Off." The sub–headline read, "Canceled to avoid 'unfortunate incident' if two negroes opposed the Floridians." Further reading of the story revealed that officials of both schools agreed that cancellation of the game would be the judicious thing to do. The president of Miami University, Dr. Bowman P. Ashe, wrote to Penn State, according to the *New York Times*, "Probably the best thing to do would be for each of us to seek another opponent and not catapult very important, not well–understood interracial problems into a football game." Dr. Carl P. Schott, Dean of Physical Education and Athletics at Penn State, said cancellation followed month–long correspondence between the schools and was in keeping with the policy of Penn State to compete only under circumstances that would permit the playing of all members of its athletic teams. A Penn State college spokesman was quoted as saying, "It's fairly obvious the student body and team are in accord with the action taken by the athletic authorities."

Some older Penn State alumni might remember that there were two black players on the squad, Wallace Triplett, III, who went on to a successful pro career with the Detroit Lions, and recently retired as a public school official, and Dennie Hoggard who, after law school, became a lawyer in the Philadelphia area. With so many skilled black athletic stars on practically every team in America today, can you imagine one major university writing to another asking that black athletes not participate in a game? Can you imagine the level of play? Can you guess attendance at such a game?

That Miami game is not the only incident in which Penn State was a pioneer in integrated sports. A few years after that cancellation, Penn State's boxing team (boxing was a major college sport in those days, if boxing ever was truly a "sport") was invited to participate in a boxing tournament as part of the program of the festivities surrounding the Sugar Bowl. Even though Penn State's football team was not playing in the bowl, which incidentally was closed to black players, and Penn State had no black boxers on its team, university athletic officials declined to allow our boxers to compete in the event because they didn't want Penn State participating in a segregated sports carnival.

There have been other instances when the participation of black athletes in the game itself was not in question, but other segments of society were involved. When Penn State played in the Cotton Bowl in 1948, the Lions were forced to stay at a U.S. Navy air station outside of Dallas because hotel accommodations were not available for our black athletes. Discrimination in sports continued for many years beyond the 1954 U.S. Supreme Court decision in *Brown v. Board of Education* that outlawed segregation in education. Even as late as 1961, when Penn State met Georgia Tech in the Gator Bowl in Jacksonville, the Penn State team was housed in a hotel in St. Augustine (the hotel was opened out–of–season to accommodate the team) because of the difficulty in finding housing in Jacksonville for a team with black players.

In 1966, Penn State scheduled a game at East Lansing, Michigan, against the powerhouse Michigan State team. The Spartans were loaded with talent that year and easily beat the Lions 42-8. That was Joe Paterno's first season as head coach and facing such a powerful team early in the season was a tough test. Michigan State had Bubba Smith, an all–time university star for the Spartans, as one of its ends. They had George Webster, who went on to star in the NFL, at one of the linebacking spots. They had several outstanding linemen led by George Thornhill. Clint Jones, later a star with the Minnesota Vikings, was one of the halfbacks, and Bon Apisa was an outstanding fullback. They had a great placekicker, Nick Kenney, who came from Hawaii. Their quarterback was Jimmy Raye, who had a long career as a coach in the NFL, and they had many other outstanding players.

Friday afternoon before the game, following the Michigan State practice, Spartans Coach Duffy Daugherty invited the press to his home for an informal press conference and buffet. Duffy, as many sports fans know, was a great storyteller, and I'll repeat one of his stories to point out the limited opportunities for black players in some southern schools that continued to offer athletic scholarships on a segregated basis even after the court decision.

He told us that he had called Peahead Walker, long–time coach at Clemson in South Carolina, to say he was coming south to scout a star halfback he hoped to persuade to come to Michigan State. Walker told Duffy he was wasting his time in visiting the halfback, who Walker described as being just okay. He told Duffy the high school player he really should recruit was George Webster from Anderson, South Carolina, and said Webster was as good a player as he had ever seen.

When Duffy asked why Walker wasn't recruiting him himself, the answer was that since Webster was black, he couldn't play at Clemson. Duffy said he called Webster's mother and asked if he could visit her home to talk to her and her son, George. He received an invitation and was able to secure use of a plane from an executive in the Oldsmobile plant in East Lansing to fly down to Anderson to take a look at George. Duffy described a very small, very neat house on the outskirts of Anderson. He said there were three people living in the house, George, his mother, and his grandmother. He told us that George Webster was as imposing looking a high school athlete as he had ever seen in all his years of coaching. He stood 6'3" or even taller and weighed around 220 pounds.

Duffy said he told the boy's mother and grandmother of all the virtues of playing at a Big Ten school, of Duffy's contacts in the NFL that would assure George high consideration if he decided on a professional career, and all of the industry contacts in the East Lansing area that would assure George plenty of opportunities when he was ready to enter the professional workforce.

At some point during his sales pitch, George's mother left the room. When she returned, she was carrying a suitcase. She handed the suitcase to Duffy and said, "Mr. Daugherty, I've decided to let you have my boy if you'll take good care of him." Duffy said this happened during the month of May, right at the end of the school year and he, of course, didn't want George on the Michigan State campus until the team assembled in late August or early September. But he said he took another look at this magnificent physical specimen and could visualize him playing for another team against the Spartans. He said, "I figured I'd better take him while I could." So, Duffy said, George kissed his mother and grandmother and they headed for the airport. Duffy said Webster had never flown before, and he sat behind the pilot and endured a very white–knuckled flight. Duffy finished his story with, "So I took George back to East Lansing, got him a job for the summer, and as far as I know, he ain't been back to Anderson since."

As more and more colleges began integrating their campuses and teams, the college athletic talent began to disburse all over the country. There continue to be fine teams at historically black schools and, in addition, schools all over the south are obviously deep in talent with both black and white players. Some years ago, northern schools were the beneficiaries of the segregation rules of southern teams. Schools like Michigan State, Minnesota, Purdue, and others, attracted fine black athletes from the south because of their limited opportunities at home. As this has changed, many such athletes are now starring at schools closer to home. If you watch television or look at the All–America teams, you realize how many outstanding black football players are enrolled in southern colleges and universities.

In my experience at Penn State, the university has always tried to attract both black and white players who were not only talented athletes but who also demonstrated a willingness and ability to handle an academic class schedule, as well as the demands of Division I competition. As a result, Penn State has compiled an impressive and enviable graduation rate for its athletes and has a long list of loyal alumni among its former athletes.

Two Great Ideas

The instant the college football bowl match–ups are announced, Penn State fans begin making plans to see the big game, either in person or on television at some sort of bowl party. It doesn't matter who the opponent is or if the game will have any bearing on the national championship picture. It also doesn't matter when the game will be played or which bowl has invited the Lions; the "big" bowl game is the one in which the Lions are playing and their fans will either be there or else in front of a large TV set.

If the plan is to be in the television audience, many important questions have to be answered: Do we plan to be at home for the game? If so, should we plan a TV party or wait to be invited to someone else's house. If we will be at a friend's house, are they serious football fans or are they likely to serve dinner while the game is on? If they are likely to serve dinner, can we watch the game from the dining room? If not, how mad will they get if I keep leaving the table for a quick trip to the TV set in the kitchen or some other room so I can keep track of the game? Might we plan a trip and end up being on the highway at game time? If we are going to stop and eat, can we plan to stop at a restaurant that has a TV set and be confident that it will be tuned to the Penn State game and that our table will allow us to see the game? Also, we have to ask the management to make sure that no other customer tries to change the channel to another game. If they do, they are to be told that I own the restaurant and the television set, and that I will fire anyone who allows the channel to be changed.

I'm sure such bowl plans are reviewed with the same fervor by college football fans at Ohio State, Alabama, Nebraska, Notre Dame, Florida State, and other schools where football has become almost a way of life. These are critical questions at our house because for the past several years we have been away over the New Year's Day holiday, and have seen the telecasts of Penn State's games in a wide variety of locations. For a number of years, we have spent the holiday week visiting an old and dear friend I met when we were freshmen at Penn State. His name is Mike Grossman, and he spends most of the winter months at his home in Woodstock, Vermont.

The only trouble with this visit is the difficulty in receiving the broadcast of the Penn State game. Mike lives a couple of miles outside of town and doesn't want a satellite dish, even though his TV can only receive one network channel. I can't recall any year that the Penn State game was on the one station that he can receive, so over the years he has become very inventive to ensure that we get to see the game. One year, he reserved a room at a country club that had a very tall antenna and could receive several stations. Other years, we have gone to a restaurant and managed to see the entire game through an extended meal that we somehow made last for about three hours. Several years ago, he came up with what I considered to be an idea of pure genius.

When we arrived in Woodstock several days before the game, we asked our usual question: "How are we going to see the game?" The answer was, "Don't worry about it. We're not only going to see the game, but we're going to have a big tailgate just like you are used to at home games at Beaver Stadium." Mike had several other guests who were interested in games other than Penn State's; some were Notre Dame fans and others wanted to see Boston College play. Mike told all of them they were invited to tailgate and see a wonderful game.

As game times approached, we loaded up the station wagon with all the food and drink for the tailgate. We still didn't know where we were going. We drove two or three miles out of town and were signaled into a commercial building's parking lot. We went into the building and on the front wall saw 10 or more television sets, ranging from one of the largest sets I had ever seen through all the various sizes on the market. They were all turned on and each had a perfect color signal. Three or four of the sets were tuned to the Penn State game, while others were showing Notre Dame or Boston College. Our host had rented a retail television showroom, and all the sets were tied into a very tall tower in the parking lot. It was warm in the building, there were lots of chairs spread around, the retail counters were perfect for our tailgate, and we all got to watch our favorite games. Pure genius!

One of the couples at the party had brought along their houseguest, a man from South Africa who knew everything about cricket but had no idea how we played football, never having seen a game live or on television. When he looked at the maze of television sets in the room, he was utterly confused.

Just before kickoff, the couple hosting the South African came to my corner of the room and said that one of the other guests had told them of my interest in football and background as a former football broadcaster. Since neither of them knew anything about football they asked, "Would you be willing to have our guest sit with you and explain the game and answer any questions he might have?" Although I hate to be distracted during a game, what could I say? The visitor seemed to be a personable guy, and I certainly didn't want to be boorish by refusing to sit with him. So I invited him to sit with me and said he should feel free to ask questions about anything he didn't understand. Boy, did he have questions!

"Who are the men in the striped shirts and why do they need so many?" " Why do they sometimes throw the ball and sometimes kick it?" "Why did the team in white get the ball, the other team just had it?" "One side seems to be sending more players into the game than the other side is—are they allowed to do that?" "One team has had the ball for a long time. When does the other team get a chance?" Those were just a few of his questions. Making it worse was the back–and–forth game being played. The final score was 50-39 in favor of Penn State. It was the kind of game that is usually described as "the team that has the ball last will probably win."

The lead swung back and forth until a Penn State defensive back, Gary Brown, who is now a running back with the San Diego Chargers, came on a blitz and literally took the ball right off the hand of Ty Detmer as he was getting ready to pass. Gary ran 53 yards with what is officially listed in the Penn State record book as a fumble. I don't remember how I explained that play, since I had never seen it happen before. I do remember that after the play was over and I gave my "student" the only explanation I could, he then asked me to explain the explanation I had given. Most Penn Staters will probably remember that this was the 1989 Holiday Bowl in San Diego against Brigham Young.

When the game was over, I finally was asked a question I didn't even try to answer. I was afraid that if I had tried to answer, I would have burst out laughing. The man from South Africa didn't know anything about American football, but did know that Joe Paterno was the Lions' coach. The final questions went something like this: "Do you know Joe Paterno?" I told him that I did. "Do you ever see Joe Paterno?" I said that I often did. "Would you ask him something for me?" I said that I would. "Ask Mr. Paterno why his team does something that doesn't make sense to me. Every time his player runs with the ball, he always seems to run right into a pile of players from the other side and he gets tackled. Ask him why he doesn't tell his players not to run to the side where the other team has all its players. Why don't they run over to the other side where the other team doesn't have any players? If his runner does that, he can probably run a long way before the other team catches up. Doesn't that make more sense than the way you're doing it?" I was speechless and certainly didn't want to laugh. All I could say was, "When I see him, I'll ask him."

I didn't see Joe until next fall at the new season's first Quarterback Club meeting in September. I could hardly wait to ask him the question posed by the man from South Africa. When I did, Joe seemed speechless and looked at me a long time without saying anything. Finally he looked at me through his trademark glasses and said, "That's a hell of an idea, Mickey." Then he walked away. As he left, I thought I could see him shaking his head.

All–American, Heisman Candidate, # 1 NFL Draftee, University Graduate

College and professional football have drifted closer and closer together. With the media, especially television, growing in size and number, more and more attention is being paid to the sport. Early in the fall, you can see and read about the most outstanding college players and how likely they are to leave school to get their share of the signing bonus dollars and salary money that seems to be theirs for the taking.

As the season unfolds, you begin to learn what the "experts" think about next season's football needs for the professional teams and which college players likely can fill those needs. Football fans can hardly wait until the professional draft takes place. The draft is a national television production that attracts larger and larger viewing audiences that anxiously wait to learn which professional team or teams have an interest in their favorite players. Prior to the draft, if you are interested, you can learn how your favorite players tested out under the microscope of the professional scouts who want to know how high a player can jump, how much weight he can lift, how fast he can run a 40–yard dash, and how well he can score on various mental and attitude tests.

More and more star players choose to skip these opportunities to perform, not wishing to chance lowering their rating by performing head–to–head with possibly hundreds and hundreds of other players. These highly sought–after players have their agents arrange for personal testing. According to news reports, where do the scouts test these players? At the player's home campus, using the university's space and facilities. As a side note, does it make sense for a growing number of college coaches and athletic administrators to keep complaining, in print, that the professional league is doing a disservice to college players by drafting them earlier and earlier in their college careers while they still have eligibility remaining and then throwing open their doors and offering use of their facilities to make the league's job easier?

Professional sports used to be a place for a player to make some money, compete for a few years and then, using his recognized name, get a "real" job. Not any longer. Today a professional career offers the possibility of making a great deal of money, qualifying for a handsome pension, earning signing bonus and endorsement money that can be kept whether a player is injured or even whether he makes the team. Professional sports have become an end in themselves, and you would be hard pressed not to claim these "goodies" as soon as you can. So outstanding players, or those who believe they are outstanding, are leaving school earlier and earlier. It is not uncommon for a player to select the school that he believes will best qualify him for a professional career.

That's why you'll hear about a quarterback, for instance, who selects a certain school because they run a pro–type offense, or

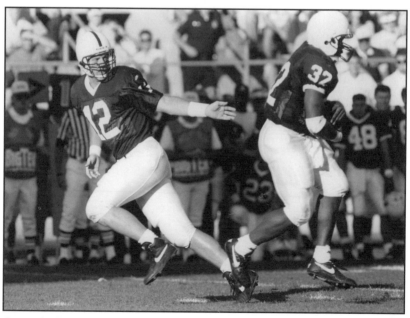

Quarterback Kerry Collins (number 12) hands off to Ki-Jana Carter during a game in the 1994 season.

have a former pro quarterback or former pro coach working with the quarterbacks. There are still some families that use their influence to be sure their son doesn't leave school without a diploma, but these families seem to be shrinking in number. It is not impossible for a player to play football at a top–level school, graduate, and still qualify for a professional career. This is assuming that the player is in his senior year and has made normal academic progress through his first three years on the campus. Many players, of course, are at schools that don't monitor their progress or the number of credits earned and aren't remotely in range of earning a degree in four or even five years. That's a different problem and one that also is too widespread. Although there undoubtedly are a considerable number of players with similar dedication and an appropriate appreciation for an academic degree, let me discuss Ki–Jana Carter.

Ki–Jana came to Penn State as a highly sought after running back. Barring serious injury, he was a good bet for an outstanding college career and a lucrative professional career. After a red–shirt freshman year, Ki–Jana rushed for a three–year total of 2,829 yards (averaging 7.2 yards per carry), scored 34 touchdowns, and holds the Lions' season record for the most games in which he got 100 yards rushing—nine in his senior year. Ki–Jana was a serious Heisman trophy candidate his senior year and was the first player taken in the 1995 NFL draft. He was selected by the Cincinnati Bengals and signed a contract that called for a signing bonus in the millions of dollars as well as a multi–year agreement worth many more millions.

Since he didn't play his freshman year, he still had an additional year of eligibility remaining. He chose to forego his final year and sign with Cincinnati, where he suffered a serious knee injury during the pre–season and sat out the entire 1995 season. In the two seasons since his injury, he still hasn't reached his pre–injury form.

This story, however, isn't about his contract or the tough luck injury he suffered. What it is about is the fact that despite the millions of dollars he would earn and the temptation to drop out of school and rest before reporting to the Bengals, Ki–Jana chose to graduate in four years. To earn his degree in four years, he had to complete 21 credits (seven courses) his final semester, play in post–season all–star games, attend the various camps and combines run by the professional teams and the NFL, and work with his agent. How did he do it?

Ki–Jana was a marketing major, and so the odds were high that sooner or later he would be enrolled in one or more of the classes I teach. As it turned out, he was enrolled in two of my classes his final semester. I was glad to have him. First, he is a very pleasant young man. Second, he is someone who always has a wonderful smile on his face, and he brightened up the entire room, especially during our 8 a.m. class. One of the problems in teaching classes that are made up largely of graduating seniors is their preoccupation with job interviews on campus and, they hope, invitations to visit the plant or offices of the interviewing company. This creates a problem for completing course work. Since the job interviews are so important to the students, it always seemed to me that class attendance during the final term was the teacher's problem and not the student's. So students are told that it is appropriate for them to be away from the campus as part of their job search, but in return they are expected to complete the assignments that are missed within a reasonable time after their return. That seems fair, and it has always worked out for my students.

If you accept the premise, as I do, that an athlete's being away to play in an all–star game, where they have a chance to impress the professional scouts, is a part of his job search, just like attendance at NFL camps and combines, how can this be handled? Simply by laying down the same rules that you expect all other graduating seniors to follow. The class assignment—a written case to be submitted or a paper to be prepared—must be completed within 48 or 72 hours of returning to campus.

Does this present a heavy workload between travel and class assignments. Of course it does, and it should. Can a player do it? Of course he can. Ki–Jana and others have done it. What is their secret? No secret. As the cliché goes, you have to want it. In Carter's case, he must really have wanted it. I told him when the assignment he missed would be due. Right on time, he handed in the assignment, and it was properly prepared and presented. When the semester was completed, Ki–Jana earned a respectable passing grade in each course. I don't know how his other professors handled his absences and assignments. I assume that Ki–Jana worked out some arrangement to enable him to graduate on time.

There was only one negative to having him in class. I have always insisted that students attend class when they are on campus and that they arrive for class on time. Many classes start late for a variety of reasons. Students often arrive late and blame it on the weather. The fact that I am there on time, and most of the other students are there on time, doesn't seem to make an impression on the late arrivals. Sometimes, we have to wait until all the baseball caps have been removed. The most usual reason for delaying the start of the class is the difficulty in getting the students to put away the morning campus newspaper that they can't seem to delay reading. The semester I had Ki–Jana in class was the only semester, in approximately 40 years of teaching, that a class was often late in starting because there were so many students gathered around a seat asking for an autograph.

The Second Mile

Many of us have our own special dream, something we want to accomplish or build, some profession we aspire to join, some important societal change we want to accomplish. Some of us accomplish our objectives and realize our dreams, while others never are able to bring their dream to fruition. In State College, we have had the opportunity to see one man begin his dream and help it grow. The dream is called the Second Mile, and the dreamer is Penn State's very successful defensive coordinator on Joe Paterno's staff—Jerry Sandusky. Jerry's story and his dream have been an inspiration to all who have had dreams but have not been able to see them become a reality.

Jerry Sandusky grew up in Washington, Pennsylvania, the son of Art and Evelyn Sandusky. His parents operated a youth center where the family lived. Jerry and his family have always been involved with foster children, children who need a hand, young people who need adults to offer them hope and help. And so it should come as no surprise that Jerry has always had empathy for the underdogs. It also should come as no surprise that Jerry would marry someone who shared his feelings for the less fortunate and was willing to share her heart and her home. Dottie and Jerry have five adopted children and have been foster parents to several more. That should be all one needs to know about the Sanduskys and their dedication to the goals and ideals of the Second Mile.

The Second Mile was incorporated in 1977. The name of the organization offers an invitation to anyone who is willing to travel the "second mile" to help young people who need their help if they are to grow into adults with a fair and equal chance to become useful and contributing members of our country's society.

In 1982, the foundation for the Second Mile was built: a residential facility a short distance from the Penn State campus. The young people who live there attend schools in the State College area, are supervised by live–in adults, and receive caring support from members of the Friends program. Originally, these Friends were largely Penn State athletes, mostly from the football team, but the program has expanded to include people outside of the athletic programs. The home was made possible with donations from private organizations and individuals, as are almost all the programs that have been added since the home was built.

Officials of the Second Mile have said it is scary to build a program that depends completely upon the goodwill and generosity of private donations. The decision not to seek government funding means that the program is not beholden to any agency and is not subject to cutbacks that could terminate a program. At the moment, most of the organization's monies come from private individuals, private businesses and corporations, foundations, and special events such as the Second Mile Celebrity Golf Classic, which raised $219,735 in 1997.

One story about the Friends program bears repeating because it captures the essence of the program and describes the emotional attachments that are formed between those who act as big brothers and the young people in the program. During his years at Penn State, Todd Blackledge, the quarterback who led the Lions to the 1982 national championship, was actively involved with the program and formed a close relationship with one of the young men in it. The young man, a resident of State College, was being raised by his mother alone. He and Todd became close friends, and Todd called him every time Penn State finished a game on the road, to assure him that he was physically okay, so that the youth could go to bed without worrying. One particular act of kindness is worth telling. When Todd learned that this young man had rarely been out of town and never had the experience of a big city hotel, Todd took him to Pittsburgh, as his guest, so he could spend a night in a hotel and experience a visit to a big city.

There are many, many other stories of the friendships and kindness of Friends of the Second Mile. In 1982, the program was serving 41 kids with two programs. Now, with eight or more programs, the effort involves more than 100,000 kids. The programs are wide–ranging and far–reaching. There are chapters in other parts of the state and Second Mile offices in other communities. The Penn State Alumni Association has become actively involved. One of the most visible and widely distributed efforts is a video entitled, "The Choice of Champions." Public school counselors were asking for a way to involve young people in their schools. The Second Mile produced the video that is shown to schools throughout the Pennsylvania, using Penn State athletes to talk to the students about peer pressures.

Another unique program is the Nittany Lion Tips. These are sports trading cards with pictures of Penn State athletes on the front. The backs of the cards carry inspirational messages from the athletes to the young students. School counselors use the cards to "break the ice" with reluctant young people and effectively use them as rewards for improved behavior and as reinforcements for behavioral changes.

The Second Mile also offers a Summer Challenge that provides camping experiences at three sites in the state. There are many, many success stories of young people who have turned their futures around because of the camp experience.

The programs described here give you just a quick look at the extent of the work of the Second Mile. Under the direction of Jerry Sandusky, who is chairman of the board of the organization, and Dr. Jack Raykovits, a Penn State graduate who earned a doctorate in school psychology and is executive director, the list of programs continues to grow. There are counseling and referral services, a Children's Fund to provide for the financial needs of referred children, and other assistance programs.

All of this happened since 1982 and if you know Dottie and Jerry Sandusky and all of the others who have helped them achieve their dream, you know there is lots more still to come.

Do We Still Have Heroes? Do They Deserve to be Heroes?

It is a well–worn cliché to say that "nothing is forever." Cliches become cliches because they are true. If you look at our society, you see few areas of our daily lives that haven't changed. There are dramatic changes in the family, the government, our educational system, the makeup of the workforce, and in technology and how we use these changes. There also are changes in sports, and in how we view the teams we root for and the players on those teams. Because of the many changes in sports, it has become difficult for fans to look at teams and players as we once did.

Take professional baseball for example. Sports fans of all ages were pretty much the same. They had a favorite league and usually very little interest in the other league. Your favorite league was determined by the league in which your favorite team played. Even as you had your favorite teams, there were teams that you hated. If you were a New York Giants fan, you were not a Brooklyn Dodgers fan. If you rooted for the Chicago Cubs, you had absolutely no interest in the White Sox. The teams you hated often were in the same league as your favorites and were usually teams that had lots of success against your team.

We all had our favorite players, too. But then along came free agency and fans have been confused ever since. Your favorite player could be traded to a team you hated or, even more likely, to a team in the other league that you had never followed. There are rules laying out conditions under which a player can sell his services to the highest bidder. So it is hard these days to have a real baseball hero. Professional football and basketball have followed the same pattern and it has been equally hard to keep track of who plays for whom. As a result, it has become much harder for fans to have sports heroes to whom they are loyal over the years.

If hero worship is still in style, it's different than it used to be, and for good reason. It's hard to idolize a player when he has been arrested or indicted, or is serving time in jail for abusing his spouse or girlfriend, rape, illegal drug use, or causing death or serious injury while driving under the influence of drugs or alcohol. There is at least one player who has been suspended multiple times for repeated drug use. We read about present and past stars being cited for income tax evasion because they failed to report income they pocketed from autograph sessions at baseball card shows. Even younger fans know that any money you earn is supposed to be reported.

This is not to ignore the fact that the great majority of athletes are good citizens and caring spouses and parents and are involved in devoting time or lending their name to various charities. But sports have been tainted, and the pedestal upon which we used to place our sports heroes is broken or at least tottering. A few years ago, the sports hero's image was further tarnished by the sight of baseball players who earn salaries in the millions of dollars giving up half a season and the sacred World Series because they are on strike. Millionaires on strike? A baseball season without a World Series?

Remember when there used to be eight or nine boxing world champions? Now, even a boxing fan cannot name all the weight divisions or organizations that sanction a "world champion" in boxing. Why all the divisions and all the champions? Obviously, so there can be multiple "world championship" fights to sell. And if a young boy still thinks of fighters as heroes, he cannot see his heroes fight without paying for an expensive television show or asking his family to take him to an arena with a special television hookup at a high price.

Is it important that there be sports heroes? We cannot know for sure. We do know, however, that with the growth in single–parent families, role models are in decline and there should be some in public life to fill that void. It may be that sports are overblown these days. Maybe the entire world of sports has been given too much importance. Maybe one of these days young people will begin to turn their attention in other directions. I doubt it. At least for now, I continue to think that wholesome sports heroes are important to our youth. Where can we find them? And even if we do find them, we'd better pick them very carefully and hope that they don't disappoint both their older and younger fans. As we all realize, recent scandals, court trials, drug violations, and problems of abuse have the same effect on the public and all prove the same point—heroes don't last forever, much as we might want them to. We must be sure they don't also prove the point that illegal and immoral behavior can be considered okay since it is practiced by our heroes.

Love and Guts

My wife, Betty, and I had three children. Our oldest son, Andrew is an instructor in marketing at Penn State and a marketing communications consultant for Altec–Lansing Technologies, Inc. Andrew received his undergraduate degree from Penn State and his master's degree from the University of Maryland. His younger brother, Michael, received both his undergraduate degree and his Master's of Fine Arts from Penn State and is the managing editor of a fine literary journal at Bard College. Our youngest child, Nan, who was born with a brain injury, is the sadness of our family's life.

Unless you have been the parent of a handicapped child, you cannot understand how difficult it is to accept not only the disability that the child faces, but also the realization that the disability will last for a lifetime.

We sought whatever medical advice was available. Everyone told us the same thing, "Take this child home and love her as long as you can, because you will receive very little in return." If you think that was the end of it, you don't know my wife. She would not accept that verdict as final and kept asking and looking. One day I came home from the office and my wife told me that the neurosurgeon who had operated on Nan had made an appointment for us with Glenn Doman, Director of the Institute for the

Achievement of Human Potential, which is located in the Chestnut Hill section of Philadelphia. Perhaps you have heard or read about Glenn. He is not a medical doctor, but he is a teacher, a therapist, an innovator, a visionary, and an inspiration.

Space will not permit me to tell you everything I know about Glenn. I will tell you that he is the man who gave birth to the "patterning" method that has helped hordes of brain–injured children who could not walk or even turn over to first creep, then crawl, then stand, and finally walk. Without attempting to offer a complicated description of the rationale for Glenn's patterning process, I will simply tell you that it is based on the belief that undamaged areas of the brain can be taught to take over the functions of damaged brain cells. Glenn, along with Dr. Carl Delacato, taught many, many brain–injured children to read at very early ages despite their injuries.

When we first went to see Glenn, Nan could not turn over and had already undergone drastic brain surgery. We talked to Glenn and he promised us that Nan would not only creep and crawl, but that patterning would someday make it possible for her to walk. In addition, he and Carl and my wife taught Nan to read before she could speak. It wasn't easy but Nan's mother and our family, friends, and neighbors pulled it off.

The central part of the program called for three people to "pattern" Nan four times a day in addition to dozens of other movements and therapies that Betty would do with and for Nan. After our meeting with Glenn, we drove the Pennsylvania Turnpike from Philadelphia to Harrisburg and Betty asked, "Where are we going to get all the people we will need to pattern Nan eight times a day?" "Eight times a day?" I said. "Glenn said four times a day." You don't know my wife. She said, "If four times is good, eight times is better."

It seemed almost an impossible task. After we arrived home we spread the word throughout the neighborhood that we were going to begin a program we hoped would help Nan to creep, crawl, and walk. We asked friends and neighbors to come to our home for a meeting. After explaining the theory and purpose of the program we said, "If you are willing to volunteer to help us, you are undertaking a task that will need real dedication. This program must be done eight times a day, seven days a week, 365 days a year. We will have to ask you to be responsible either for filling your time slot or arranging for a substitute. Betty won't have time to call around looking for substitutes. She'll be doing other therapies that will take all the time she will have." We went on to say, "We have no idea how long this might take. It could be years. And the worst part of it is that it might not work!"

Approximately 15 of our friends and neighbors agreed to take on the task. Our two sons, of course, also pitched in. I will not describe all the therapies that were required. As an example, we had a crawling tunnel, and when Nan progressed to the point that she could crawl, my wife stretched out the tunnel on a hot summer sidewalk and together they crawled through the tunnel 300 times every day. There were other therapies just as difficult and time consuming and hot.

Our neighbors who helped Betty and Nan really deserve to have their names on our family's honor roll along with family members. The program lasted approximately six years. At the beginning, Nan could not even turn over. When we stopped patterning, she could walk. She had a slightly rolling gate, but <u>she could walk!</u> Can you imagine our neighborhood when the word flew around that "Nan walked yesterday"? Some of our helpers hadn't missed more than an occasional session for six years. There was a point when we decided that Betty needed a vacation. I went along, but it was Betty's vacation. We left Nan and our two sons at home, but the program had to go on. We had a chart with 168 patterning time slots that had to be filled, and we asked our friends to sign up for as many sessions as they could. The 168 slots were filled—every one of them—before day's end. So we went off on a much-needed respite for Betty, knowing that not one therapy session would be missed.

What did Nan achieve? First, she received a high school diploma. We know that she didn't really fulfill all the requirements for a diploma. Special education students are treated with charity and kindness. But she rode a van to and from school every day. She reads as well as I do, and I'm a college professor. She spells better than most people I know, including my university students. She types her own letters and makes no mistakes in spelling or typing. She can ride a three–wheeled bicycle and swim.

Is she perfect? I wish I could tell you that she is, but she is not. She still suffers from occasional seizures. But she rides the bus home from the residential school where she now lives, she calls her brothers and us on the phone, and she has the very best memory of anyone I have ever known.

By Pennsylvania law, Nan received her diploma with the rest of her class. Our local high school's graduation ceremonies are held in Rec Hall on the Penn State campus. When Nan came forward to receive her diploma, there were approximately 15 of her friends, of all ages, sitting up in the balcony at the fieldhouse who knew that without them, Nan would not be there in the graduation line. Whether she actually owned a "real" diploma doesn't matter. What matters is that she walked down the aisle in the Penn State fieldhouse where her high school graduation was held and received her diploma.

Which group would you have rather joined? Would you have been proud to join the group that said, "Take her home and love her because you will receive very little in return," or would you rather have been one of our family's friends who said, "Let's give it a try, it might just work." Thank God it did!

In 1991, I was invited to make three different presentations to agents of the Connecticut Mutual Life Insurance Company. The audiences were made up of the company's agents who had reached various levels of insurance sales during the preceding year. I spoke to one group in Phoenix, one in Puerto Rico, and a third in San Diego. One of the other speakers at all three events was an agent of the company who had achieved notable success in life insurance sales. When I first heard him speak, I thought immediately of the efforts expended by my wife, other members of our family, and our friends during the therapy program for our daughter that I have just described.

The speaker told the audiences that his son, who was of Little League age, was a pretty good baseball player. In the words of his father, "My son was not a great player, but he was pretty good. I didn't get many chances to see my son play because my work kept me on the road and away from home during many of the summer weeks." He went on to say that he found himself at home one mid-week afternoon when his son's team had a workout, and he thought this was an opportunity to at least see his son play in an intra–squad game. He went to the field early and watched the pre–game workout. The team's coach was a former pitcher for the University of Michigan, and he was pitching batting practice to the squad. The father said, "The coach was a fairly young man of pretty fair size, and he threw hard to the team's young players, but he couldn't throw the ball past my son. My son hit the ball to all fields, and I was impressed. When the coach tired, he turned the pitching over to his assistant coach, who had been a high school pitcher, and he too threw the ball pretty hard. He had no more luck than the head coach in trying to strike out my son. My son wasn't afraid to stand in there, and he hit almost every pitch that was in the strike zone. After about 30 minutes of batting practice, the coach divided the team into two squads, and they got ready to play a nine inning practice game."

The speaker told us that he settled in the bleachers and prepared to see his son hit the ball all over the lot. He said, "Now, the pitcher was a regular member of the team's pitching staff. His name, as I recall, was Albert. Albert struck out my son three straight times, and my son didn't come close to hitting the ball. When he did hit it, it didn't get out of the infield." The father told us how puzzled he had been to see his son hit nothing but line drives against the hard–throwing coaches and hit nothing but air or weak ground balls against the team's pitcher who was the same age.

The man and his son got into the car after the practice game and headed for home. The father said that his son seemed downcast, apparently because of his poor showing in front of his father. The father, while recognizing that this probably wasn't the best time to talk about his son's performance, said he couldn't help bringing up his son's batting futility. He said to the boy, "I'm really curious. When I got to the ballpark, you were hitting against the head coach and you were hitting nothing but solid line drives. When the assistant coach started throwing, you were even better. You hit some sharp line drives and you hit a couple of fly balls to the outfield. When the game started and the pitcher wasn't any older or bigger than you were, you seemed like a different hitter. You either struck out or hit weak infield ground balls. You seemed like a different hitter. Why do you think you could hit the coaches and you had no luck hitting Albert, who is your own age? What is it about Albert that keeps you from hitting anything solid against him?"

His son answered, "I can't hit Albert because he's a better ball player than I am." The father thought and then responded, "If you say you can or you say you can't, in either case you're probably right." Remember when you were a kid and probably read a book or two that made this point? In my case, the popular book was about a small steam engine pulling a long line of railroad cars up a steep hill with great difficulty. The book was called "The Little Engine That Could."

In the case of my daughter Nan and the therapy program directed by her mother, I am absolutely certain that my wife embraces the philosophy, "If you say you can or you say you can't, in either case you're probably right." I am sure of one thing. My wife did not allow herself to say or even think the word "can't." She would not allow herself to think of failure. The program was too hard and too testing for her to even think of the possibility that it might not work. If she had, it would have been too easy to stop crawling through that tunnel wearing her basketball shin guards hot day after hot day. I'm absolutely positive that Betty never, ever doubted that our daughter would walk. The only question she allowed was "when," never "if."

Note: This chapter was finished shortly before Nan Bergstein passed away on March 7, 1997, at age 35, of causes unrelated to her birth defect. The descriptions of her progress and of the person she became were left in the present tense as a tribute to her courage and perseverance.

In the Matter of Grades

Let me make it clear that I enjoy college athletics and believe that they play an important part in the life of many in the student body, and certainly in the lives of the alumni who live and die with the fortune of their school's athletic teams, especially the football and basketball teams. I am not tired of college athletics, but I am tired of coaches and athletic administrators and other university officials at so many schools pretending that all of their athletes are just like the rest of the student body, that they combine their academics and athletics without special treatment, and that they are regular students who just happen to play a major sport.

Fortunately, I have seen no evidence that such an attitude exists at Penn State. Penn State athletes receive the help they need to maintain normal progress toward their degree, and there are adequate academic advisers to monitor their progress. Penn State players, as at many schools, try to arrange their schedules so they can meet class obligations and still find adequate time for team practice. This, of course, is not always possible, and Joe Paterno often must begin or end important practices without key players who have a late class or exam responsibilities.

Too many schools, I am afraid, pay far too little attention to an athlete's learning responsibilities; if large numbers of fans ever lose their interest in and support for college athletics, these types of schools will have driven them away.

We all hope that sane athletic programs continue to offer as much entertainment and fun as they do. Isn't it time that less sane programs stop deluding everyone about what they do to attract and hold some of their athletes? If they don't, they make a mockery of the term student–athlete. It might be more accurate for those schools to reverse the words and talk about athlete–students. When I think of the special help that schools with high visibility athletic programs give their athletes, I am reminded of an incident that involved Penn State football players. This happened many years ago, long before coaches Rip Engle and Joe Paterno arrived on our campus. In those days, money for scholarships and help for athletes did not come easily, and coaches and athletic administrators had to beg and scratch for help. Penn State's football program did not enjoy anything close to the reputation it enjoys today. If there was money for scholarships, it wasn't very much, and many of the players on the team had to work hard at jobs to meet their expenses.

At that time, our football players were given, in addition to whatever minor perks were available, free textbooks. Actually, instead of being given free textbooks, they were given free use of textbooks. The proprietor of a State College bookstore was our textbook "angel." Once a player had registered for his courses, he took his registration form to the bookstore and was loaned the books he would need for his courses. When the semester or term was over, he was expected to return his textbooks. When he registered the following term, he repeated the process. It worked out for everyone. A player was sure to have the books he needed each semester, and the bookstore owner could place the books in his used book pile and sell them to other students. It seemed to be a low–cost yet effective way to help the members of the football squad.

The bookstore owner who provided this service told me some years ago what happened one year to disrupt the smooth working system. At that time, most of the football players lived in the same dormitory on campus. (Penn State abandoned that practice a long time ago.) One of the players, who shall remain nameless, decided that he needed some spending money and apparently went from room to room, gathering a pile of textbooks, that he then sold. The bookstore owner knew nothing about it since the books were sold to a different bookstore. He only learned about it when there weren't very many textbooks returned at the end of the semester. Apparently, it took that long to discover the theft because none of the other players had noticed that any books were missing and therefore had no reason to report a problem. I have no idea whether the players who didn't open their textbooks passed their courses. If they did, that's a pretty good trick.

Joe Paterno has said many times that if Penn State ever contemplated establishing a football dormitory, as many schools have, he wouldn't have anything to do with it and would not continue as coach. He has always believed that a normal campus experience includes living in a fraternity house, apartment, or wherever a player chooses to live, and that he ought to have a chance to live with other students on campus, not just his teammates, so he can interact with a cross–section of students with different interests, different academic areas, and different cultural backgrounds.

If you are concerned about academic standards and graduation rates, it would have been upsetting to read an NCAA news release a year or so ago that announced that increasingly high admission standards seem to be working since, during the preceding year, graduation rates for football players on aid, all over the country, were higher than graduation rates for the general student body—58 percent of the players graduated within six years of their enrollment year, while the graduation rate for the general student body was only 57 percent. It seemed to show academic progress for those on athletic aid since their 58 percent graduation rate was higher than the last time a survey was taken. The story also indicated that Proposition 48, which requires minimum test scores before an athlete can be admitted and be eligible to play, was working and contributed to the increased graduation rates.

There probably are several things to consider if we are to take that news release seriously. Let me first say that I salute any program that helps raise the graduation rates, however small the increase, as long as the rates continue to rise. While I still am not sure that Proposition 48, as presently written, is the very best way to extend opportunity for a college education to deprived young men and women who need and deserve a break, if it plays a part in any increase in graduation rates for athletes, we have to be pleased with those parts of the program that are working.

My objection to the NCAA trumpeting the increase in graduation rates lies in the comparison of the rate of athletes to that of the general student body, and the implication that somehow athletes are either smarter or work harder than students without athletic abilities or scholarships. In other words, I would suggest that the cliché "comparing apples to oranges" holds true here, and I think it is unfortunate that such a comparison was made.

While it is true that there is scholarship help available for students who qualify, the level of scholarship help for most students, compared to an athletic grant–in–aid, is not worth much. What do you think would happen to graduation rates for the general student body if every student received full tuition, room, board, books, easy access to tutors, availability of a counseling center, supervised study halls, and a structure to monitor their academic progress in the event that academic help is needed? That, I think, is a fair listing of the help available to scholarship athletes. I find no fault with any parts of this program.

Participating in a major sport at a Division I college or university while maintaining normal academic progress is a very difficult assignment. Not only is time required for athletic participation, but can you imagine how hard it is to complete academic assignments when friends constantly want to talk about last week's game or this week's opponent. Then, add in all the time an athlete spends in the training room receiving treatment for game and practice injuries and you have a full schedule. It is no wonder that relatively few major college athletes complete their academic careers in four years.

In looking at graduation rates, I don't understand why the NCAA uses a six–year time frame when a five–year period should be a true measure of their accomplishment, given the fact that five years includes a full redshirt year when a player is held out of competition. In reality, given that players receive a financial grant–in–aid and all the academic help they should normally need to keep abreast of their academic requirements, it could be considered embarrassing that only 58 percent earn their diplomas in six years. The latest Penn State figures show a graduation rate of 81 percent in all sports.

I am not sure how other schools and coaches view their responsibility for their players' graduation once their eligibility is used up, but I can tell you how Penn State's Joe Paterno feels about his players and their obligations to earn a diploma. One spring semester, I was teaching a large lecture class, and in looking over the classroom I recognized a very large young man who had played for Penn State about a year before this semester. Since I assumed that he had graduated, and this was an undergraduate class, I wondered how and why he had enrolled. I knew that he had been out of school for at least a year, and that he had spent at least a year on the roster of the NFL's New York Jets.

When class was over, I asked the student to stop by my desk, and then asked him why he was scheduled in this undergraduate class. He told me that when he left Penn State, he was one semester shy of graduation, and that he had intended to return when the Jets' football schedule was completed. For one reason or another, he had neglected to return to school for the final semester. He said that his phone had rung one evening and, to his surprise, it was Joe Paterno calling. He told me that Joe had asked him to remember what Joe had promised the player's mother when he was recruited. The player said that Joe had promised his mother that her son would be given every opportunity to graduate from the university. Joe asked him if he had received all of the academic opportunities he needed. When the player agreed that he had, Joe told him that he expected him to enroll in the spring semester to complete his remaining credits. The player told me that Joe also reminded him that he had received a substantial professional salary the past season, and there was no reason he could not afford to come back to school. The player promised Joe that he would enroll.

Two weeks later, according to the player, his phone rang and Joe's secretary was on the line. She said that Joe had asked her to call the admissions office to see if the player had enrolled. When she found out that he hadn't, Joe asked her to call the player to tell him that Joe was angry at his broken promise and again remind him of his obligation to earn a degree. The player then told me, "I figured I better get back here and get my degree or Joe will keep calling me until I do."

This player could no longer help Penn State's football team or Joe Paterno in any way. His eligibility was gone, and he could easily have remained on the "failed to graduate" list. But realizing the value the degree would have for the player after his pro career, Joe pushed him into earning his diploma. I have a hunch that if more football coaches followed their players after they left the campus and encouraged them to earn a degree, the graduation rate that the NCAA talks about would be significantly higher than 58 percent.

Command Presence in the Military and Elsewhere

Anyone who has sat in a classroom, or been in the military, especially in combat, or been a member of an athletic team, recognizes presence when he or she sees it. In the military, they call this air of leadership "command presence."

The dictionary defines presence as "a way of carrying oneself...bearing...the quality of self–assurance and confidence." In teaching my classes and talking about what is needed for success, I often talk about command presence. I used to suggest ways of attaining it, but I gave up that effort some time ago. I'm not sure that talking about it is productive because I don't believe that it can be taught, only demonstrated. So I would point out role models and hope that students might someday learn to emulate them.

Command presence is not limited to the military, of course, but military leaders who possess it are widely recognized because of the exposure they receive, largely on television. Think back to the coverage given to the military operation called Desert Storm and the immediate fame that Gen. Norman Schwartzkopf achieved largely because of his dynamic style during televised news conferences and briefings. I am sure that only a handful of Americans even knew the general's name before that exposure. I also am sure that he became universally recognized almost immediately once he was exposed to the public eye.

I am sure that Lee Iacocca, former chairman of Chrysler Corporation, never would have agreed to do his company's television commercials without being sure that his presence would help sell the product. And the late President John F. Kennedy was widely described as having charisma, but I am sure we would also credit him with a sense of command presence.

At Penn State, Joe Paterno's presence has been extremely important to his success in selling himself and Penn State's football program to potential players , their parents, and their coaches, as well as to the media and the general public. I thought of Paterno's sense of presence recently when one of his former players visited the campus for a team reunion. I was on an early morning flight with the player and asked him about the reunion. He said, "We were having a great time reminiscing about our team's experiences and there was conversation everywhere. All of a sudden, as if on a signal, the conversation stopped. What happened? Joe had come into the room!" He then told me what many fans suspect and what Joe himself is quick to admit. "Whether you especially like Coach Paterno or not, you respect and admire him as a coach and for his personal and professional record." I suspect that not too many coaches would get that immediate reaction if they walked into a crowded room.

Many successful players, especially quarterbacks, have demonstrated the air of being in charge. Joe Montana, long–time quarterback of the San Francisco 49ers, obviously had it. Former Pittsburgh Steelers quarterback Bobby Layne was noted for his command of his team and air of command presence. I've been told that a receiver who dropped a Bobby Layne pass often was afraid to go back into the huddle to face Layne. I also have been told that sometimes Bobby Layne could strip the skin off a careless receiver by just giving him what the Steelers called the "Layne look."

Think back to teachers you had in grade school, high school, or college, and remember who had command presence and who did not. Some teachers walk into a classroom, open their notebook or textbook, look at the class, and there is immediate quiet. That's command presence. We all have had other teachers who never really got control of the class. In those classes, there always was a faint hum of whispers, turning of newspaper pages, and lots of shifting around in chairs and shuffling of feet. It doesn't matter how competent the teacher is or how well recognized in his or her field. Without the control I'm talking about, there has to be diminished learning.

At Penn State, I always thought that the Lions' All–American quarterback Richie Lucas had that intangible ingredient of leadership. Richie never went into the huddle during team timeouts. He always walked some distance away from the rest of the squad, knelt down and took off his helmet. His teammates will tell you that when Richie rejoined the huddle, he was immediately in charge and everyone knew it. Another Penn State quarterback, Kerry Collins, a first round draft choice of the Carolina Panthers, demonstrated that kind of confidence and leadership when he took the undefeated 1994 team on drives down the field.

One person in my life who had outstanding command of his job and was a walking and breathing example of executive command presence was Lt. Col. Robert Williams, the executive regimental commander who served under Col. Harry Liversedge, commander of the 28th Marine Corps regiment, who lost his life during the battle of Iwo Jima.

We landed under heavy fire at the base of Mt. Suribachi. Our landing area was designated as Green Beach, the leftmost landing beach. We had ocean to our rear and ocean to our left since Suribachi rose at the very end of the island. Although I didn't see Col. Williams during the landing, I was told later than he came onto the beach ramrod straight. As he started up the beach, an enlisted man who was down on the sand yelled at the colonel, "Get down. There's a sniper over there." The colonel called back to the enlisted man, "I suggest you shoot him for me!" I also was told that, under fire, Col. Williams shaved every morning on Iwo Jima and that he shaved with a straight razor. Talk about confidence building. Talk about leadership. Talk about command presence.

When the Iwo Jima monument was dedicated 10 years after World War II, the Marine Corps invited all of the officers from the 28th regiment to come to Washington for the dedication ceremonies and related activities. Although I had little to do with winning the battle because I was wounded on the beach on the day of the landing, I still wanted to be a part of the dedication. I knew the men who had raised the flag at the site and actually had shared a tent in Hawaii with Lt. Harold Schrier, the officer who led the contingent to the top of the mountain. He is not shown in the famous picture because, as one Marine told me later, he was engaging snipers while his men raised the flag.

We gathered at the Army–Navy Club in Washington the night before the dedication for a dinner that would follow Marine Corps ritual. It began with a series of toasts beginning, as I recall, "Gentlemen, a toast to the President of the United States." This was followed by, "Gentlemen, a toast to the Commandant of the Marine Corps." Following the prescribed ritual meant that various officers had to be selected to say and do specific things during the dinner. Col. Williams had arranged the dinner and assigned roles.

I will never forget when the colonel made his entrance. The entire room was full of men who were now civilians, except for General Haynes who had been a captain on Iwo Jima and was still on active duty and wearing his dress blues. Col. Williams was retired and wore a beautifully–cut suit that, to my eye, he wore like a uniform. Perhaps I had that impression because I had never seen him out of uniform and, as always, he was impeccably dressed. When he entered the room, I saw a perfect example of command presence. Although we were all civilians and had no official contact with the Marine Corps, other than an occasional newsletter, as the colonel entered the room, every man automatically rose as one man.

The colonel went from one man to the next, handing out slips of paper on which he had written instructions for their role in the ritual. Every single one, upon accepting his assignment, responded, "Yes, sir" to the colonel. If you had entered the room and looked over the large gathering of men in suits, and I had asked you to tell who was in charge, I am confident that you would have immediately pointed to Col. Williams. As the years passed, he had retained his command presence. And if he walked into my office today, I am sure I would stand at attention and call him "Sir."

Even though I never got to know the colonel personally, I am conscious of him every day. As I sit at my typewriter, I face a wall covered with artwork, various memorabilia, and several photos that are important to me. As I type these words, I can raise my eyes and look at two photos of Col. Williams. Several years after the war, while he was still on active duty, the colonel returned to Iwo Jima to lay a wreath at the monument that has been placed with appropriate inscription on the spot where the original flag had been placed, under fire, on the top of Mr. Suribachi.

With the American flag and the flag of the U.S. Marine Corps being held by the color guard, Col. Williams is placing a wreath at the base of the monument. I can't remember who sent me the photos, but I have had them framed, and I look at them several times a day as I sit typing. If you could see Col. Williams standing ramrod straight in one of those photos as he salutes at the monument in memory of the men he helped command, you would know what I mean by command presence.

Maybe some day we'll learn how to teach young people how to acquire command presence, but when I look at the picture of Col. Williams, I doubt that what he had can be taught. ■

12

Final Reflections

Most people have little or no say in the matter of retirement. If you work for someone else, especially in a mid–size to large company, the retirement decision is made for you. That decision can be part of corporate policy or, as is often the case these days, can be a financial decision in keeping with the current move toward downsizing, or "rightsizing."

Companies seem to prefer the term "rightsizing" because "downsizing" can imply that the organization was too big to begin with and stockholders may wonder how it became that way in the first place. Rightsizing sounds much more professional and implies that the company is right on top of things and is in the process of making sure that they are the "right" size and are constantly reviewing their employee force with an eye on the competition and economic conditions.

The retirement decision often is made by offering individuals inducements to accept an early retirement. As a result, there are many former corporate executives, probably somewhere in their mid– to late–50s, carrying business cards that identify them as "consultant." This is often a face–saving gesture that covers over the fact that a consultant without clients is no consultant at all.

As the economies of this country and the world change in keeping with new trade alliances and the removal of trade barriers, I suspect that more and more people will find themselves in the early retirement category. I think this is sad, but most of us can't do very much about it. What about people whose career success depends on their ability to deliver their talents to audiences that are willing to pay for them well beyond what is called the "normal" retirement years. You see this in athletics and the media and in show business with people whose name and reputation have sustained them.

When I see someone in the entertainment business continuing to perform long after their talents have eroded, and often disappeared, I wonder what sustains them. Why do they keep working? Why don't they quit? I am quite sure that we all know entertainers who find themselves in this category. We all are aware, too, of entertainers who leave their careers almost at the peak of their popularity and simply move into their retirement years or into other fields. Some must feel a need to stay in the spotlight; others are content to take their bows and exit stage left or right.

About a 14 or 15 years ago, I picked up our local newspaper and read a story that said that Bob Hope would be appearing as the featured performer at the Clearfield County Fair.

Clearfield is a small town and its fairgrounds look the way a county fairgrounds should look. They have the standard trotting track surrounded by the standard fence and the standard grandstand. I don't know how many people a star performer might draw there, but I guarantee you that Bob Hope wasn't attracted by the size of the audience. Hope is reputed to be an extremely wealthy man, and I am fairly certain that he wasn't attracted by his fee. At the time, he was in his 80s, and I know the trip to and from Clearfield had to be physically demanding.

We all can suggest answers as to why performers continue to perform. The most usual is that they don't want people to forget who they used to be, and don't want to become another faceless person as their career fades into the past. About a year after reading about Bob Hope and his appearance in our area, I knew for sure why he came to Clearfield and why he continues to perform even now that he is in his 90s.

At that time, I was presenting a considerable number of speeches for the IBM Corporation. I received an assignment to deliver a speech to an audience of IBM employees at the Texas Heritage Center in Austin. IBM had an Austin plant largely devoted to production of the IBM personal computer, and their employee force numbered somewhere around 6,500. The company had scheduled an event to salute the employees for their work on the personal computer.

The program included a company vice president; Drew Pearson, then a Dallas Cowboys star; the performer who played the giant synthesizer at Epcot Center in Orlando (they disassembled the massive instrument and shipped it to Austin for reassembling); and other entertainers. I was asked to make a speech in the middle of all this, although I wasn't sure why. About a month before the event, I had a call from a production company in Atlanta asking if I could contact the Penn State Blue Band and ask for the sheet music for a Penn State fight song that their program band could perform for the Texas audience. The director of the Blue Band gave me the music, and I forwarded it to Atlanta.

The Texas Heritage Center where the program was held is a very large arena that is used for all sorts of events, including rodeos. No one had told me that the audience would number about 3,500. They had simply said there would be a "large audience." They made me comfortable in their version of the "Green Room," the place where performers relax prior to going on stage. Someone stuck his head in the door and said, "Ten minutes, Professor Bergstein." He counted down the minutes for me and then said, "You're on!" They headed me down an Astroturf ramp that led to the stage, which looked like it was a quarter mile away. As I ran down the ramp, I looked up and saw the entire front of the arena was covered with about 10 large screens.

Right about then, I heard myself being introduced to the audience and the pit band struck up the Penn State fight song. The screens were dark, and then my name started to flash all over the 10 screens, over and over again. By this time, I had reached the stage and there were 3,500 people in a semi–circle, row after row, reaching all the way to the back of the hall and to the ceiling, and all looking right at me! Because of the size of the arena, there was a large television camera below me and out of sight of the audience that projected my image onto four or five giant screens mounted high above me so that the audience in the higher rows could see me as well, or better, than those down front. The stage was bathed in bright lights for the television cameras, and the audience seated in the darkness was one big blur.

I never use a script for my talks, but on this occasion I had decided in advance what my opening lines would be. I knew, from experience, that a speech before a large audience always rises or falls on the opening minute of the talk. If you don't grab the attention of the back half of the audience immediately, you probably won't ever get it. But when I turned to face the audience and all I could see were cowboy boots and Levi jeans, I changed my opening on the spot.

Three weeks before, Penn State had played the University of Texas at Giant Stadium in New Jersey (this was the 1984 season) and the Longhorns had beaten us 28-3. Knowing how rabid Texans are about football, I waited until the music and applause had died down and stepped forward when the hall was absolutely quiet. Then I said, "Thank you for that warm Texas welcome, but it didn't surprise me. Everywhere I go I hear about the warm and gracious welcome one always receives when visiting Texas. But, I have a hunch that perhaps your welcome was a little warmer and more enthusiastic than usual since three weeks ago your football team kicked the hell out of my team 28-3." I must have picked the right opening line. The audience came to its feet with a roar, and 3,500 people put their fingers in the air in the traditional symbol of horns and started to chant, "Hook 'em horns…hook 'em horns." When they finally were seated, I knew I had them with me.

All of a sudden, right in the middle of my talk, I knew for certain why Bob Hope went to the Clearfield County Fair and why other famous stars continue to perform. Positive feedback from audiences is a wonderful thing and working for their approval really starts the adrenaline flowing. It's a feeling that cannot be described; you have to experience it. I had never experienced it before, and I haven't performed for an audience of that size and enthusiasm since. Your inner excitement doesn't mean that you are scared, it only means that your whole system seems to be tuned to a higher level than you are used to and you are on some sort of a "high."

I finished my talk and headed up the ramp to the strains of the Penn State fight song. When I reached the Green Room, I knew without a doubt what keeps any performer—actor, musician, speaker, or athlete—going as long as, in their mind, they are able to perform. It is a feeling hard to describe, and I only experienced it this one time, but "real" stars must experience it every time they perform. Think how hard it would be to walk away and never experience that feeling again.

I am not a person who perspires very much, but I set a record that day. I was so hyped that when I took off my shoes, I was actually able to wring out my socks, which were as wet as if I had fallen into a swimming pool. My shirt collar was wet, my tie was soaked, and I felt wonderful!

Is this why so many athletes try to stay on beyond their time of talent? Is this why they try to stick with the team just one more year, even though they have had multiple injuries and many operations? Money may be part of it, but I think that being cheered by the crowd and interviewed by the press and recognized on the street also must be part of it, because they know how much they will miss it.

I recently heard of a former great college All–America star and a long–time All–Pro who put this feeling into sad, almost tragic perspective. He said, "I was a star all of my life. I was "all–everything" in high school, in college, and for a couple of decades in the pros. Five years ago, for the first time in my life, I had to buy a ticket to a football game because no one wanted me in the locker room, on the sidelines, in the press box, or sitting with the owner and his guests. I guess that will be it from now on."

Does this have any relationship to Penn State or other colleges and universities? In a different way, teaching is a kind of ego trip, and I don't mean that negatively. In addition to the importance of dispensing learning, teaching is a form of performing, especially to a large class. If you don't enjoy performing, I don't think you will enjoy teaching. Isn't it ego–satisfying to offer facts, or your opinion, and have everyone write it down in a notebook?

I include this here because, in a way, that may be one reason why professors don't usually quit, especially if they enjoy standing in front of a class. In a way, many teachers these days might find themselves feeling as do performers and athletes who feel that they no longer have an audience, although they believe they can still perform as well as ever. Whether they really can perform as well as before doesn't matter to them; it is only important that they think they can.

The average adult in our country now lives approximately 11 years longer than when Social Security was initiated. This means a long retirement for many, perhaps too long! Doesn't this place new emphasis on receiving a solid education? Wouldn't it be a good guess that a good education will prepare you to find additional alternatives for premature retirement? For some, retirement can be fulfilling and rewarding. For others, it can mean an unhappy letdown when they turn off your personal spotlight. When they do turn your light off, how will you feel when you return to your office, or other workplace, after 35 or 40 years of service, and a new, young, recently hired secretary doesn't recognize you and asks, "What can I do for you, sir?"

It Hardly Seems That Long

I have had a long and full career. I began as an adjunct instructor (part–time, in addition to my radio station employment) in the latter part of the 1940s, and was replaced in the lineup and sent to the bench in the spring of 1995. During my time on the Penn State team from the 1940s through the 1990s, I think I have taught somewhere between 15,000 and 16,000 students.

As I matured as a teacher and gained work experience in a wide range of fields, I found myself more freely sharing with the students my ideas about how they should feel about work, and their employers, and their peers at work, and their superiors. In short, in addition to the material in the textbooks, I wanted them to know why I believe that their attitudes and relationships with their employer, their customers, and the people they work with will play the most important role in their efforts and desires to move "up the ladder."

I will not presume to tell you all the things I tried to teach my students. Perhaps I will leave that for future writing. But I would like to share one story that I always shared with my students and always will share with any young person who asks me for career advice.

When I was growing up, I used to read many of the Horatio Alger books and stories. I never had the money to buy one, but you could find many, many of these books in the library. Practically none of my students know anything about Horatio Alger or why there is still an award in his name. (I referred to this annual award in the section about Eric Walker when he was president of Penn State.)

Horatio Alger was the son of a poor minister and became an ordained minister himself. Alger was a young man who worked especially hard at whatever job he held or was assigned. He did all the right things that an ambitious young person does if he is determined to reach the top. Along the way, he managed to write 135 books about energetic young men who, through dint of hard work and focused ambition, eventually reached the goals they had set for themselves.

After reading all of these stories, and deciding that almost anything was possible, I resolved that I, too, would try to follow the formula to work hard and rise to the top. I never reached the top, but I <u>have</u> reached enough varied goals to believe that I have been modestly successful. One day, I began to read a business magazine that carried the picture of a mature and handsome man on the cover. Under the photo was this intriguing and eye-catching caption: "From Janitor to Chairman of the Board."

Realizing that he had accomplished a feat worth reading about, I turned to the inside pages and read his story. It might well have been the shortest article ever written. The reporter asked the interviewee the most obvious question, "How did you rise from janitor to become chairman of the board of this large and famous company." The chairman answered, "It was really very simple. I rose because of a game I constantly played with myself."

The writer asked, "Would you be willing to explain the game?" The chairman's answer is probably the greatest formula for success ever said or written. He said, "The game is called <u>I always pretend that I own the company.</u> Everything I did while working for the company, every suggestion or recommendation I ever made, every penny I suggested be spent, every facility or product I recommended be built, I always asked myself a question before I offered the recommendation. Would I say what I am about to say, would I recommend what I am about to recommend, would I spend the money I am going to suggest we spend, would I make this suggestion or suggest that we hire this person or recommend this course of action if I owned the entire company and every penny's worth of this company was mine? If I answered yes, I spoke up and offered the suggestion or approval of the action taken. If I said no, that's the way I always voted. If you get the chance, try and play the same game. I'll bet you win."

How Deeply Do I Care?

Two questions I am asked these days are, "What's next?" and "Now, what?" These are probably questions that are asked of anyone who has recently retired. My answer to these questions is something like, "I really don't know. But I do know that there is a difference between retiring and quitting."

Once I get used to the idea that I don't "have" to be somewhere, I am sure that I will find something or somewhere where I can make a meaningful contribution. I have to continue trying to be of useful service because of how I feel about this country and its institutions and what they have made possible for my family and me. I never have taken for granted what has been given to us, and I never shall.

In America, regardless of who you are, rich or poor, do or do not pay taxes, regardless of your race or national origin, do or do not have parents, regardless of the religion you practice, irrespective of your gender, you not only get to go to school, you have to go to school. Many people take this for granted. I don't and never did. I believe that our public school system built this country. That's why so many, many immigrant families knew that if you "work hard and take advantage of your education, in an economic sense, you can easily outdo your 'old man.'"

Our educational system provided me with 12 years of public schooling, made it possible for me, for relatively few dollars, to graduate from a tax–supported state university, helped me earn a graduate degree from the same institution, and prepared me to teach at one of our nation's finest state universities. All this has relatively little to do with me; it was the system that made this possible.

If you search the entire campus, you will not find a single plaque that extols my outstanding academic average. I was, and am, just an average student who took advantage of the most generous educational opportunities in the world. I have to believe that, coming from my original background, there is probably no other country in the world where I could have wound up as a college professor!

What do you suppose would happen if the United Nations passed a unanimous resolution that said that for a selected period of time, all national barriers must be removed and there could be unrestricted immigration all over the world? How many Americans would choose to leave and go elsewhere? How many people from other countries would choose to come here?

Finally, I would like to tell you about a meaningful gift that I received one day. The gift was from the late Eric Walker who, at the time he gave it to me, was preparing to retire from the presidency of the university. We were at Rec Hall, and he asked me to stop in his office in Old Main. At this time, I was still an adjunct professor, teaching two courses a semester.

As I left my class the next afternoon, I went to the president's office and told his secretary that the president had asked me to stop by. She said that he was in a meeting with a trustee and wouldn't be able to talk with me as he probably would have liked to do, but she knew he would want to know that I was there.

Dr. Walker came out of the meeting, apologized for not being able to spend some time with me, and handed me a gift–wrapped package. I was surprised because it wasn't my birthday and, as I mentioned, I was not yet a full–time faculty member. He said, "I want you to have this gift from me." With that, we shook hands and he went back into his office.

When I returned to my office at the radio station, I opened the package. Inside there was a wonderful book that had just been published entitled *This is Penn State*. I opened the book and it was inscribed by Eric Walker: "To Mickey Bergstein, who helped build this place!"

I cannot tell you how moved I was to receive that book and to read the inscription from the university president. Whatever I have done at and for the university was done because of what the university has meant in the lives of my family and me, and I never considered that I had done anything special. I still don't think there was anything special in what I did, but I am very glad that Eric Walker believed that I had made a special contribution, and I treasure the book that he gave me. As I said in my note to the president, "I am grateful for the book. I hope I deserve the inscription."

And now, as I used to say in my earlier radio days, "Thanks for listening." ▪

Index

C

D

Dartmouth University, 65
Daugherty, Duffy, 251
Davis, Ernie, 228, 232-234
Delacato, Carl, 267
Derogatis, Al, 87-89
Detmer, Ty, 256
Doman, Glenn, 266
Donora, Pennsylvania, 208-209
Dorney, Keith, 22
Dozier, D.J., 23
Drazenovich, Chuck, 23, 101
Drum, Bob, 228-229
Dunn, Jerry, 103

E

Ebersole, John, 23, 86
Economos, Jack, 26
Eisenhower, Dr. Milton S., 109-113, 235
Engle, Rip, 10, 85, 125, 129, 138, 156, 164, 230, 272
Engram, Bobby, 22
Enis, Curtis, 1-3, 23

F

Farrell, Sean, 23
Fiesta Bowl, 12, 140
Florida State University, 9-10, 134
Fritz, John, 103
Fusina, Chuck, 22

G

Gabor, Billy, 54
Garagiola, Joe, 75-76
Garrity, Greg, 160
Gator Bowl, 9, 26, 134, 251
Georgetown University, 173, 205-208
Georgia, University of, 160, 169
Georgia Tech University, 20, 251
Giftopolous, Pete, 13, 16
Gladstone, Art, 146-148
Gola, Tom, 58
Goldberg, Marshall, 223
Grazier, Bunny, 156
Grier, Roosevelt, 22, 194-196

K

Kalin, Arnold, 201
Kalin, Bill, 201-202
Kammer, Angie, 184
Kansas, University of, 87
Kates, Jim, 86
Kennedy, John F., 277
Kennedy, Robert F. 195
Kenney, Nick, 251
Kentucky, University of, 63
Kochman, Roger, 22, 203, 232
Kwalick, Ted, 22

L

LaSalle University, 58
Lawther, John, 51-57
Layne, Bobby, 229, 278
Lenkaitis, Bill, 23
Little, Floyd, 228
Liversedge, Col. Harry, 278
Lombardi, Vince, 193-195
Lorenzo, Rich, 103
Loughran, Tommy, 29, 92
Louisiana State University, 58
Lucas, Richie, 22, 232, 278

M

Markovich, Mark, 23
Mautino, Fred, 230
McConnell, Suzie, 180
McCoy, Ernie, 156
McDuffie, O.J., 23
McHugh, Roy, 134
Medlar, Chuck, 154
Meredith, Bill, 60
Meredith, Don, 77-79
Miami, University of, 6, 11-15, 86, 140, 250
Michigan, University of, 175
Michigan State University, 251
Millen, Matt, 22, 150, 166
Miller, John, 8-9
Milot, Rich, 5
Minnesota, University of, 100
Missouri, University of, 135, 162
Mitchell, Lydell, 5, 6-7, 22

Mitinger, Bob, 22
Miyagawa, Dick, 102
Monessen, Pennsylvania, 25, 41
Montana, Joe, 278
Moore, Lenny, 16-20, 22, 129-130, 231
Morris, J.T., 154
Munchack, Mike, 22

N

Navy, *See U.S. Naval Academy*
North Carolina State University, 63, 168
Notre Dame University, 58, 168

O

Ohio State University, 155, 175
Onkotz, Dennis, 5, 22, 86
Orange Bowl, 87, 135
Oregon, University of, 175
Oswald, Dr. John, 27-29, 238
Owens, Jesse, 187-193

P

Palmer, Arnold, 229
Pankey, Irv, 23
Parkhill, Bruce, 103
Parsons, Bob, 7, 80
Paterno, Joe, 2-4, 6-11, 14, 71, 80-81, 83, 86, 125-148, 166, 171-174, 251, 256-257, 272-273, 275-277
Paterno, Scott, 143
Paterno, Sue, 138-139, 144-145
Patrick, Frank, 223-226
Pearson, Drew, 283
Pei, I.M., 239
Pelton, William, 121-123
Perez, Larry, 237
Perry, Darren, 23
Pettit, Bob, 58
Pittman, Charlie, 22, 88
Pitts, Stephen, 153-155
Pittsburgh, University of, 56, 168, 173, 175, 223
Pittsburgh *Press*, 134
Portland, Rene, 180
Prince, Bob, 161-162, 209-219
Princeton University, 66-67
Prothro, Tommy, 82-84

Q

Qualiey, Stu, 25

R

Rackley, Ralph, 237
Radecic, Scott, 23
Rafferty, Tom, 22
Ramsey, Frank, 63
Raye, Jimmy, 251
Raykovits, Jack, 263
Reid, Mike, 22, 86, 149-153
Ressler, Glenn, 23
Riley, Ridge, 48, 231
Robinson, Dave, 20, 22
Robinson, Mark, 22
Robinson, Susan, 180
Rogel, Francis, 222
Rohland, Bob, 57
Rose Bowl, 175, 226
Rose, Russ, 180-181
Rosenthal, Dick, 58
Rosewell, Rosey, 59-60, 212
Rupp, Adolph, 64-65

S

Sandusky, Jerry, 14, 261-264
Schott, Carl P., 250
Schreyer, William, 240-243
Schwartz, Robert, 235
Schwartzkopf, Gen. Norman, 277
Schwartzwalder, Ben, 227, 230
Second Mile, The, 261-264
Seitz, Ellery, 161
Seton Hall University, 173
Shafer, Gov. Raymond, 127-128
Sherry, Jack, 17, 57, 63
Shuler, Mickey, 23
Simpson, Jim, 87-89
Skorupan, John, 22
Smear, Steve, 22, 86, 150
Smith, Bubba, 251
Smith, Neal, 23
Soose, Billy, 91
Southeast Conference, 175
Southern Methodist University, 85

Celebrate Pennsylvania!

Order Today!
For fastest service, Call 1/800-497-1427 or from Harrisburg 232-7944
Call between 8:30 a.m. - 5:00 p.m. M-F or FAX: 717/238-3280 anytime

RB BOOKS
"...richly beautiful"

Featuring stunning color photos by Blair Seitz

PENNSYLVANIA'S CAPITOL takes you through this "Palace of Art" in Harrisburg. Enjoy the paintings, sculpture and stained glass. 8½" x 11" hc 80 photos $19.95

PHILADELPHIA AND ITS COUNTRYSIDE portrays historic and scenic attractions of Pennsylvania's Southeast. 8½" x 11" hc 180 photos $29.95

PENNSYLVANIA'S NATURAL BEAUTY invites you to the serene but wild beauty of Pennsylvania's state parks and forests—all four seasons. 8½" x 11" hc 120 photos $24.95

SUSQUEHANNA HEARTLAND shows you the reasons why the people of Harrisburg, York and Lancaster love living in the Susquehanna Valley. 8½" x 11" hc 180 photos $24.95

PITTSBURGH uncovers the distinctions of the Three Rivers City—its museums, its topography, its festivals. 8½" x 11" hc 125 photos $29.95

AMISH WAYS opens your window to Amish faith and culture through ordinary happenings. 8½"x 11" hc 150 photos $24.95

PENNSYLVANIA'S TAPESTRY: SCENES FROM THE AIR will thrill you with aerial views of Pennsylvania's farms, forests, and waterways. 8½" x 11" hc 90 photos $24.95

SAVE OUR LAND; SAVE OUR TOWNS lays out an easy-to-grasp blueprint for comunities to thrive while preserving the earth. 8½" x 11" p 150 photos $24.95

Insights Series

AMISH VALUES: WISDOM THAT WORKS describes how ten insights benefit these "plain people" and could enhance your life. 5½" x 8½" p color photos $9.95

GETTYSBURG: CIVIL WAR MEMORIES takes you back to this battle as experienced by ten-year-old Charles McCurdy and other civilians. Photos of battle relics published for the first time. 5½" x 8½" p color photos $9.95

Detach this portion prior to mailing

Return your order to: RB Books
1006 N. 2nd Street, Harrisburg, PA 17102

Name _____

Address _____

City _____ State _____ Zip _____

Phone _____

Method of Payment

☐ Check (Make payable to "RB Books")

☐ Visa   ☐ MasterCard

Card Number _____ Exp. _____

Signature _____

Satisfaction Guaranteed

Quantity	Book Title	Special Price	Total
____	Amish Ways	$24.95	____
____	Pennsylvania's Capitol	19.95	____
____	Pennsylvania's Natural Beauty	24.95	____
____	Philadelphia	29.95	____
____	Pittsburgh	29.95	____
____	Save Our Land/Towns	29.95	____
____	Susquehanna Heartland	24.95	____
____	Amish Values	9.95	____
____	Gettysburg	9.95	____
____	Pennsylvania's Tapestry: Scenes from the Air	24.95	____
____	Penn State Sports Stories	19.95	____
		Sub-total A.	____
	Shipping & Handling($5.95 first book, $3 2nd book, $1 each additional)	B.	____
		Sub-total C.	____
	PA Sales Tax/Pennsylvania Residents (Sub-total C x 6%)	D.	____
		Total Enclosed (C+D)	____

Celebrate Pennsylvania!

Order Today!
For fastest service, Call 1/800-497-1427 or from Harrisburg 232-7944
Call between 8:30 a.m. - 5:00 p.m. M-F or FAX: 717/238-3280 anytime

Featuring stunning color photos by Blair Seitz

PENNSYLVANIA'S CAPITOL takes you through this "Palace of Art" in Harrisburg. Enjoy the paintings, sculpture and stained glass. 8½" x 11" hc 80 photos $19.95

PHILADELPHIA AND ITS COUNTRYSIDE portrays historic and scenic attractions of Pennsylvania's Southeast. 8½" x 11" hc 180 photos $29.95

PENNSYLVANIA'S NATURAL BEAUTY invites you to the serene but wild beauty of Pennsylvania's state parks and forests—all four seasons. 8½" x 11" hc 120 photos $24.95

SUSQUEHANNA HEARTLAND shows you the reasons why the people of Harrisburg, York and Lancaster love living in the Susquehanna Valley. 8½" x 11" hc 180 photos $24.95

PITTSBURGH uncovers the distinctions of the Three Rivers City—its museums, its topography, its festivals. 8½" x 11" hc 125 photos $29.95

AMISH WAYS opens your window to Amish faith and culture through ordinary happenings. 8½"x 11" hc 150 photos $24.95

PENNSYLVANIA'S TAPESTRY: SCENES FROM THE AIR will thrill you with aerial views of Pennsylvania's farms, forests, and waterways. 8½" x 11" hc 90 photos $24.95

SAVE OUR LAND; SAVE OUR TOWNS lays out an easy-to-grasp blueprint for comunities to thrive while preserving the earth. 8½" x 11" p 150 photos $24.95

Insights Series

AMISH VALUES: WISDOM THAT WORKS describes how ten insights benefit these "plain people" and could enhance your life. 5½" x 8½" p color photos $9.95

GETTYSBURG: CIVIL WAR MEMORIES takes you back to this battle as experienced by ten-year-old Charles McCurdy and other civilians. Photos of battle relics published for the first time. 5½" x 8½" p color photos $9.95

— — — — — — — — — — — *Detach this portion prior to mailing* — — — — — — — — —

Return your order to: RB Books
1006 N. 2nd Street, Harrisburg, PA 17102

Name _____

Address _____

City _____ State _____ Zip _____

Phone _____

Method of Payment
☐ Check (Make payable to "RB Books")
☐ Visa   ☐ MasterCard
Card Number _____ Exp. _____

Signature _____

Satisfaction Guaranteed

Quantity	Book Title	Special Price	Total
_____	Amish Ways	$24.95	_____
_____	Pennsylvania's Capitol	19.95	_____
_____	Pennsylvania's Natural Beauty	24.95	_____
_____	Philadelphia	29.95	_____
_____	Pittsburgh	29.95	_____
_____	Save Our Land/Towns	29.95	_____
_____	Susquehanna Heartland	24.95	_____
_____	Amish Values	9.95	_____
_____	Gettysburg	9.95	_____
_____	Pennsylvania's Tapestry: Scenes from the Air	24.95	_____
_____	Penn State Sports Stories	19.95	_____

Sub-total A. _____

Shipping & Handling($5.95 first book, $3 2nd book, $1 each additional) B. _____

Sub-total C. _____

PA Sales Tax/Pennsylvania Residents (Sub-total C x 6%) D. _____

Total Enclosed (C+D) _____